THROUGH AUSTRALIAN EYES
Colonial Perceptions of Imperial Britain

Through Australian Eyes

Colonial Perceptions of Imperial Britain

ANDREW HASSAM

sussex
ACADEMIC
PRESS

BRIGHTON • PORTLAND

The right of Andrew Hassam to be identified as author of this work has been asserted in accordance with the Copyright, Designs and Patents Act 1988.

DU
113.5
.G7
H37
2000

2 4 6 8 10 9 7 5 3 1

First published 2000 in Great Britain by
SUSSEX ACADEMIC PRESS
PO Box 2950
Brighton BN2 5SP

and in the United States of America by
SUSSEX ACADEMIC PRESS
5804 N.E. Hassalo St.
Portland, Oregon 97213-3644

British Library Cataloguing in Publication Data
A CIP catalogue record for this book is available from the British Library.

Library of Congress Cataloging-in-Publication Data
Hassam, Andrew.
Through Australian eyes : colonial perception of imperial Britain / Andrew Hassam.
p. cm.
Includes bibliographical references (p.) and index.
ISBN 1–902210–62–X (acid-free paper)
1. Australia—Relations—Great Britain.   2. Great Britain—Foreign public opinion,
Australian.   3. Great Britain—Relations—Australia.   4. Imperialism—Public opinion—
Australia.   5. National characteristics, Australian.   6. Public opinion—Australia.
7. Australians—Diaries. 8. Travelers' writings, Australian.   I. Title.
DU113.5.G7 H37   2001
303.48'241094—dc21   00–041301

Printed by Biddles Ltd, Guildford and King's Lynn
This book is printed on acid-free paper

Contents

List of Illustrations

―――――

The author and publisher gratefully acknowledge the following for permission to reproduce copyright material:

Cover picture: George Bernard O'Neill's 'The Return from Australia', courtesy of The Fine Art Society, PLC, London.

'A Contrast – Christmastide in England and in Australia.' *Illustrated Sydney News*, 22 December 1877.

Margaret Tripp. From the Toorak College Archives. Reproduced by kind permission of Toorak College.

Patterson Street, South Melbourne, c.1950. From *Early Melbourne Architecture, 1840 to 1888*. Melbourne: Oxford University Press, 1953.

'The Great Palm House, Kew Gardens.' *Illustrated London News*, 7 August 1852.

Interior of the Crystal Palace, Sydenham. From Henry Russell Hitchcock, *Early Victorian Architecture in Britain*. New Haven, CT: Yale University Press, 1954.

The Queensland Annexe at the London International Exhibition, 1872. From the collection of the John Oxley Library, Brisbane. Reproduced by kind permission of the Library Board of Queensland.

South Kensington Museum, London. From Henry Russell Hitchcock, *Early Victorian Architecture in Britain*. New Haven, CT: Yale University Press, 1954.

'The Mob Pulling Down the Railings in Park-Lane.' *Illustrated London News*, 4 August 1866.

Thomas Lodge Murray-Prior. From the collection of the John Oxley Library, Brisbane. Reproduced by kind permission of the Library Board of Queensland.

'Australian Nurses for the Front.' *British-Australasian*, 1 July 1915. From

The publisher apologises for any errors or omissions in the above list and would be grateful to be notified of any corrections that should be incorporated in the next edtion or reprint of this book.

Acknowledgements

Most of the research for this project was carried out in 1995 while I was the C. H. Currey Memorial Fellow at the State Library of New South Wales, and I am grateful to the Library Council of New South Wales for their support at a key moment in the project. Alan Ventress, the Mitchell Librarian, Jennifer Broomhead, Martin Beckett and many others provided invaluable help. The award of a Visiting Fellowship, also in 1995, by the Centre for British Studies at the University of Adelaide gave me the opportunity to extend my research to the State Library of South Australia and I am grateful to Dr Michael Tolley for his hospitality, as well as to the staff, especially Neil Thomas, at the State Library in Adelaide. Staff at the State Library of Victoria, the State Library of Queensland, the Australian National Maritime Museum and the National Library of Australia all provided much needed assistance; once again I am greatly in debt to Mr Graeme Powell and all the staff in the Manuscripts Reading Room of the National Library in Canberra for providing such a convivial working environment.

In 1998, I was fortunate in being awarded a Visiting Fellowship within the History Program at the RSSS, the Australian National University, to finish writing up, for which thanks are due to the late Professor Paul Bourke, a sadly missed beacon in the world of Australian History. While at the ANU I was greatly encouraged by conversations with Professor Pat Jalland, Sue Allan, Dr Sue Rickard and Dr Margaret Stephen, while Bev Gallina, Janice Aldridge, and Anthea Bundock all contributed to the fun and effectiveness of my stay in Canberra. The Menzies Centre for Australian Studies in London gave me the opportunity on several occasions to present papers to a stimulating audience, and the Centre remains an invaluable resource for all those working in Australian Studies in Europe.

Acknowledging the help I have received in the five years of working on this project is a humbling process. So many people have given generously of their time and thoughts. While I was researching in Sydney, Marion Flynn took pity on me and invited me to stay with her, an act of generosity which led to Marion sharing not only her home with me but her experiences of living in Britain and Germany in the late 1960s and early 1970s. Marion also accompanied me on a memorable visit to Mrs Nancy Cranna whom I had identified as the writer of an anonymous diary lodged in the State Library of New South Wales. Over tea, Mrs Cranna spoke of her experience of a trip to Britain in 1939 and afterwards arranged for me to have copies of the diary of her sister, Kathleen Bate, who had accompanied her on the trip, and of their mother, Ethel Reid, who had visited Britain as a young woman in 1900.

Professor Elizabeth Webby arranged for me to occupy an office in the English Department of the University of Sydney while I was working in the State Library of NSW. Elizabeth shared with me her thoughts on my topic, as did Dr Richard White, also of Sydney University, whose work in the area of Australians in Europe has been more inspiring than my endnotes suggest. Dr Chris Tiffin, of the University of Queensland, shared with me his knowledge of the nineteenth century and of Thomas Lodge Murray-Prior, while Dr Ian Britain, of Monash University, supplied both intellectual stimulation and, as ever, excellent hospitality. My greatest debt is to Mrs Ros Shennan who, in return for a meagre supply of Thornton's Treacle Toffee, unfailingly retrieved from the depths of the archives vital and reliable biographical information about any diarist or letter writer I cared to name. To Ros, for her astounding expertise, total conscientiousness and persistent good humour, I dedicate this book. I would it were a life's supply of Thornton's Treacle Toffee.

The following people generously gave me copies of diaries in their keeping: Janice Aldridge (for Henry Aldridge); Elizabeth Southan (for Alice Andreas); Nancy Cranna (for Kathleen Bate, Nancy Newell and Ethel Rose Reid); Mr M. B. Morrisby (for Richard Crocker); Annette Cunliffe (for T. J. J. Cunliffe); Marion Flynn; Sharon Bakewell (for Henry Pilcher). Mrs Ann Ashby shared with me the family history of her relative, Henry Pilcher.

Earlier versions of sections of this work appeared in the following journals and books, and I am indebted to their editors for allowing me to share my preliminary thoughts with the academic community: *Journal of Australian Studies*; *Prose Studies*; *Imperial Cities: Space, Landscape & Performance*, edited by Felix Driver and David Gilbert (Manchester: Manchester University Press, 1999).

Introduction

Researchers rarely acknowledge the source of their interest in their subjects. Perhaps, in Freudian fashion, they need to undergo therapy and scholarly counter-transference to understand the depths of their academic psyches. Perhaps such matters can never be fully understood. My own interest in British colonial identity does not so much originate in, as relate to, my own 'expatriate' condition. I was brought up in a very English part of Surrey, a semi-rural suburb inhabited predominantly by professionals working in London. They commuted daily, setting off at 7 o'clock in the morning to return at 7 o'clock in the evening. Some wore bowler hats and swung umbrellas as they marched to and from the railway station. Rail strikes provided the only disruption to routine.

In an attempt to escape from the suburbia of my childhood, I took a flat in London, only to find myself at the very hub of the suburban railway network and among a whole city of bowler hats and umbrellas. I fled again, this time to the Midlands, looking for the simple life living on a canal boat. The simple life, without running water or electricity, proved to be as hard a life as I could have wanted, though it had its compensations, I'm sure, and I am proud of the fact that I never once fell into the canal. After a brief stint as relief ferryman at Stratford-on-Avon, I drifted into an office job and a reminder of just how much I disliked working from 9.00 to 5.30 five days a week. So I became an undergraduate in Wales, finding among the sheep a more pleasant combination of a rural life and sociable working hours. I have remained here, on and off, ever since.

I will say little of the Welsh people I know, except to say that among them are the most generous individuals I have ever met. But Wales also contains the most bigoted of people, especially when it comes to the English. At best the racism comes in the form of being refused a drink in a pub. I imagine most English people in rural Wales have, like me, been sworn at, and a number have suffered worse. Having experienced the gratuitous abuse of the bowler hatted English Tories as a teenager in the 1960s and then the bigotry of rural Wales in the 1980s, I am keen to regard myself as neither English nor Welsh. I am content to be called British, if Britishness can be emptied of its imperialist associations. Ideally I would like to be called a European and have done with the whole problem.

Being British is for me both a more inclusive identity and a more elusive identity than being English or Welsh. Stereotypes of the English, the Welsh and the Scots are pervasive in television comedy, but a British stereotype springs less easily to mind. At times of national crisis, Britishness has been represented as Britannia ruling the waves, as a lion mauling Britannia's enemies on land, and as John Bull, the yeoman farmer, exemplifying civil freedom. The composition of the Home Guard platoon in the television series, *Dad's Army*, offered a representative cross section of the British in the 1940s, and the platoon included men from the upper, middle and lower classes, as well as a Scot. But none of them was more British than the other. Even the Union flag that cheekily defied the Nazi swastika in the opening credits is a composite of three separate national flags.

I was attracted to examining an Australian colonial identity for similar reasons, namely, a positive combination of inclusivity and elusiveness. The British in the nineteenth century are not remembered for their inclusivity, and to prevent what they saw as racial pollution they erected strictly maintained racial boundaries even among those formally defined as British subjects. We are all aware of the use of racial difference to justify the dispossession of indigenous populations. Yet Britishness had a broader definition than it does today, and Australians, New Zealanders, Canadians and South Africans could all regard themselves as British and be welcomed in Britain as such. Between Britain and the settler colonies, at least, what was and what was not foreign was difficult to define, and I wanted to understand better how people can associate with two nations without having to choose between them.

The diaries of Australian colonial visitors to Britain offered a means of examining the inclusiveness of being British in the nineteenth century, though partly because of the limited nature and size of my sources, my study is not a history of Australian visitors to Britain. Many Australians came to Britain to take up more or less permanent residence, returned colonists made good or Australian men intent on following careers in finance, the law or politics. Rather than write their history, I have tended to ignore such people, my interest falling on those less well-known Australians who, while they may have worked in Britain and may even have stayed for more than a year, never regarded themselves as expatriates; they intended to visit for a short while and they returned. Such visitors made the journey for a number of reasons, and we see them sightseeing, inspecting factories, taking music lessons and consulting doctors. Thomas Padman, for example, visited Britain in 1863 to order goods for his hardware business in South Australia, to visit his mother and brothers and sisters still living in Britain, and, as a lay preacher, to attend a Methodist Conference in Sheffield. It would be difficult to identify Padman's main purpose for visiting Britain, but it is clear that here, as in perhaps the majority of cases, emotional ties were an important factor in the decision to return Home.

I have managed to trace and read about seventy accounts of such trips to Britain from Australia in the nineteenth century. For obvious reasons, the number of accounts increases towards the end of the century, and a quarter of them fall in the 1880s. If there were something like 200,000 arrivals from Australia and New Zealand between 1876 and the end of the century, seventy accounts is a small number indeed, far smaller than the number of voyage out diaries existing for that period. A history based on such a small sample would hardly be comprehensive, though the sample is representative in terms of social class. Of the seventy accounts, only two or three are by working people; most are by relatively affluent members of the colonial bourgeoisie. About a quarter are by women, probably a reflection of the fewer number of women making the trip than of any male predilection for keeping a diary. To help readers, I have provided short biographies for the main writers discussed.

Letters and diaries written by Australian visitors to Britain are a rich and yet undervalued primary source for the investigation of the cultural histories of both Britain and its former settler colonies. Cultural historians have looked in some detail at the relationship between British and English identities within Australia, at the maintenance of specific migrant identities, and at the shifts in Australian national identity. My own project differs by studying the construction of Australianness outside Australia and in stressing the plurality of cultural identity. Colonial visitors to Britain maintained, in addition to gender and class identities, divergent national identities, regarding themselves as, say, Scottish, British, or Australian depending on context. Nineteenth-century British culture was already a product of complex social relationships and paradoxically the uncertain loyalties of being both British in Australia and Australian in Britain enabled Australian visitors to Britain to negotiate hidden tensions and create a sense of being Australian. My assumption is that the cultural displacement of travelling abroad was a necessary part of the process of forming an Australian cultural identity.

Angela Woollacott's study of Australian women living in London between 1870 to 1940 is one of a growing number of studies that demonstrate the importance of displacement in the construction of a cultural identity. As Woollacott demonstrates, the voyage Home, with its ports of call in other imperial possessions like Ceylon, India, Aden and Egypt, could teach Australians their place within the empire: 'For Australian passengers, learning more about the empire, its constituent parts and the interconnections among them, was in part a process of learning specific dimensions to Australia's location within the empire.'[1] Others have written about nineteenth-century travellers to Britain from the United States, Canada, and India, and the ways in which such travellers also formulated and tested their various national identities. In *Anglo-American Landscapes: A Study of Nineteenth-Century Anglo-American Travel Literature* (1983), Christopher Mulvey has considered literary accounts of Britain by American writers, concentrating on published travel books for their value 'more as imaginative statement than as documentary evidence'.[2] From this perspective, it would seem that most Americans were blind to any evidence, such as industrialisation, that might have prevented them from experiencing the romantic England of their American imaginations. Eva-Marie Kröller, in *Canadian Travellers in Europe, 1851–1900* (1987), has studied published and unpublished accounts of both French and (what she calls) English-Canadian travellers. Her account, especially as it relates to English-Canadians, confirms Britain as a site for the formulation of a complex colonial identity, apparent in the metaphor of parent and child, though it also confirms that Canadians disliked American tourists as much as the Australians in my own study appeared to dislike them. Indian visitors to London may not have felt so strongly about American tourists, but as Antoinette Burton argues in *At the Heart of Empire: Indians and the Colonial Encounter in Late-Victorian Britain* (1998), their presence in Britain allows us to 'more fully appreciate some of the ways imperial power relations were challenged and remade by colonial subjects not just in the far-flung territories of empire but more centrally, in the social spaces of "domestic" Victorian imperial culture itself'.[3] The position of Indians in Britain was far more circumscribed than that of Australians or Canadians, and Indians could not choose to merge with the British, but Britain proved no less a site for the formulation of a colonial identity; as Burton puts it: 'In many respects, "being Indian" was something to be learned by travel to Britain – a performance to be tested, a habitus to be tried out and reinvented on a regular basis, especially given the fact that "India" was not considered to be a coherent national political entity in the late-Victorian period.'[4]

All such studies of colonial encounters 'within' the imperial metropolis tell us a great deal not only about colonial identities but about the Britishness of the inhabitants of Britain itself. Australian historians have tended to see colonial culture as a negotiation and adaptation of British culture, without considering how British culture was already a negotiation of conflicts and tensions. Yet if we adopt a modern outlook and maintain a strict division between Australian and British cultural identities, we blinker ourselves to the ways in which the unstable identity of the colonial visitor makes visible cultural uncertainties within metropolitan Britain. If we accept that Britain itself was in a state of cultural flux, then the study of an Australian colonial identity can be as revealing of British culture as it is of Australian culture. To be aware that British culture was produced out of colonial encounters as much 'within' as without is to challenge by implication the imperial geography of centre and periphery.

As a way of reading rather than a history, therefore, this study concentrates on a selective, though broadly representative, group of Australian visitors, and considers varying responses to the regions of the British Isles and to a diversity of cultural sites, among them Westminster Abbey, the Thames Embankment, the Crystal Palace and Epsom Downs. Different cultural sites produced a range of responses even within individual accounts, and in combining close textual analysis with historical analysis, my readings are sensitive to those textual hesitations when cultural models clash, and when, through revision or awkward phrasing, the writer tries to negotiate conflicting identities.

Plan of the Book

The substance of this book takes the form of five illustrative essays devoted to particular themes; these essays are presented as chapters within a broadly chronological structure.

Chapter One, *'Neither English nor Foreign,'* examines the difficulties of separating an Australian colonial identity from a British identity, especially in a period in which Britishness was itself undergoing changes as a result of British imperial expansion and contact with new peoples and new environments. Although Australian visitors to Britain were made aware of their Australianness, they also found the places and culture of Britain familiar and thought of themselves as racially British. Australian commentators have tended to dismiss colonial Australians as not distinctively Australian, yet this is to ignore the challenge of understanding the fluidity of a colonial identity. Their awareness of being British but not of Britain meant that colonial Australians were and were not British. They were the same and yet different.

Chapter Two, *'Familiar and Yet Strange,'* considers the experiences of Australians newly arrived in Britain. Although Australian visitors sought recognition by relatives and incorporation into their homes, this desired homecoming was disturbed by the operation of difference. First impressions of Britain were a mixture of the familiar and the unfamiliar: the familiar came from the cultural models on which Australians had been brought up, the unfamiliar from the ways in which the cultural models were deficient. The effect was dreamlike, or, to use a slippery Freudian term, *unheimlich* (unhomely). The case of the Tichborne claimant in the 1870s, who was both like and unlike the person he claimed to be, highlighted the uncertain identity of the Australian in Britain.

In **Chapter Three**, *'Aborigines at the Crystal Palace,'* I turn to uncertain spaces. The 1850s saw a number of portable iron structures of British manufacture erected in Australia and other imperial possessions in response to local conditions. Such structures suggest that colonial culture was a mobile culture, the buildings enabling both the migration and adaptation of cultural values. This mobility and adaptation, however, was also a feature of the metropolitan centre, witness the removal of the Crystal Palace to Sydenham, its much expanded and more cluttered interior emphasising 'colonial' spatialities. In particular, Paxton's combination of heating and exotic plants made the Sydenham Crystal Palace much more of a botanical hothouse than the 1851 structure, and the use of the south transept to display ethnography and natural history combined the imperial, collecting impulse of glass houses like those at Kew Gardens with the confusion of the tropical forest and the confounding of the imperial gaze. In these ways, the Sydenham Crystal Palace was an uncertain space which questioned, even as it celebrated, imperialism.

Chapter Four, *'Roast Beef and the Epsom Derby,'* looks at the ambivalent attitude of Australians towards symbols of Britishness. Because it attracted both royalty and the working classes, Derby Day was celebrated by the British as an example of social cohesion, an occasion on which the nation could not only be imagined but be seen. Middle-class Australians were disappointed by the races and the race course, yet their accounts of Derby Day still managed to celebrate the British nation. Accounts of the Derby condemned the race course in terms of Australian courses, and condemned the event in terms of its working-class crowd; yet, in turn, visiting Australians identified with the British social élite and expressed loyalty to those members of the royal family present. Caught between the fair ground and the grandstand, middle-class Australians attending Derby Day used social status in a complex way to negotiate a literal displacement. And in so doing, they gave voice to the social dissatisfaction of the industrial middle-classes of Britain.

In London, Australians went in search of their heritage, and **Chapter Five, '*Cleopatra's Needle: Antiquity, History and Modernity in Britain and the USA,*'** analyses what they found. Those very sites whose history was offered to the colonial visitor 'as his own,' served as witnesses not so much to a historical continuity, but to present discontinuities and to the social, cultural and national diversity already present in any nineteenth-century Britishness. Australian perceptions of the prestigious Thames Embankment highlighted the tension between the modernising impulse of civic improvement and the creation of an imperial capital that could demonstrate its historical lineage. The attempt to provide the sanction of antiquity to the imperial capital by erecting Cleopatra's Needle on the Thames Embankment in 1878 was undermined because many Australians had first-hand knowledge of Egypt's greater antiquity from having sailed via the Suez Canal. Australians travelling through the USA could more easily praise America's modernity than Britain's, yet this praise was tempered by an appeal to their British heritage, an appeal less problematic to them in the USA than in Britain itself.

Chapter Six, '*A Disgusting Climate,*' considers how Australians reacted to Wales, Ireland and Scotland. When they travelled to Britain, Australians travelled to London. London was the seat of Empire, and if their ship docked at Liverpool or one of the South Coast ports instead of London, they were swiftly transferred to the metropolis by express train. But not all of them remained there. Wales, Scotland and Ireland were easy to reach by train from London, and the tourist routes were well travelled. For those of English descent, visiting Wales, Scotland and Ireland drew from them the ways in which they regarded themselves as English. For those of Scottish or Irish descent, Scotland and Ireland increased their awareness of being Australian. For all of them, the return to 'sunny Australia' brought with it a new sense of their Australian identity, an identity based on their experiences of having been an Australian abroad.

As a conclusion, **Chapter Seven**, *'Australia has more of a Continental Atmosphere,'* looks at continuities between nineteenth-century accounts and the ways in which twentieth-century visitors wrote about Britain. Social commentators have repeatedly defined the growth of a distinctive Australian identity according to a model of human development, with Australia growing beyond a nineteenth-century infancy towards a coming of age and maturity. Colonial identity has been dismissed as not being 'distinctively Australian.' Yet a comparison of accounts by twentieth-century Australian visitors to Britain with accounts by nineteenth-century Australians reveals a continuity in definitions of Australianness. Rather than becoming 'distinctively Australian,' Australian visitors have become less British, both because of the growth of the cheap conducted tour which has prevented them from experiencing Britain as insiders; and because, with large-scale postwar migration from Continental Europe to Australia, Australians find European culture equally familiar. From Federation to the New Millennium, Australia has spent the twentieth century apparently on the brink of 'coming of age' without ever attaining maturity, a failure more of the rhetoric of national maturity, perhaps, than of seeing Britain through 'distinctively Australian' eyes.

ONE

Neither English nor Foreign: Australian Colonial Identity

From my house overlooking the Teifi valley in West Wales, I can trace the route of a disused railway line that was closed as part of the rationalization of the British railway network in the early 1960s. A line of trees, about a mile or so away on the other side of the river, marks where the track once followed the contours of the valley, weaving its way northwards from Carmarthen to Lampeter and Aberystwyth. It was along this stretch of track that John Rae travelled in August 1879, emerging from Pencader tunnel in the cutting on my right and disappearing from view two or three miles to my left behind the church tower at Maesycrugiau, a short walk from where the road crosses the River Teifi at Pont Llwni:

> *Passed Pencader and Port Lonie [Pont Llwni].* Fine undulating open country, hills without timber & cultivated to the summit. At Strata Florida rougher country rocky mountains & tree clad hills – less cultivation. Before reaching Pencader passed through a Tunnel 1 mile long, now passing through deep rocky cuttings. Grander scenery as we advance. A magnificent scene like Glen Tilt – but smaller – with stream rushing through lighted up by the evening sun, & large extended Plains dotted with trees & cropped by sheep. On either side thickly timbered hills – all very enchanting. The long shadows cast by trees and mountains improve the prospect. Beautiful England! Where shall we find such trees, such verdure, such color and beauty. (23 August 1879)*

* Square brackets are used to indicate where punctuation or explanation has been added to the original source. Manuscript material has been transcribed as closely as possible, except with regard to underlined words which have been set in italics where the quotation is in roman font, or in roman font where the quotation has been set in italics. Original spelling has been retained.

I first read this account in the reading room of the Mitchell Library in Sydney, and apart from the understandable, and admittedly self-indulgent, pleasure at recognising the journey Rae was describing, I was amused to find myself implicated in John Rae's own cultural displacement. Rae had been born in Aberdeen in 1813 and had migrated to Sydney in 1839. Forty years later, towards the end of a career in the public service, Rae had taken twelve months leave of absence to visit the United States, Britain and Europe. On his return to New South Wales in 1880, Rae had written up an account of his travels from notes, and it was this account which in 1995 and having recently arrived from Britain, I read in the Mitchell Library. Another British-Australian exchange had taken place.

One reason I became interested in nineteenth-century accounts of Britain by Australian visitors was that I hoped my Britishness, however it might be defined, would help me to read these old, and sometimes almost illegible, diaries and letters in a different way from the way in which an Australian might read them. What particularly amused me about translating Rae's elegantly transcribed 'Port Lonie' into Pont Llwni was that here was a quite specific example of my own cultural displacement working to my advantage. Yet this is not in reality a simple case of a British researcher reading an account of a trip abroad by an Australian. Rae's sense of his own national identity was complex and was constructed out of a range of displacements, clues to which we can see in his description of Wales quoted above. Here is part of it again:

Grander scenery as we advance. A magnificent scene like Glen Tilt – but smaller – with stream rushing through lighted up by the evening sun, & large extended Plains dotted with trees & cropped by sheep. On either side thickly timbered hills – all very enchanting. The long shadows cast by trees and mountains improve the prospect. Beautiful England! Where shall we find such trees, such verdure, such color and beauty. (23 August 1879)

Through whose eyes is Wales here being described? The aesthetics of the piece, the highly pictorial composition and the references to its picturesque beauty and enchantment, are typical of a certain kind of travel writing, and the land is described impersonally though the eyes of a tourist. More personal to Rae is his comparison of Wales with Scotland: 'Grander scenery as we advance. A magnificent scene like Glen Tilt – but smaller.' Rae himself grew up in Aberdeen, and Glen Tilt is in central Scotland, running north from Blair Atholl in Perthshire. Rae is therefore seeing Wales both through the eyes of a tourist in search of the picturesque and through the eyes of a Highlander. Yet Rae is not just a Highlander on a tour of Britain, he has been away from Britain for forty years and his journey northwards through Wales is a prelude to his homecoming to Scotland. Rae's eulogy to Wales and to England is also an expression of the delight of the returned migrant: 'Beautiful England! Where shall we find such trees, such verdure, such color and beauty.' Implicitly, the comparison is with New South Wales. Rae is not, of course, mistaking Wales for England; in the nineteenth century, the whole of Britain was commonly referred to as England, a usage still common in Australia today. Yet his pride in Britain would seem to beg the question of whether it is derived from his upbringing in Scotland or from his forty years living in Australia. Is Rae seeing Wales through British eyes (the comparison between Wales and Scotland) or through Australian eyes (the comparison between Wales and NSW)?

Yet to try to separate Rae's British identity from an Australian identity is to make two unhistorical assumptions, that there is a natural, coherent, and timeless notion of Britishness, and that being British and being Australian were mutually exclusive categories. In terms of their geographical coherence, the British may be defined as the inhabitants of the British Isles, a region which shared a common sovereignty in the nineteenth century as the United Kingdom. Historically, the United Kingdom was a consequence of the gradual amalgamation of different realms: England and Wales were united in 1536, Scotland was added to produce Great Britain in 1707, and the United Kingdom was formally created out of the union between Great Britain and Ireland in 1800. The United Kingdom therefore contained within it at least four separate potential modern nations, the Irish Republic being the first to gain independence.

The United Kingdom also contained a much greater number of diverse regional loyalties, and we can gain a sense of these from reading the shipboard diaries of migrants to Australia. Will Sayer's account of dissension on board the *Samuel Plimsoll* sailing from London to Sydney in 1876 gives a flavour of the regional diversity of British migrants and the practical complications of forming a mess:

I will now tell you about our mess[.] we have agread better than any mess in the ship[.] we have not had A miss word all the time while the next mess to we have A row every meal and some times two[.] they will fall out how they shall cook the meat or meals and then as soon as they have eaten it they will begin hoo wash up is it and they have had blows several

times[.] thear [they're] one north country man one welsh man one west
and one as been at work near alton tows [Alton Towers] and them two
chaps from hednesford and Alfred Joins[.] he is the cakey dofey half baked
slopey cakey headed fool I hever seed[.] they will find falt with one another
twang especly the Durham mans language[.] it is A very rong thing to
mak game of another twang[,] it will cause A row sooner than any thing
else[.] (Will Sayer 22 August 1876)

Will Sayer's Staffordshire dialect demonstrates one of the many vari-
eties of English that were being spoken on board migrant ships and
which could lead to members of a mess falling out: 'it is A very rong
thing to mak game of another twang[,] it will cause A row sooner than
any thing else.' On board a migrant ship and perhaps for the first time
away from their regional homes, many migrants, all of whom might be
British, would have discovered that they had no common variety of
English by which to communicate.

If the British spoke no common language, they might nonetheless be
defined through a set of common values. For example, we might associate the British with a belief in tolerance, expressed constitutionally as
belief in a liberal democracy and those institutions associated with
democracy such as a parliament and an independent judiciary. Yet
Britishness is not a timeless essence and any catalogue of British values
must be related to an historical context. The historian Linda Colley, for
example, has argued that the Britishness produced in the eighteenth
century following the political formation of Great Britain in 1707 developed out of recurring warfare with France:

> *Time and time again, war with France brought Britons, whether they*
> *hailed from Wales or Scotland or England, into confrontation with an*
> *obviously hostile Other and encouraged them to define themselves collec-*
> *tively against it. They defined themselves as Protestants struggling for*
> *survival against the world's foremost Catholic Power. They defined them-*
> *selves against the French as they imagined them to be, superstitious,*
> *militarist, decadent and unfree.*[1]

For Colley, being British in the eighteenth century was primarily a case
of being not French. But she also notes the way in which this development of Britishness was influenced by imperial expansion:

> *And, increasingly as the wars went on, they [the Britons] defined them-*
> *selves in contrast to the colonial peoples they conquered, peoples who were*

manifestly alien in terms of culture, religion and colour. . . . They came to define themselves as a single people not because of any political or cultural consensus at home, but rather in reaction to the Other beyond their shores.[2]

In their wars with the French, the British found themselves acquiring Canada, India and the West Indies. Being British meant not being French, but it also meant being white and not black.

Colley is keen to stress, however, that whatever definitions that emerged from this contact with various Others, new national identities did not supplant older loyalties:

Identities are not like hats. Human beings can and do put on several at a time. Great Britain did not emerge by way of a 'blending' of the different regional or older national cultures contained within its boundaries as is sometimes maintained, nor is its genesis to be explained primarily in terms of an English 'core' imposing its cultural and political hegemony on a helpless and defrauded Celtic periphery. As even the briefest acquaintance with Great Britain will confirm, the Welsh, the Scottish and the English remain in many ways distinct peoples in cultural terms, just as all three countries continue to be conspicuously sub-divided into different regions.[3]

As the passage from Will Sayer's diary demonstrates, the development of a British national identity did not invalidate a sense of being Welsh or from Staffordshire.

The imperial historian, P. J. Marshall, also argues that the experience of empire contributed to the development of Britishness: 'In the late eighteenth century, some merging of identities between the peoples of the United Kingdom of Great Britain and Ireland was producing a new sense of "Britishness". . . . But empire did more than reflect the Britishness of the British in Britain; it helped to focus and develop it.'[4] Yet if Marshall, unlike Colley, accepts that Britishness was produced out of a 'blending' of the constituent national loyalties of the United Kingdom, he goes further than Colley in arguing that the Britishness of the settler colonies was produced from a greater degree of blending. Pointing out that in the colonies neither the Scots, the Welsh, the Irish nor the English were able to impose their identity on any of the others, Marshall notes: 'Those who had settled the empire generally experienced a greater sense of undifferentiated Britishness than those who stayed at home and emigrants who returned to Britain no doubt brought that sense of Britishness with them.'[5] If Marshall is correct that a blending of national loyalties in the colonies produced 'a greater sense of undifferentiated Britishness,' then it would mean that the inhabitants of nineteenth-century Australia were in fact more British than the inhabitants of Britain itself, where individuals might still regard themselves primarily as English or Scottish. As James Jupp points out: 'Australia had become by 1940 what no other nation in the world could claim to be – a truly British, Anglo-Celtic society. Britain, although increasingly dominated by the English and then by the southern English, has never attained such a degree of homogenisation and uniformity.'[6]

The extent to which Britishness was more evenly developed in Australia, New Zealand and Canada is an intriguing question. From an Australian perspective, the argument is more usually that any blending of identities in Australia produced an Australian and not a British identity. As Percy Rowland argued in 1902: 'as the old provincial sentiments and characteristics die out, new ones are formed to take their place. The more the Englishman ceases to feel himself a Yorkshireman or a Devonian, the more he begins to feel himself an Australian.'[7] Such arguments prompt the question: in comparison with the inhabitants of Britain, were visitors from Australia more British or more Australian? The evidence of their diaries and letters is inconclusive because for them being British and being Australian were not such mutually exclusive categories as they are assumed to be today. Despite the ways in which Australia and Australians were represented as the opposite of Britain and the British, it would be quite wrong to regard Britain and Australia in the nineteenth century as though they were in some form of antipodean relationship: the British respecters of rank, the Australians egalitarian; the British reserved, the Australians frank; the British bad tempered, the Australian good-humoured; and so on. Colley may be correct about the relationship between the British and the French in the eighteenth-century, but in the nineteenth century, as today, there were too many similarities between the inhabitants of Australia and Britain for Australians to be regarded by the British as their antithesis.

In John Rae's case, the overlap between a British and an Australian identity is inherent in Rae's background as a migrant from Scotland. But many Australian-born visitors to Britain had an equally strong sense of their Britishness. Mary Kater, daughter of a former New South Wales Premier, was born in Australia and, accompanied by her husband, she made her first trip to Europe in 1875. For Kater, as for many Australians travelling abroad for the first time, the voyage to Europe made her aware of herself as an Australian in new ways. After changing ship in

Galle, Kater noted in her diary how she as an Australian differed from the British returning from India: 'I have come to the conclusion that our Australian climate is not quite so bad after all – We Australians can stand both heat and cold much better than the Indian passengers' (4 February 1875). Passing overland from Suez to Alexandria, Kater sailed to Brindisi to tour Italy and to head for London via Switzerland and France. In Rome, Kater compared the Papal city with Naples in terms of the differing perceptions of the English and Australians: 'It is an old saying "See Naples and then die" – but I would much rather give up my remembrance of Naples than of Rome – Of course it is the scenery, the natural beauties, of Naples that people go into raptures over – The Bay is very lovely and seems to strike English eyes as very beautiful, but then they have never seen *Sydney Harbour'* (21 March 1875). In her determination to assert a distinct Australian identity, Kater may well be oversimplifying. But she is nonetheless aware of the need to assert a difference between seeing Naples through English and through Australian eyes.

And yet, although Kater was Australian born, England was immediately familiar to her, and her arrival in London came as a welcome relief from Continental languages, cultures and cooking:

> *By rail to Calais, & then across the Channel and on to London – It was so pleasant to feel oneself in an English speaking country again – We felt at home at once at the railway-station and all the officials are so much more polite than they are on the Continent – We reached the 'Great Western Hotel['] between six and seven and Harry [her husband] went round to see Mrs Kater after dinner[.] We enjoyed an English Beef steak so much after the French dishes – they dont know how to cook meat in the English fashion and if you ask for Roast Beef they give you 'Fillet de Boeuf' which is meat first partially boiled, in order to extract the goodness out of it to make soup of, and just browned before the fire[,] of course it is a very economical way of using the meat[.] (15 April)*

Having travelled halfway around the world, Mary Kater had arrived in an overseas country which her upbringing and education had prepared her to call 'home'. In this way, the voyage Home strengthened not only her sense of being Australian by offering the contrasting experiences of the British, the familiarity of Britain itself strengthened her sense of being British. As Philip Phillips expressed it in 1889: 'soon found ourselves in Trafalgar Square[.] Spotted St Pauls in the distance & felt *at home'* (19 April).

One indication of the difficulty of defining the Britishness of nine-teenth-century Australians is that there is no satisfactory term to describe them. The inhabitants of the six Australian colonies have been variously described as Colonials, Anglo-Colonials, Colonial Australians, United Kingdom colonists, Australian Britons, Southern Britons and British Australians. It is often easier to refer to them simply as Australians, though this disguises the fact that being Australian in the nineteenth century was not the same as being Australian today. In any case, the plain term Australian is often replaced in multicultural Australia as Anglo-Australian, Anglo-Saxon or Anglo-Celtic, terms which complicate (and possibly racialize) rather than simplify the def-inition of Australians of British or Irish descent. A key problem is that we have no term for an inhabitant of the United Kingdom, a term which, if it existed, could be widely used because it includes the Irish in a way in which the term 'British' may not. But then not all the Irish would have wanted to be associated with the English under the one heading.

The truth is, of course, that there is no such thing as the British, if by 'British' we mean a people with a common culture, religion, language and social structure. There is not even a common British law, Scotland having its own judicial system. For the same reason, there is no such thing as a Yugoslav or a Malaysian. It might be better to use terms refer-ring to nationality to indicate citizenship of a political entity, and say that citizens of the Australian colonies were also citizens of the United Kingdom. This definition accords with the free movement of travellers in both directions, and the fact that passports issued to Australians did not distinguish between British and Australian citizenship until the Chifley Government's Nationality and Citizenship Act 1948, which came into effect on Australia Day 1949. In terms of their nationality as travellers, nineteenth-century Australians were British citizens.

But they were also British according to a more fundamental notion of Britishness. Mary Kater felt at home in London because she spoke English, she recognised certain forms of behaviour, she could enjoy the kinds of food she was used to, and other family members lived there. In other words, by and large she was culturally at home. But British iden-tity in Kater's time was considered not simply a matter of culture, or even of citizenship; it was considered a matter of race. The humanitari-anism that lay behind the abolition of slavery at the beginning of the nineteenth century gradually hardened into a theory, or more properly a collection of theories, which asserted that the cultural and industrial superiority of the British was a manifestation of the superiority of the

British as a race. Colonial settlement was therefore concerned with transplanting the British race abroad, as Mary Kater herself notes in her diary: 'England seems to be too full – and Australia seems to be the natural outlet for the teeming population, and it seems to me that she must have a wonderful future before her as the home of the English race who cannot live for ever in this little island already too small for them' (14 June 1875). Of course, for settlement to be successful, the British race must reproduce itself, and do so without degenerating into the savagery, both racial and moral, of the indigenous peoples. Women of the settler colonies of Australia, New Zealand and Canada were specifically charged with the reproduction of the British race abroad; and in sporting competitions, such as rowing or cricket, their sons had to test themselves against the young men of Britain, a test that was as much a test of racial purity as of sporting capabilities. As James Thomson, the Secretary of the Victorian Commission at the 1886 Colonial and Indian Exhibition in London, put it: while the inhabitants of Victoria are proud of their colony, 'they are also proud of being Australians of British blood'. And he added: 'that the British race in Victoria does not suffer deterioration is amply proved by the fact that in each of the University boats in the memorable race of the Third of April last was a Victorian born oarsman'.[8]

In this sense, the British as a nation exceeded any geographical identity. People were British, however that may have been defined, not by living in Britain and sharing a common culture, but by feeling British. Although many saw themselves as racially British, whether or not they supported that by any particular racial theory, the important point is that it enabled them to imagine themselves as part of a wider or Greater Britain. To be a Briton was not only to claim an ancient heritage traceable to the so-called ancient Britons, the inhabitants of Britain before the Roman conquest, but to claim a racial identity as an inhabitant of the British Empire.

From our vantage point of the late twentieth century, we can see that the inhabitants of Britain were in fact a rag bag of overlapping language groups, ethnic groups, social groups, and so on. The nineteenth-century racial theorists nonetheless tried to isolate the characteristics of what they regarded as the constituent racial groups, the Anglo-Saxons coming out on top, the Celts hardly registering, their traits being described by the eugenicist Robert Knox in 1862 as: 'Furious fanaticism; a love of war and disorder; a hatred for order and patient industry; no accumulative habits; restless, treacherous, uncertain: look at Ireland.'[9] Given such a diverse population, it is unsurprising that definitions of

Britishness change over time and are themselves the product of struggle and debate, both between and within the diverse interest groups that constitute a society. However, this is not to say that that there were no agreed markers of Britishness in the late nineteenth century. On the contrary, the more diverse a population, the more necessary the symbols indicating commonality may be. Statues of Queen Victoria were erected in public spaces right around the empire. The British stood to attention before their national flag and throughout the playing of their national anthem. Monarchs, flags and anthems were the stuff of the European nation state; and in the development of red areas on the imperial maps, they became the stuff of the British colonies as well.

Those red areas of the British imperial map which seemed to assert a uniform Britishness were another means of creating a sense of feeling British. Maps, flags, and portraits of the monarch were part of the furniture of the late nineteenth-century school. But British maps denoted, above all, material possession: possession by an imperial power of the peoples and the wealth of lands beyond Great Britain. In the imagined geography of empire, Britain was the mother country, the colonies her children. The model of empire in the later nineteenth century was that of a metropolis distributing civilization and economic investment through its agents and migrants, while receiving in return a tribute in the form of raw materials for its factories; the mills of Britain were dependent on imports of colonial wool and cotton. In this model, there was a dominant centre and a dependent periphery, with the sea and British naval supremacy providing a symbolic cordon sanitaire against unwelcome foreign influences. The British Empire may have been celebrated for its geographical diversity, but it depended on a clear geographical centre and a clear sense of us versus them. In order to maintain that sense of territorial integrity essential to the modern nation state, the Other needed to be clearly demarcated as Other.

Always problematic, since 1945 it has become even more difficult to define nations geographically. In Britain, the 1950s saw the beginnings of large-scale migration, first from the Caribbean and then from the Indian sub-continent, as Britain sought to support postwar economic growth by increasing its labour force. In Australia and for a similar underlying reason, the Labor government of the immediate postwar period facilitated the migration of large numbers of people displaced by the war in Europe, most notably from eastern and southern Europe. In both countries, it was clear by the 1970s that policies of assimilation, whereby migrants rapidly became indistinguishable from the dominant cultural identity, would not work. Being British or Australian did not exclude a continuing sense of being Jamaican or Indian, Serbian or Greek. And not only have geographical divisions between peoples with differing ethnicities now been resituated within the nation, the globalization of capital, telecommunications and the media has caused a diminishing of the influence of the nation state over the national economy and national cultural production. In reaction to what many regard as an erosion of national identity, it is not surprising that images of a 'purer' nationhood continue to be evoked, be they images of a pedigree British royal family or images of Anzac service men and women fighting abroad.

The political and intellectual pressures to reappraise the idea of the nation since the 1970s has led to a historical reassessment of the Britishness of both Britain and Australia in the nineteenth century. In Australia, for example, historians have been keen to stress the ethnic diversity of nineteenth-century Australia, and to gauge the influence of European migrants, such as migrants from Germany and Scandinavia, on the development of Australian society. There has also been greater recognition of the history of the Chinese in Australia, though the phrase 'the Chinese in Australia' is one to which Jan Ryan, for good reason, objects:

> *Where are the Chinese in the history books of Australia? There is a proliferation of ethnic histories of Chinese, Japanese, Irish, Hungarian, Italians in Australia. There are local studies on Chinese in Australia (or Chinese in Victoria or in New South Wales), but the Chinese are not there in our grand national histories and the token fragments that are included retain familiar stereotypes of Chinese as a homogeneous 'race', a detached entity, with a separate and alien identity. By such inclusion they remain excluded.*[10]

Revised histories are clearly important in reappraising the contemporary nature of Australian society, and in this context, the treatment of the Aboriginal peoples of Australia and their long and hard won recognition to be regarded as indigenous Australians cannot be forgotten. As the 1997 'Bringing them Home' report into the Stolen Generations emphasised, reconciliation between indigenous and non-indigenous Australians cannot be satisfactorily achieved without a wider understanding of the history of the dispossession of the original inhabitants of Australia.

In terms of the Britishness of Great Britain, the work of British historian Catherine Hall has been exemplary in demonstrating ways in which the histories of the Caribbean or Australia are connected to the histories of industrial British cities such as Birmingham.[11] What such pioneering work calls for is no less than a history of Britain as a postcolonial nation. To the extent that the term 'postcolonial' is more often used to refer to colonies that have achieved a sovereign independence, such a definition retains the geographical division between us and them, between (ex-)imperial centre and (ex-)colonial periphery. A postcolonial history of Britain, on the other hand, will not only enable British people descended from the peoples of the so-called periphery to find their history within Britain, it will enable us to see how nineteenth-century Britain was itself shaped by the experience of empire, sometimes literally so in the shape of the built environment.[12] There were numerous ways in which Britain was moulded by empire, and in sketching these, historians may have to consider writing histories that no longer take the nation state for granted. As Antoinette Burton puts it in her study of Indians in Britain: 'Few can escape the struggle over geography, and British history in an age of postcoloniality is no exception. If narratives of geography are at stake in narratives of history, then in the end making colonial people in Victorian England subjects of history may mean displacing nation-states like Britain and even India from center stage.'[13] If empire was a globalizing force, then the histories of empire also need to be global.

The British people most directly influenced by contact with non-European societies and environments were those British men and women who were themselves displaced and who spent periods abroad, as soldiers, colonial administrators, missionaries, migrants, and so on. Catherine Hall cites the example of Edward Eyre (1815–1901), whose career as squatter, explorer and colonial administrator took him to Australia, New Zealand and the Caribbean. Hall plots Eyre's changing attitudes towards black people, from one of intellectual equality (when he lived in Australia) to one of intellectual inferiority (when he lived in Jamaica), and relates this progression not only to Eyre himself but to broader changes in definitions of Britishness.[14] Elsewhere Hall considers how the Australian experiences of Robert Lowe (1811–92) not only influenced Lowe himself but were later used by Lowe, as a Member of the British Parliament, to argue against an extension of the franchise in 1867. Lowe argued against universal suffrage on the grounds that if such rights existed, 'they are as much the property of the Australian savage and the Hottentot of the Cape as of the educated and refined Englishman'.[15]

The experiences of the British abroad in this way indirectly influenced those who remained in Britain, as Daniel Matthews from Victoria noted while visiting his childhood home in Cornwall in 1869:

Made a call at my old school. The master kindly allowed me to pass through, and conversed with me for more than an hour about the colonies. The system of results, that has been for six years employed in the colony of Victoria, is now in vogue in England, and was introduced by Robert Lowe, one of the colonial senators, but now a member of parliament in England, and Chancellor of the Exchequer. (8 September 1869)

In this way, ideas and practices that were developed within the empire fed back into the ideas and practices of Britain.

Mary Louise Pratt has reversed the ethnographic concept of transculturation, the selection and reinvention of metropolitan culture by those on the imperial periphery, to examine the effects of the periphery on the metropolis: 'While the imperial metropolis tends to understand itself as determining the periphery (in the emanating glow of the civilizing mission or the cash flow of development, for example), it habitually blinds itself to the ways in which the periphery determines the metropolis.'[16] Gillian Whitlock has applied this notion of transculturation to books of household management written by colonial women, such as Lady Barker (1831–1911) who was born in Jamaica and kept house in India, New Zealand, Natal, Mauritius and Western Australia. Barker published eight books, among them *A Year's Housekeeping in South Africa* (1880), and while living in England she served as Lady Superintendent of the new National School of Cookery. Whitlock concludes that: 'Traffic between the imperial centre and the colonies was two way: ideas of domestic order and hygiene which were taught to the English population were in part produced overseas and imported back "home".'[17]

There were more material results of reverse transculturation. The imperial historian, John MacKenzie, has examined the numerous ways in which exotic artefacts encountered through imperial expansion influenced British design and architecture in the nineteenth and early twentieth century. Of Victorian and Edwardian artists, MacKenzie has written: 'Theirs was the first age in which almost all the cultures of the world had been made available through writings, illustrations, museums, photography (later film) and increased opportunities for safe travel itself.'[18] Exotic artefacts themselves were most often to be found in ethnological collections in museums, stimulating debates about human evolution and the place of the British in the world. The 1851

Great Exhibition and its successor, the Sydenham Crystal Palace, displayed artefacts from British imperial possessions in such a way as to depict human development as a gradual evolution from the Aboriginal Tasmanian to the middle-class Englishman.

The great paradox of imperial transculturation, then, is that on the one hand the British saw themselves as racially distinct from the peoples of the Empire, protected from the savagery of the periphery by distance and their own civilized and civilising values. On the other hand, British culture was itself developed out of contact with other societies, and was dependent on the presence within Britain of numerous traces of the empire. Traces of Australia, for example, were avidly noted by Australian visitors in their diaries and letters. They sniffed the wattle blossom in botanical glasshouses, they bought Australian beef, wool and Tasmanian apples, and they spotted gum trees just about everywhere. They found Australian birds and snakes at the zoo. They noted illustrations and the produce of Australia at exhibitions. In 1883, Emma Walker found Australian birds in the York Museum alongside Roman relics: 'In the afternoon visited with Mr G the Museum, where I saw a few familiar birds from South Australia, and from the other colonies, and countries. For the first time in my life I saw the skeleton of the earliest bird of New Zealand – the Moa – a great deal larger than an Ostrich' (20 July 1883).

Yet more subtly, Australian visitors themselves were evidence of transculturation. They exchanged cooees with other Australians, sought out Australian entries in visitors books and brought fresh news to friends or family members who had returned to live in Britain. In describing Australia to the British, they often acted as unofficial migration agents. And many men combined visiting family with visiting factories where they ordered goods, anything from a piano to a railway carriage, to take back to Australia with them; they participated in an imperial economy which generated a constant circulation of credit, produce, and people. British imperial territories could not be kept at arms length, and the global dynamics of empire ensured that the Britishness of the inhabitants of Britain was fundamentally influenced by visible and invisible forms of cultural exchange. Strange peoples and environments could not be contained on what was regarded as the periphery of empire and, like the returned convict Magwitch in *Great Expectations*, such peoples could very often be found much nearer to home.

Magwitch, though, was hardly a representative figure of the returned Australian. Until the Great War, the cost of the trip back Home limited visitors to members of the upper middle class. Thomas Anderson returned to his native Scotland in 1851 after an absence of nine years, during which time he seems to have prospered as a squatter near Mount Elephant in what is now western Victoria. In December 1850 and in his late thirties, Anderson married Joan McLaurin, a young woman twenty years younger than himself who had arrived from Scotland only a year previously. Both Joan and Thomas kept diaries of their trip Home, but Anderson also kept a detailed and revealing set of accounts. The passage from Melbourne to London on the *Nelson* cost £140, though there were many additional expenses, such as Anderson's diary (3 shillings) and the purchase of 'chest of drawers for own use on board' (£4 6s), expenses that brought the total cost of getting the two of them married and then to London to more or less £300. The cost of the three weeks they spent in London before they went north to Scotland was a further £120, and they spent £230 in the following twelve months. Overall, the cost of the trip would have been over £700. To give an idea of the scale of the expense, the average yearly wage of an agricultural worker in England was about £25 to £30.

Joan and Thomas Anderson remained in Britain for sixteen months, during which time Joan gave birth to their first child, Tommy, and though they generally stayed with relatives, the cost of such a trip would have been well beyond most of the Australian population throughout the nineteenth century. The cost decreased with the coming of steamers, but the volume of Australian visitors to Britain was never large, and the number of British citizens arriving in British ports from Australia and New Zealand was no more than 2,000 in 1876. From 1876 to 1887 the numbers of arrivals, which also included short-term British visitors to Australia and migrants returning permanently to Britain, increased from 2,000 to 10,000, the number remaining steady to the end of the century.[19] As Richard White has shown, the first opportunity for working-class Australians to experience Britain in any number was during the Great War, when 330,000 Australian men out of an Australian population of 5,000,000 served in Europe.[20]

Because only the social elite of Australia was able to afford the trip to Britain, the kind of experience to be found in the diaries and letters of the time reflected the culture and general outlook of the colonial haute bourgeoisie for whom a trip Home could be seen as a rite of passage into a select social group. As the historian Ros Pesman notes, because of its cost the trip Home had social prestige 'as a ritual event, a rite-of-passage, a convention in Australian middle-class social and cultural life, an event that had its beginnings in the first return voyages from Sydney Cove to Plymouth.'[21] The class nature of the voyage to Britain has been cited as one reason why nineteenth-century Australian travel writing has been to a great extent ignored by both historians and literary critics: 'For most of Australia's history, travel has been the preserve of the middle class, a middle class often seen as not being particularly relevant to the creation of Australian culture or society, least of all when enjoying the frivolity of leisurely overseas travel.'[22] Yet if, as Linda Colley and P. J. Marshall both argued, British national identity was formed through contact with those peoples and environments lying beyond the shores of Britain, then Australian identity was in the same way formed by Australians travelling abroad. The point is made by Ros Pesman herself:

> *To place Australian experience in a wider framework is not to reject Australian nationality and culture, but to emphasise their connections with the rest of the world, their porous and permeable qualities. Identity and nationality are, like everything else, not fixed structures, but processes in the making. There is no Australian 'identity', only 'identities', and these have been forged abroad as well as at home, in contact and collision with others, as well as in isolation.*[23]

Such a role for middle-class colonial Australians has been overshadowed not only by an assumption that middle-class experience is not part of an Australian culture, but by the commonplace that Australia achieved its nationhood through young working-class Australians fighting alongside first the British and later the Americans in overseas wars. According to this model, following the birth of the Australian nation in 1901, subsequent stages of national maturity have been marked by the landings at Gallipoli in 1915 or the fighting along the Kokoda Trail in Papua New Guinea in 1942, with conception having occurred in the Sudan in 1885 or in southern Africa between 1899 and 1902, depending on your choice of war.

However, the relative lack of interest in Australians travelling abroad in the nineteenth century is not due solely to the social status of the travellers, and many Australians still regard colonial Australia as essentially British. Post-Federation nationalism has gradually replaced earlier symbols of the birth of Australia, the landings of James Cook in 1770 or Arthur Phillip in 1788, with twentieth-century anniversaries, such as Anzac Day, and Ros Pesman appears to concur with Walker and White in viewing nineteenth-century travel writing as pre-Australian:

Australian Colonial Identity

Throughout the nineteenth century, most Australians overseas saw themselves simply as British travellers, making no great distinction between their reactions and what they imagined were those of the British abroad. If they did think of themselves as diverging from the norm, it was in being a colonial variant rather than being distinctively Australian.[24]

This view of the nineteenth century as a prelude to a fuller and more authentic Australianness begs a number of questions.

Many Australian travellers in the nineteenth century certainly did regard themselves as colonials, and they also thought of themselves, by and large, as British. But that did not mean they had no idea of themselves as distinctively Australian. Take, for example, Mary Kater negotiating with her landlady for some lodgings:

Before we went there [their Albion Street lodgings] the old woman Mrs Baker was rather nervous about taking children, she said they did so much mischief, and she was still more uneasy about having a servant, as she said nurses and ladies-maids were generally such fine ladies that they wanted more waiting on than their mistresses, and waiting on in London houses is no sinecure, if they have to go from the kitchen four pairs of stairs to the very top of the house, for the nursery was at the top of the house, just above our room – However when I said Lizzie was no fine lady, but an Australian girl who was not used to be waited upon, and could have her meals in the kitchen, she seemed to look at things in a different light. (24 May 1875)

Mary Kater regarded herself as English, but, as in her preference for Rome over Naples, she used her diary to assert what she regarded as distinct Australian characteristics and a distinctly Australian way of viewing the world.

This sense of being an Australian has been too easily ignored. An Australian colonial identity is seen as either a British identity contaminated by living in Australia, or an Australian identity contaminated by an adherence to British cultural values. It is viewed as a variant of something else and therefore not authentic. This may partly stem from an anxiety about Australia's British heritage, an unease with the idea that an Australian identity may still today share aspects of a British identity. Yet the Australianness of 'the colonial variant' can be recovered by reference to Australia's multicultural and postcolonial condition. Ros Pesman in stating that 'There is no Australian "identity", only 'identities",' voices a modern suspicion held by many Australians, predominantly of the political left, that images of a typical Australian male, such as the Digger, disguise the multicultural nature of contemporary society. I should stress that I am not arguing that we can recoup a middle-class colonial identity under the banner of multiculturalism, yet there are clear continuities between the colonial and the postcolonial; as Stoler and Cooper put it: 'the current emphasis on the hybridities and fractured identities of the postcolonial moment looks far less distinctive when the interstitiality of colonial lives is brought back into sharper relief.'[25] The complexities of colonial identities should not be dismissed merely because, like multicultural or postcolonial identities, they appear to be 'variants' or hybrids. If we cannot dismiss other loyalties in the late twentieth century, why should we continue to do so for the late nineteenth century?

The challenge is in trying to comprehend what it meant to think of oneself as Australian in the nineteenth century. In their diaries and letters home, Australians wrote of the similarities and differences they noticed between Britain and Australia and in so doing they enacted a sense of their own Australianness. Again we can quote Mary Kater:

> *People certainly live in great comfort, not to say luxury in England[.] I remember Miss Badcock who had spent one year in Australia in the bush, telling me that the one thing that would strike me most in England would be the comfort in which people lived, and certainly it does strike me. They are able to make themselves so comfortable – With all the quiet, and the thousand charms of a country life they can have every luxury they wish for[.] (14 June)*

Mary Kater maps out for herself an Australian identity by noting in her diary how the English differ. Richard Hannan does much the same thing seventeen years later in 1892:

> *there was nothing extraordinary to relate about today but I have noticed a few things while walking about London which would seem rather strange to an Australian. . . . I have often been told about the want of Urinals in Australian Cities & that London is better supplied with these very necessary accommodations even if they are a bit obnoxious to the fastidious taste. London might be better supplied than an Australian City for there are plenty of posts in the city & cab wheels are not scarce, both of which I have seen used in broad daylight & in busy throughfares. in fact the cabman that drove Mr Dibbs luggage from Fenchurch St Station to Metropole gave me my first surprise. I will endeavour to relate*

*now. There was a crush at Station [sic] everyone was trying to get lug-
gage in cabs & carriages which were scarce. it was a case of you must
first catch your cab & then get your luggage. well after some little delay
I captured cab but it had no driver. a street Arab informed me he had just
gone round er corner ter ave er drink. at last he arrived a real beer eater
as they say in Australia. We shoved some of the luggage on & I thought
it was better for me to stand by as the sailors say as there was some queer
looking fellows about & I have heard some stories of how quick a London
theif [sic] is. The driver had mounted his box when all of a sudden down
he walked. I was standing on the kerb & I could see him through the win-
dow looking very intently at his boots so I walked round & there he was
in the middle of the crowded street as if it was a dark night in the bush.
but I soon got used to that sort of thing. I don't know how much hard he
would have got for it if he did it at Redfern Railway Station. (21 June
1892)*

Australians expressed in their diaries and letters ways in which they
were Australian, and in so doing these accounts became a powerful
medium for reflecting on what it meant to be Australian. Indeed, the act
of writing home itself could move the writer to affirm a national identity. Thomas Lloyd migrated as a young man in the mid 1850s, and
having referred to Britain as home for 27 years, he discovered through
visiting Britain that Australia was now his home: 'I spent this forenoon
in writing home. It seems strange to call Australia home. But so it is to
me' (8 September 1883).

Visitors to Britain like Mary Kater, Richard Hannan and Thomas
Lloyd came to realise that being Australian and being British were not
necessarily the same thing. Yet they nonetheless retained a belief in
themselves as both Australian and British; having a hybrid identity is
not the same as relinquishing loyalty to a place or nation. The
complexity of being a colonial Australian is captured by Thomas Lodge
Murray-Prior's response to a question asked him at his hotel in London:
'An old clergyman sitting near me asked me a question – if I was a
foreigner. but telling him no[,] an Australian' (14 June 1882). Australians
were therefore outsiders who were also on the inside; they regarded
themselves as something more than mere sightseers, a term they applied
especially to Americans, yet they were aware that they were not of
Britain. As Margaret Tripp put it on arriving in London in 1872: the
places of London 'had so long had an imaginary being in one's mind,
that it was strange to see them translated into a drab bricks and mortar'
(2 May 1872). This awareness of being British but not of Britain meant

that Australians were and were not British. They were the same and yet different.

It was this element of difference that made an Australian identity unlike a British regional identity. Being Welsh, Scottish or, as in Will Sayer's case, from Staffordshire did not make one less British, yet being Australian could clash with being British in a way in which being Welsh or Scottish did not. Inside Australia, and excluding the distinction between the Irish and the British, this was perhaps less of a problem, but visiting Britain had the potential to make Australians aware of their differing loyalties and their hybrid identities. Margaret Tripp found herself being shown round London by two 'orientals,' as she calls them, both of whom were amused by knowing London better than Tripp: 'Tafar especially was very affable, & we talked a good deal, he pointing out to me all the buildings of note that we passed, and, until the cause of my benighted ignorance was explained, opening his eyes at meeting with an English person who did not know Nelson's monument' (2 May 1872). In being both English and yet not quite English, Margaret Tripp was made conscious of the 'benighted ignorance' of being Australian.

Being Australian in nineteenth-century Britain could therefore be discomforting; Australians might share the security of being British in Britain, but they also suffered the dilemma of not knowing quite where their Britishness stopped and their Australianness began. Being British and being Australian were not antipodean opposites, were not defined against each other like summer and winter, and there was no clear line of demarcation. Australians could be British or not British depending on context, and they might on occasion believe themselves to be both. Today we might view their dilemma as the result of a failure to be fully Australian, a symptom of an immature Australian national identity. Yet the inclusivity of an identity that could, like John Rae's, be Scottish, British and Australian questions the essentialism implicit in late twentieth-century national identities, questions the assumption that to belong to one nation one must abandon other national loyalties. A colonial identity had its disadvantages, and at least some of the praise of Australia to be heard in the letters and diaries of Australians in Britain must have been a reaction to the snobbery displayed towards colonials. But the colonial Australian was a product of cultural displacement, a displacement that paradoxically allowed Australians to visit Britain and still feel at home. Australians could feel at home in either hemisphere, and indeed, it may well be that Australia was defined as much by Australians travelling north as by those who remained in the south.

As I have already indicated, there are continuities between a colonial and a post-colonial Australian identity. But there is also something to be learned from a British perspective; there are, if we follow Catherine Hall, ways of re-thinking the British Empire that point to the possibility of replacing the divisive exclusivity of contemporary nationalism with something more inclusive:

> *If it is to be possible to construct myths which could bind Europeans together in ways that are inclusive not exclusive, not reminiscent of 'Fortress Europe' with its boundaries firmly in place against brown, black and yellow migrants, then we need to begin the work of remembering empires differently. Such a project might begin from the recognition of inter-connection and inter-dependence, albeit structured through power, rather than a notion of hierarchy with the 'centre' firmly in place and the 'peripheries' marginalised.*[26]

Read in a certain way, the accounts of Australians in imperial Britain stress the importance of cultural displacement in the creation of national identity and offer us an alternative to dividing the peoples of the world into those of the centre and those of the periphery. And with luck, we may take from them an understanding of the continuing place of Australia within Europe and Europe within Australia.

TWO

Familiar and Yet Strange: First Experiences of Britain

'even my brothers are unknown to me'

It was about one PM of Wednesday the 23rd day of September, 1846 – a day as beautiful as any the sun ever shone on, that I left the 'Royal George' & boarded a small boat of about ten tons, being at that time about forty miles off the Isle of Wight – this was after a long voyage of better than five months from Port Phillip New South Wales round that never to be forgotten scene of horrors Cape Horn – but however I must not go back-wards in my journal or but poor progrefs* will be made – the day as I said before was fine but the wind evidently was brewing for bad weather – the appearance of Old England after an absence of more than seven years was thrilling – beyond anything & my heart beat high with anticipation as our gallant little boat stemmed the now rapidly rising sea – first to fsed on the top of one wave and then thrown into the bottom of another – whilst far off in the distance was that fine old ship the Royal George in which I had spent so many days – one cannot help feeling sorry at leaving a home – for verily it had been a home though a stormy and dangerous one, yet still it was home.

In the decades that followed William Postlethwaite's passage from Port Phillip on the *Royal George*, the voyage to Europe became quicker and less dangerous, but the experience of the voyage, be it a voyage of five months under sail round Cape Horn or six weeks by steam through the Suez Canal, frequently resulted in passengers forming an attachment to the vessel. The ship provided food, accommodation, and a

---

* The long *s* as in *progrefs* and *tofsed* that was a common feature of English handwriting until the late nineteenth century has been retained in quotations.

relatively safe environment; but it also provided companionship and a diversity of social spaces, such as cabins, dining rooms and promenade decks, in which cultural identities could be practised and maintained. The ship was home because its physical spaces had become familiar social spaces.

When the time came to leave that home, many travellers understandably felt uneasy or vulnerable; and when they disembarked at one of the southern English ports such as Plymouth or Portsmouth, they tended to stay in a group, either to go sightseeing or to travel straight on to London. Such behaviour is in one way unremarkable, and package tours today often display a similar group psychology. But for Australians reaching Britain, the traveller's uneasiness in a strange environment was compounded by deeper fears of a loss of identity.

After spending the night in Portsmouth, Postlethwaite and his companions looked over Nelson's flagship, the *Victory*, and were shown round the naval dockyards. In his journal, Postlethwaite dramatises his signing of the visitors book:

after I had entered my name in the book I observed a second column for the calling of the individual signing – Now not knowing exactly what to put down I turned to one of my friends and asked him to clear me of the difficulty – he jocosely answered 'why you cannot call yourself a gentleman, therefore put down your true calling without prevarication – write – squatter' *– Now I must here observe that the room was filled with visitors all waiting for the book to enter their names, and after mine was duly inserted & it is no little one either – the old man who acts as Clerk or Porter at the gate – (a man who the moment you looked at him reminded you of Roast Beef or an alderman) took up the Book to see what I was – for they are very particular as to who visits the Yards – Foreigners not being allowed to enter at all – Well the old man looked first straight at the Book – then sideways – then crofsways – then put it under him – then took out his glafses – still no better – & whilst he rubbed them, he cast his little eyes up to me, I suppose to see whether there was anything in my countenance that indicated humbug – he was apparently satisfied & by this time the glafses were clean, and again placed acrofs the nose[.] Still the word appeared to bother him – again he tried this time spelling it S.Q.U.A.T. Squat – Ter – ter 'Squatter' said he – Yes – said I – 'What does that mean' – Bushman I answered – '& What's that' said the old man again – Why Stockholder – returned I again. 'And what the Devil is that' said the little pompous man – Why a Backwoodsman said I – By this time the company were drawing near us, enjoying the fun most*

*heartily [–] the girls tittered, the gentlemen laughed outright – so did I –
for I was but just ashore and determined to be amused with everything –
the old man found that it was uselefs asking any further questions &
whether he has ever discovered the meaning of the entry in his Book – viz.
W. Postlethwaite. Squatter. P.P. New South Wales is now as great a
mystery to me – as it was to that jolly looking – though very snappish old
gentleman, on that eventful morning – (24 September 1846)*

As a young man just turned twenty-seven years old, Postlethwaite
was clearly intent on having a young man's fun. Yet the joke against the
clerk at the dockyard is double-edged. The clerk recognises
Postlethwaite's social standing, yet is unable to place him because of the
ambivalence of his Australian identity: as a squatter from New South
Wales, Postlethwaite is both foreign and English. When they signed visitors books at cultural sites, Australians were generally quick to note the
signatures of previous Australian visitors; and they were uneasy about
the guardian's reaction.

Questions of cultural identity became more serious when they
affected the relationship between the visitors and their British families.
Postlethwaite was born in Lancashire in 1819 and migrated to Australia
in 1839. Having been away for seven years, he was very warmly
received by his brother, James:

*I need not repeat how glad he & Annie were to see me – but I may with
propriety remark that there was a young man in the room who appeared
to addrefs me with a great deal of familiarity & who I did not know in
the slightest – 'do you know me said he?' – No, I returned – 'I am your
brother Tom' – Surely it is a pity I thought to return to a Land where I
am even forgotten by my friends & where even my brothers are unknown
to me – (25 September)*

Tom had evidently been quite young when his brother had migrated,
and this failure of recognition was clearly embarrassing and unpleasant
to both brothers. It was an embarrassment that became increasingly
disagreeable to Postlethwaite with each successive failure of recognition:

*In the afternoon called on my Cousins the Mifs Postlethwaites – here
again I had to make myself known – this I find is growing too disagreeable – none can understand the feeling excepting they who have
experienced it – to remedy it – I shall invariably send in my Card & have*

Port Phillip printed on it – this will remedy one half of the error – remove their difficulty – & my half of the unpleasantnefs I must fight through as best I can – (3 October)

What was a joking matter the day after his arrival in Britain becomes irritation enough for Postlethwaite to take the trouble to announce his identity before meeting his relatives and friends. But, as he admitted, such a strategy did not entirely solve his own difficulties, and even on the steamer from Fleetwood to his home in Dalton he finds himself having to go to absurd lengths to avoid embarrassment:

There was a gentleman on board her whose countenance I imagined was familiar to me – his voice too, sounded as that of an old friend – I hunted over his luggage – there was no name there – on going down to the Cuddy, there I found a hat box belonging to this mysterious individual – with the name in full upon it – 'C. D. Archibald' – here was a discovery – & yet it was something to be sorry for – I involuntarily asked myself the question – 'are we both so much changed that old friends cannot even recognize each other? – do seven short years work such wonderful changes? – it is but too true. (22 October)

For Australians visiting Britain, there seemed to be a very real danger that they would not be recognised and so not be incorporated into the British social world to which they felt they belonged.

The Princess on the Pea

For Australian women travelling alone, the need for recognition was especially important. While Postlethwaite could at least find words to describe his profession, such women generally had no 'calling' by which to describe themselves; their identities were linked to those of their fathers, making it imperative they should be accepted by male relatives and be incorporated into a family home. Without such an incorporation they might well have risked their claim to respectability.

Margaret Tripp was born in Somerset in 1838 and migrated to Victoria with her parents in 1850, when she was eleven years old. At the beginning of 1872, Tripp, then thirty-three years old, returned to Britain alone to visit relatives and to travel around Europe. The Tripps were a well-connected family in both Victoria and England (Margaret's father was a solicitor, her mother ran a school in Melbourne), and on 28

February, having arrived in England only a few days before, Tripp sat down to write home and announce her arrival at her Uncle's house in Beaminster, Dorset:

My dearest Mother,
It is indeed delightful to be writing to you from this house where I am enjoying myself immensely and they are all so wonderfully kind; but, I suppose now, I must try & give you an orderly account of my travels from the time when I posted a letter to you at Gibraltar. (28 February 1872)

Having established herself in Beaminster, Tripp uses the occasion of writing home to add to her previous letters and complete the narrative of her voyage. She tells how she was met on board ship in Southampton by her Aunt Meg:

I heard some one ask for me. I felt quite bewildered, the voice was familiar & yet strange, & I had quite made up my mind no one would come until Monday. I went down into the knot of people & saw some one who pushed back her hat and said 'you do not know me'. 'Yes' I said 'Aunt Margaret, come into my cabin' and off I rushed in what I am afraid must have seemed a very unfeeling manner. (28 February)

As if to emphasise the symbolism of the moment, Tripp herself admits a few sentences later that 'I felt so bewildered and excited that now I cannot recall the very first words she said to me.' Despite this deficiency, the episode is still narrated, and that initial moment of recognition is rehearsed and documented as evidence that she has maintained her identity.

Tripp disembarked the following day and joined her Aunt at Radley's Hotel where together, over breakfast, they validated that initial moment of recognition: 'You may imagine how Aunt Margaret & I talked & how every minute I recognised and enjoyed her more. Aunt Margaret treated me like a real princess, I must say, without even the intervention of the parched pea under the 20 mattresses and 20 eider-down quilts.' Then, after clearing her luggage through customs, Tripp set off with her Aunt by train to Dorset, making the final stage of the journey from Maiden Newton station to Beaminster by fly. They arrived late in the afternoon to find a welcoming party and another affirmation of Tripp's identity: 'Ah, dear Mother, there was Aunt Peter, & her kiss and voice had the most homely feeling that I had felt since I left Melbourne. There too was Frances, like & not like what I had expected to find and Uncle Peter, whose face was like a flash of recollection making me feel like a child again' (28 February). This account owes a debt to Romantic poetry, especially in the relationship between flashes of recollection and childhood, but here I merely want to stress the narrative movement in Tripp's letters from arrival, through recognition, to incorporation. Incorporation into Uncle Peter's house gives Tripp that 'homely feeling,' a signal that the temporary home of the ship has been substituted for a home which, though also temporary, more closely resembles the family home left behind in Victoria. The home becomes a suitable site for ending her narrative of the voyage to Britain, and incorporation into the home provides a narrative closure that allays the anxiety of a possible failure of recognition. As in the fairy story of the Princess on the pea, Tripp's identity has been validated and publicly acknowledged.

"Tis Roger'

Margaret Tripp's anxiety about being recognised and accepted was undoubtedly exacerbated by the case of the Tichborne Claimant. The case of the Tichborne Claimant began in earnest in January 1867 when a claimant to the Tichborne baronetcy and estates arrived in England from Australia and was recognised by the Dowager Lady Tichborne as the son who went missing on a voyage from South America to the Caribbean in 1854.[1] The rest of the family, however, refused to recognise the Claimant as the real Roger Charles Doughty Tichborne, and in May 1871 a civil case was commenced in the Court of Common Pleas to test the identity of the Claimant. This case was followed daily with growing interest by newspaper readers in both Australia and Britain, who delighted in such courtroom exchanges as this one between Major-General Custance, C. B., who had known Roger Tichborne in his youth, and Mr Hawkins, Q. C., defending counsel:

CUSTANCE: *Nobody could go abroad for so long without being changed, but I never saw any change so great as that in the claimant's case. His face is double what Roger Tichborne's was, as far as fat and cheeks go.*
HAWKINS: *As far as fat and cheek go? (Laughter)*
CUSTANCE: *Well, no, cheeks. I really cannot explain his nose.*
HAWKINS: *I don't want you to explain it. Only to describe it.*
CUSTANCE: *I can't explain his ears, or the shape of his head. There was a peculiar expression in his eye, but I can't explain it.[2]*

The civil case reached its conclusion after 103 days of evidence on 6 March 1872, eleven days after Tripp's arrival, when the Claimant's case was withdrawn and the Claimant himself was committed to Newgate on a charge of perjury.

Tripp spent the evening of her arrival in Beaminster chatting around the fire with her rediscovered family:

> *Our old recollections were legion, and constantly when I would remember something, some past event, or old saying, Uncle Peter would cry out 'Tis Roger'. I assure you that there is something in the air of one's native land for so many things have come back into my mind, & places, before I saw them again. (28 February)*

Tripp was evidently reassured to find herself so completely accepted by her relatives, yet she continued to seek further reassurance: 'we took a walk in the town, where I was constantly and involuntarily proving myself to be the real Roger.' It would be too strong to say that Tripp was obsessed by the question of the real Roger Tichborne, but she was certainly preoccupied with the whole question of identity and memory, and she returned to the Tichborne case in a postscript:

> *All here take as much interest in the Tichborne case as we do, & I hope that you dear Mother and Frances are now admiring the discernment which Florence & I always exhibited as we heard yesterday that the Jury had said that they had heard enough evidence . . . . every one expects that the end is near & no one seems to doubt what it will be, namely, the utter discomfiture of the arch impostor. (4 March)*

If Tripp's hostility to the Claimant was due to what she sees as his audacity, it was also, I suspect, evidence of a continued anxiety about her own identity as an Australian in Britain, even after her acceptance by her relatives. Tripp concluded her account of her voyage to Britain by relating her successful incorporation into her uncle's household. Yet her continued fascination with questions of cultural identity suggests that narrative closure did no more to resolve the tensions inherent in the identity of a nineteenth-century Australian in England, than the closure of the Tichborne case resolved the identity of the Tichborne Claimant.

'Oh the oak & the ash, & the bonny ivy tree, Do flourish at home in my own countree!'

Arrival at her uncle's house in Beaminster ought to have resolved the adventure narrative of Tripp's journey Home, and in one way it did: 'Ah, dear Mother, there was Aunt Peter, & her kiss and voice had the most homely feeling that I had felt since I left Melbourne.' The adventure narrative of Tripp's journey to Britain is resolved by her entry into the female domestic space of her uncle's home. Yet, as in William Postlethwaite's account of meeting his brothers, this narrative resolution was disturbed by unfamiliarity: 'I went into the dining room feeling a good deal as if I were walking in my sleep & it was all a dream. First I looked for the picture of the poppy & the black pig; there it all was, but the room did not seem quite so large as my childish fancy had made it' (28 February). Tripp, in one sense, has arrived in her home country, and yet the home at which she has arrived is not quite the same as the home from which she had migrated.

Tripp's personal memories are inaccurate partly because of the passage of time, and it is important to remember that the colonial home imitated a home frozen in the past; migrants imagined people and places as they were at the time of migration. But this mismatch between memory and experience also had a cultural dimension. In looking for 'the picture of the poppy & the black pig,' Tripp was looking for what she expected to see; that is, she was looking for a particular sign of domesticity. When migrants returned to areas left years before, they searched for objects that had attained in their absence a significance they did not have when they left. Such objects became idealised within the culture of that particular family, and recognition of them validated their sense of having arrived home.

Of course, paintings on dining-room walls are cultural in a broader sense, both in terms of interior design and in terms of what they depict. When Kathleen Bate visited Devon in 1939, she headed for the village of Cockington, largely, it seems, because of the picture hanging in her dining-room at home in New South Wales:

The road was delightful – just wide enough for one car, and vines and flowers covering the walls each side with tall trees meeting overhead. We went for three miles along this up and down and round about, and then the most glorious sight greeted us, a little village of the loveliest thatched cottages, all in perfect order and so clean and tidy. It almost took our breath away. . . . The two coloured pictures of an English village which

are hanging in our dining room at home are of Cockington but it is even
more attractive in real life than it appears on paper. *(3 May 1939)*

Despite the fact that her father came from Belfast and her mother's
parents were Scottish, for Kathleen Bate the pictures in the dining room
verified the home country she had come to find.

Along with her personal memories, Tripp also brought with her
images of Britain, in her case images she had gleaned specifically from
books, songs, and photographs. On her journey from Southampton to
her uncle's house, Tripp was struck by the 'novelty' of the countryside:
'Every step of the drive was interesting to me and so full of *novelty* for
the whole aspect of the country is so utterly unlike anything I have been
accustomed to. How the hedges delighted me, even in their thoroughly
winter garb, & with the grey evening fast falling' (28 February). There
is a kind of double colonial inversion here in the use of the term
'novelty,' a term used often by British migrants to Australia to refer to
the inversion of their cultural expectations of how a landscape ought to
look. 'Novelty' in Australia meant the land was strange, yet Tripp's use
of the term is combined with an attempt to claim the landscape as
familiar, as harmonious and beautiful in opposition to the alienating
landscape of Australia. Her poetic diction, though, gives her away, and
the phrases 'winter garb' and 'evening fast falling' indicate that her view
of the English countryside was derived from English pastoral poetry,
and she later uses James Thomson's *The Seasons* (1726–1730) to verify
her experience of spring: 'it is so delightful to have one's dear books
made living' (23 March).

Tripp's use of cultural models is made even clearer on a drive to
Bridport: 'the green hills and the grand avenues of trees, and the
hedgerows, where the primroses and buttercups are peeping out[,]
transport me. The cottages look so *solid*, the country so well tended and
refined. "Oh the oak & the ash, & the bonny ivy tree, Do flourish at home
in my own countree!"' (4 March).[3] The imperative is to recognise her
environment by whatever means possible, though the irony here, of
course, is that in order to recognise her 'own countree,' Tripp must
resort to a folk song rather than to any personal memory. Tripp's memories are here being supplemented by a cultural memory that is preserved
in particular forms of representation, a fact Tripp, with her remarkable
ability to reflect on her own psychology, herself notes:

I cannot tell you the queer feelings I have about the country, and the new
face of every thing. I do not so much remember it, as feel as if old memo-

ries which had been dormant were reawakened in me. And whenever I go out, everything I have read of nature and her beauties crowds into my mind, as if I was verifying now with my own eyes what I had known before by recollection & imagination from constantly thinking to & of all the photos of English scenery I have seen & verifying them[,] so to speak. (2 March)

This is much the same project as that of the many Thomas Cook tourists who took guidebooks with them to verify places overseas; indeed, the rise of the guidebook in the nineteenth century suggests that this project of verification fed into the broader imperialistic project of British culture. Descriptions of Paris or Sydney Harbour were carried by travellers as much to verify the places visited as to verify the description in the guidebook; as Jon Stratton notes, the guidebook aims not only to represent places but to complete the experience of visiting them.[4] In Tripp's terms, England is England only to the degree that it is identical to its representations, a point still being made by Australian visitors to England as late as the 1950s: 'What mattered was that London should be like the London you had for so long looked forward to meeting and recognizing.'[5] Such a verification was vital to the idea of the Australian home as an imitation of an English home; if England was not English, then the whole concept of being English in Australia, Canada, India, or any other British overseas territory was in danger of collapsing.

Of course, guidebooks are necessary because places always exceed their cultural representation, but this excess must be suppressed if they are to be verified as authentic. Hence Tripp's concern to dismiss difference, and if people and places are 'familiar & yet strange' or 'like & not like,' the differences are inessential: 'at a first meeting you see the outside differences and not the inner points of identity' (28 February). The same case, of course, might be made for the Tichborne Claimant whose face was 'familiar & yet strange' and whose nose was 'like & not like' the nose of Roger Tichborne. Tripp's desire for incorporation and closure was a means of claiming her 'native' inheritance, and in this a middle-class family home with its picture of the poppy and the black pig, and a naturally beautiful countryside with 'the oak & the ash, & the bonny ivy tree,' had to be authenticated. But this suppression of difference comes perilously close to the project of the Tichborne Claimant who claimed his inheritance also by stressing similarity rather than difference. Verification required the imposition of cultural memory on the present, and 'imposition' is but a short step from 'impostor'.

'I tried the effect of an Australian cooee
à la aboriginal'

Margaret Tripp was, it must be admitted, English born and might not be representative of Australian-born visitors to Britain. Emma Walker, whose parents migrated from England to Australia in 1838, made her first voyage to Britain in 1883 at the age of thirty-two. In her diary, Emma Walker seems much more confident of her Australian identity, and there are many aspects of Australia she prefers, as in her observation of British houses: 'It seems to me that the people here are no lovers of fresh air, but keep their windows closed, indeed many of them are fixtures. To one accustomed to free circulation, as I am, this way of keeping it all out, is particularly disagreeable, and is so stuffy and sickly as to be peculiarly oppressive & offensive' (2 June 1883). Condemnation of Britain in terms of its opposition to Australia was fairly typical; in contrast to a sunny, warm and open-air Australia, Britain could be condemned as wet, cold and stuffy. Such is the sweet revenge of the antipodes.

A more complex affirmation of an Australian identity occurs on a sightseeing trip to the West Midlands when Walker is both impressed and yet also unimpressed by birds flying home to roost:

> *Coming past Lady Willoughby's at dusk, thousands of crows congregated about this spot where trees were thickest, coming home to roost perhaps 20 miles off. I have seen a large number in the colony, but nothing to be compared to this. The sky was almost black with them, and the air filled with their discordant and incessant caw, caw. The note of this English bird is merely of one sound not really so pleasant to hear as ours. (5 October)*

Despite being impressed by the number of roosting birds, Walker affirms the superiority of Australia not only by opposing Britain to Australia, but by inverting the rhetoric of British colonialism. Australians were particularly sensitive to the claim that Australian birds lacked tonality.[6] Walker's comment that, 'The note of this English bird is merely of one sound,' reverses the more usual denigration of Australian birdsong by substituting 'English' for 'Australian'.

There is a similar appropriation of Britain in Walker's identification of the birds as crows, though in this case it is less overt. The colonisation of Australia meant the renaming of many of the birds after often unrelated European models, as in the naming of magpies, cuckoo-shrikes, and robins. In the passage from Walker's diary, this misrecognition, if it can be called that, is reversed, and the birds Walker describes are not crows but rooks. As an Australian, Walker could name the birds by their similarities to Australian crows, but the term 'rook' was not available to her.

The danger of such incongruities between Australian and British cultural models lay in their power to force visitors to recognise their own colonial identities, as in this exchange in 1892 between James Boucaut, a former South Australian premier, and an unnamed Canadian in the precincts of Canterbury Cathedral: 'After going through the Cathedral I took a walk around it outside to look at its noble proportions, and I asked a gentleman who was similarly engaged whether the birds which I heard cawing were rooks or crows. Said he, "I was just wondering myself and was going to ask you. In my colony we'd call them crows."'[7] The successful identification of the rook marked the difference between an inhabitant of Britain and a colonial visitor; whether he liked it or not, Boucaut's question aligned him with the Canadian.

The day following the spectacle of the crows, Emma Walker visited Kenilworth Castle. Despite the fact that it is a rather sorry ruin, Kenilworth Castle remains, especially for the overseas tourist, a primary site of Englishness due to Elizabeth I's visit in 1575 (mediated through Sir Walter Scott's popular historical romance, *Kenilworth*, published in 1821), and its proximity to the heart of England and the Stratford of Shakespeare, whom Walker, in a contrary act of cultural affirmation, refers to as 'our great bard' (8 October). Walker uses the occasion of her visit to Kenilworth Castle to assert her Australianness:

> We had a mile to walk to the Castle through a pretty village, which I hear is now getting quite a rising place. There is a very fine echo from the building, and standing about a quarter of a mile off, I tried the effect of an Australian cooee à la aboroginal [sic], with such good result that had one of our natives been near enough, he would have responded to it immediately. (6 Oct).

The phrase 'an Australian cooee à la aboriginal' is, I admit, too complex culturally to get a firm grip on; pointing to both Aboriginal and European cultures, it falls, perhaps, more within Paul Carter's analysis of 'the sound in-between,' especially his reflections on the sound 'cooee'. Carter's interpretation early in his essay of a World War I recruiting poster, 'Cooee to Australia,' which depicts an Australian soldier overseas calling to a female Australia, seems pertinent here: 'Australia can only discover her real identity and be properly named when her own voice has been authenticated overseas and comes back to her second-hand. Thus is the colonist locked into the mirror-logic of empire, forever bound to recognise himself in his reflection elsewhere.'⁸ The 'cooee' Emma Walker sends into Kenilworth Castle is returned not by an Aboriginal but by herself, another British Australian, and goes echoing back through her diary to her imagined reader in Adelaide. 'Cooee' as a specifically white Australian signature is authenticated not by its assumed Aboriginal origin but by its use overseas; the Aboriginal who returns the call is discovered to be a white Australian in Britain.

Emma Walker's stronger sense of an Australian cultural identity, then, is not without its pitfalls. An assertion of Australianness in terms of an opposition between Australia and Britain merely reversed the oppositions by which Australia was defined. Such a move may have been strategically effective, but it locks Australianness into a dependent relationship; to appropriate Britain as Britain had appropriated Australia was to perpetuate the rhetoric of antipodes, a rhetoric that remains balanced in favour of Britain. However, the appeal to an assumed indigenous culture also had its dangers. When William Postlethwaite visited Rutland Cavern, a 400 yard cave in Matlock, Derbyshire, he noted the supernatural effect of the lighting, commenting: 'I thought that a few New Hollanders corrobarying were only wanted to make the whole resemble what the infernal regions might be imagined to be' (9 March 1847). Thirty-five years later attitudes may have softened towards what was considered a dying race, but Emma Walker still had to distance herself from the 'cooee' by the use of the modifying 'à la aboriginal'.

'Thank goodness at rest in the great world at last'

In other descriptions of Britain, Walker relied on the same kinds of British cultural models employed by Tripp. For example, like Tripp, Walker used James Thomson's poetry to validate the English country-side, in her case the view from Richmond Hill:

> *the next day, proving an extremely fine, and bright morning, we had a long stroll together till half-past one. She [Miss Hall] took me into the Park up Richmond Hill and showed me a most lovely view of the Thames below. The Park extends for miles and is a favourite resort both for eques-*

trians and pedestrians. About a mile from the town and situated upon a rise, is the lovely view of the river which the poet Thomson loved so well – a spot which has been admired, and justly by hundreds. who are not poets. (27 October)

In order to produce this guidebook description of the view, Emma Walker has to ignore the particularity of her own viewpoint; she speaks on behalf of the unidentified hundreds 'who are not poets'. The gaze is here directed towards the English landscape and results, not surprisingly, in an apparent congruence between Thomson's description and Walker's view from the top of the hill; the imaginary scene is corroborated by the reality. Thomson's *The Seasons* was one of the most popular literary works in Australia in the nineteenth century, probably because it evoked an ordered landscape for migrants uncertain how to read the Australian land, and Walker's description of the view from the top of Richmond Hill relies on an Australian audience brought up on Thomson to complete it. Writing home forces the writer to relate the land to the cultural models of the overseas audience. Yet to the extent that those cultural models were British, they served, as in the case of the British-born Margaret Tripp, to deny difference. The need for Britain to live up to the representations of Britain circulating in Australia can be found in accounts by both British and Australian-born visitors.

As I argued in the case of Tripp, the denial of difference was linked to the desire for incorporation and an anxiety that the Australian visitor might not recognise, and not be recognised by, relatives. Emma Walker, unlike Tripp, was not met by relatives, and her first night in England, which she spent with strangers in London, consequently lacked the security of narrative closure: 'I arrived at their [Mrs Champion's] house about 5 P.M. thoroughly miserable, and wishing myself safely back in Adelaide again' (18 May). Walker does some sightseeing, of course, but when a promised tour of the slums of London falls through, she abandons London and sets off to stay with her father's brother, Uncle Ben, in Lincolnshire. Like Tripp, Walker depends on cultural representations for her sense of familiarity and her sense of coming home; arriving in Boston, she notes: 'It is an old-fashioned country town, with as far as I could see not a single fine building excepting Boston Church, which I recognised from our picture before the train stopped' (2 June). Arriving finally at Uncle Ben's house, she is gratified to receive the kind of family welcome Tripp received at Beaminster:

My driver not knowing the road, took me out of it, the time lost in this

instance was greatly appreciated by me, for I spent it in admiring
Frampton scenery. At about 8 o'clock I reached uncle's house, and rec^d.
from him and [cousin] Jennie a very hearty welcome. Thank goodness at
rest in the great world at last. (2 June)

Although Australian born, Emma Walker shows the same desire for
incorporation and narrative closure as Margaret Tripp, and this need to
recognise people and places, and to be in turn recognised oneself, is
clearly shared by both categories of Australian visitor.

Other nineteenth-century travellers in Europe may well have sought
resting points, but for British Australians travelling to England, this
point of rest had two converging characteristics. First, it was the home
of relatives, and both Margaret Tripp and Emma Walker were
welcomed into the home of their respective uncles; an acceptance by
relatives was all important, and it was the refusal of relatives to recognise him that was the Tichborne Claimant's major obstacle. Second, this
home, perhaps by the very presence of relatives, became a European
equivalent of, as Emma Walker referred to it, 'my southern home' (14
June). More especially, there was a substitution of family members.
Walker's father is reproduced in her uncle, her father's brother: 'Uncle
[has?] a resemblance to my own father across the eyes and forehead,
which is made more striking by the bald head rising above it. His habits
are much the same, and his actions and little jokes, remind me more
forcibly still of his brother' (3 June). Margaret Tripp had the same experience when she transferred from Uncle Peter's house to Uncle Robert's:
'One of my great pleasures in being here is, that Uncle Robert continu-
ally reminds me of dear Papa, though he looks much older. Their voices
are so much alike' (14 March). The search was not just for relatives, but
for relatives who resembled those in Australia.

The presence of relatives in Britain made the experience of Australian
visitors quite unlike the experience of visitors from, say, the United
States. For British Australians, sightseeing, the main activity of visitors
from the United States, was subordinated to the desire for recognition
and incorporation. Australians could adopt the role of tourist, but they
seem to have done so consciously and only after the establishment of a
substitute family home. As Jane Murray Smith put it in 1864: 'I don't
consider I have seen anything yet, but I shall commence soon. We have
devoted ourselves to our relations, I think we have finished them off
now' (19 March). Relatives could be a burden, especially if the need to
visit a series of them undermined the establishment of a European
substitute home. But the disadvantages of being a tourist were greater,

as Jane Murray Smith herself was to discover seven months later: 'You will find that Annie has not seen a great many things, but we have never been a day idle, and sight seeing is enough to wear the skin off your bones' (22 October). Emma Walker also had reservations about being a tourist: 'I took a walk down the Steep Hill, and came across some funny little old passages in my wanderings; got quite tired; am afraid I should make a poor tourist' (16 July). While being a tourist was a role that British Australians could adopt, being recognised by others as a relative was fundamental. Incorporation into the family home took precedence over sightseeing.

'a new world, and yet my Native home'

Yet this mirroring of southern and European homes produced a curious and extremely unstable dynamics of doubling and reversal. If uncles doubled for fathers, then arrival at the home of the uncle permitted an enactment, for both Australian born and English born, of a return to a kind of primal patriarchal home. Certainly, Margaret Tripp's incorporation into her uncle's household involved a return to childhood, as in the description of her welcome at Beaminster: 'There too was Frances, like & not like what I had expected to find and Uncle Peter, whose face was like a flash of recollection making me feel like a child again.' The same return to childhood occurred when Tripp moved from Beaminster to Uncle Robert's house in Cornwall: 'At Beaminster I am sure I could not have remembered the name of the old clerk here, but as I drove down the lane, his name flashed into my mind. I feel almost, at times, as if I were a child again' (14 March). This nostalgic return to childhood occurred despite a recognition of ageing: 'my uncle's articulation has lost much of its distinctness, from the absence of his teeth' (14 March). Or as William Postlethwaite put it in 1846 when he finally reached home: 'Not one single individual in Ulverstone but appeared to have been touched by some magic wand – some appeared to be thinner – some stouter – but all older' (26 October).

The ageing supports the notion that a visit to England is a return to the Old Country, especially when the ageing inhabitants were located against a background of quaint antiquity. As Margaret Tripp had to get used to her relatives being older than she remembered, so the towns too appeared older: 'It was quite dark & drizzling before we reached White Street, down which we drove, my memory of the neighbourhood quickening every moment. But the cottages looked so old & so solid!' (28

February). In turn, this supported the parent/child metaphor used so often in the nineteenth century to define the relationship between Britain and its colonies. Eva-Marie Kröller in her study of nineteenth-century Canadian travel writing on Europe points out the double-sided nature of this metaphor: 'The metaphor of Canada, the child, alludes to the innocence and potential fragility of the young nation, but conversely it also points towards a youthful vigour now lost by the old countries.'[9] The colonist was therefore cast both as a child in need of protection and as an innovator of technology: 'Torn between technological progress and nostalgic idealism as national criteria, travelling Canadians could not adopt a consistent point of view.'[10] Contradictory definitions of youth, as vulnerable and as innovative, destabilised the metaphor.

But if the mirroring of southern and European homes enabled the colonial subject to return as a child to the ancestral home, it also allowed the colonial visitor to return not to the Old Country but, paradoxically, to the New Country. One of the attributes of the child, at least, the Romantic construction of the child, is its freshness of vision, a freshness that visitors like Margaret Tripp delighted in when they first arrived in England: 'Every step of the drive was interesting to me and so full of *novelty*!' (28 February). It was this same 'novelty' that allowed British Australians like Emma Walker, with her misrecognition of crows, to adopt the strategies of familiarisation adopted by British arrivals in Australia. The colonial recolonised Europe, a process R. Bennett, rejuvenated by his arrival Home in 1859, found himself forced to recognise explicitly: 'I felt more than lively after the many years I had passed in Australia, it seems to put new Life into me, to feel that I am once again about to visit the home of my Childhood'; 'in my excitement I could not find adequate words to express my emotions, coming into as it where [*sic*] "a new world["], and yet my Native home' (15 July 1859). In 1884, twenty-five years later, the same trope of Europe as a New World was used in a steamship guide to Europe: 'In a word, . . . Europe is for the educated and educating Australian a new world to conquer, and a new world rich and teeming with spoils for eye, brain and hand – spoils of direct value to the mental no less than the industrial and everyday life of the Australian colonist.'[11] To the childlike eye of the colonial visitor, Europe became the New Country.

My argument, then, is that if, as they would seem to, Australian visitors to Britain desired incorporation into an ancestral home, this involved a return to childhood that, in turn, refigured Europe as a new world. The desire for incorporation emanated from a desire for stability, for a temporary home to act as the substitute home from which the visitor could travel locally within Europe for a variety of purposes, such as sightseeing, business, or to visit medical practitioners. But the substitute home also terminated the voyage out, it is a point of narrative closure of the voyage, and it is therefore not surprising to find a similarity between the arrival of the Australian in Europe and the arrival of the British migrant in Australia. Like the Australian in Europe, the English migrant became immediately aware of the 'novelty' of the natural environment. Cultural differences between Australia and Britain were less pronounced and as Australian visitors to Britain were struck by similarities – 'Everything is looking very much like Melbourne. The people dressed much the same' (Jane Murray Smith, 25 January 1864) – so British migrants to Australia found themselves in a familiar cultural environment: 'I do not find it at all dull here everything looks so English, the fashions are the same as in England' (Louisa Timewell, 17 October 1852). And beyond the similar attitude to the physical and human environments lay the same desire by British migrants (in the context of chain migration) for incorporation, the desire, that is, for recognition of and by friends and relatives.

The structures of the voyage out and the voyage back were therefore homologous. Both voyages could be depicted as a movement from separation through a kind of liminal time and space towards a narrative closure based on recognition of and by relatives. In turn, this homology between the voyages produced a fundamental instability in the relationship between England and Australia so that it was impossible to privilege one over the other. Both voyages could be figured as a passage from the Old World to the New, or from the New World to the Old; in this, both voyages offer what Jon Stratton calls a 'double articulation' of travel, they were simultaneously a journey to and a journey from the known world.[12] Both were voyages home, and both offered the traveller changes of social status, either through ageing or rejuvenation. Because Australia and England were sites of narrative closure, and in particular narrative closure through incorporation, the tropes defining them became interchangeable, even to the extent of refiguring Australia (in this case Adelaide) as the Old Country: 'there is no pavement in the streets and you walk up to the ancles in mud. . . . If any of you lived 2 hundred years ago I think you could imagine better than I can describe what sort of a place this is' (Mary Mease, 20 July 1851). To travel to Australia was to travel back, as well as forward, in time.

'it was all a dream'

Freud's concept of the uncanny suggests that the unfamiliar is implicit in the definition of the home. Freud yokes together linguistically the familiar (*heimlich*) and the uncanny (*unheimlich*) as a means of showing how a certain anxiety is the result of the disruption of familiarity by a related strangeness: '*heimlich* is a word the meaning of which develops in the direction of ambivalence, until it finally coincides with its opposite, *unheimlich*. *Unheimlich* is in some way or other a sub-species of *heimlich*.'[13] For example, waxworks or automata produce an uncanny effect because they are human and yet not human; and to the extent that waxworks imitate known personalties, they share the uncanny effects derived from other forms of doubling, such as mirror reflections and identical twins. The uncanny is produced by the introduction of an undecidability into what is familiar, by a sliding from the 'homely' (*heimlich*) into the 'unhomely' (*unheimlich*) that demonstrates a mutual dependence of the familiar and the strange. In psychoanalytical terms, the familiar is disrupted by what the mind has hidden: 'this uncanny is in reality nothing new or alien, but something which is familiar and old-established in the mind and which has become alienated from it only through the process of repression.'[14]

The concept of the *unheimlich* has been employed outside the field of psychoanalysis by Ken Gelder and Jane M. Jacobs. In *Uncanny Australia*, Gelder and Jacobs read Freud in terms of cultural space: 'An "uncanny" experience may occur when one's home is rendered, somehow and in some sense, unfamiliar; one has the experience, in other words, of being in place and "out of place" simultaneously.'[15] Gelder and Jacobs use their reading of Freud to analyse the reaction of non-indigenous Australians to the 'Mabo' decision of the Australian High Court and the assertion by the court that Aboriginal people have continued to possess certain land rights due to prior occupation. In Freudian terms, the spatial imagination of non-indigenous Australians is disrupted by what British settlement sought to repress through the doctrine of *terra nullius*, namely that the land was already occupied. The anxiety of some non-Aboriginal Australians is caused by previously familiar places becoming unfamiliar.

Such a discussion of cultural space provides another way of viewing the experiences of Australians in Britain. The doubling of Britain and Australia as homes produced a combination of the homely and the unhomely that was impossible to separate since both 'northern' and 'southern' homes were simultaneously familiar and strange. It was less a case of Australia being an antipodean Britain than a doubling or mirroring of the home; both were homes, and as a result both were and were not familiar. Travellers in both directions looked for cultural similarities; they sought incorporation into homes that looked and felt familiar, and they sought the relatives who looked and sounded like those left behind. In this sense, they were more concerned about familial identity and less about any national identity.

It was this that produced the unease to which Gelder and Jacobs point: 'one has the experience, in other words, of being in place and "out of place" simultaneously.' Such unease is not a new sensation for non-Aboriginal Australians, and it was usually ascribed to the unstable combination of a familiar British culture being transposed to a strange Australian natural environment. But even within the human or cultural environment there was a strangeness due to the doubling of homes; and to the extent that it was its double that produced the unhomely home, we can see that what disrupted the *heimlich* was an *unheimlich* that was nonetheless familiar. The strangeness was due to familiarity, as in Margaret Tripp's account of visiting her childhood home: 'Then I went all over the house; & showed Frances where everything used to be. It was so strangely familiar! I exclaimed as I went into Papa's old dressingroom for the patchwork paper is unchanged. . . . The kitchen was as familiar to me as our own' (20 June 1872). It was precisely the familiarity that was strange, or as Freud put it: 'this uncanny is in reality nothing new or alien, but something which is familiar and old-established in the mind.'

The effect of the strangeness of familiarity was often described in terms of dreaming, as in J. I. Martin's description of visiting his home in Ireland in 1891 after a gap of twenty years: 'On the way [to see some more friends] we passed over some of our old fields, & caught a glimpse of the old Loch, bringing back remembrances of the old times. I could almost imagine the present a dream' (1 July). Hence, too, Tripp's dream sensation of a home that is both familiar and yet strange: 'I went into the dining room feeling a good deal as if I were walking in my sleep & it was all a dream. First I looked for the picture of the poppy & the black pig; there it all was, but the room did not seem quite so large as my childish fancy had made it' (28 February). Although it is clear that the experience is strange because the room is smaller, the strangest aspect of the experience is its familiarity. And while the difference between memory and experience might be denied in order to permit incorporation into the home, there was no denying the strangeness of the familiarity. The homeliness of the home was the disrupting factor.

The same was true not only of such personal memories but of the more widespread cultural representations, as when Tripp used Thomson to verify her experience of the countryside: 'treading on the brown oak leaves and listening to their *strange yet familiar* rustle was indeed realizing ones dreams' (23 March; my italics). The dreamlike sensation came not so much from the congruence between image and reality, but from the strangeness of the familiarity of the experience. The familiarity of the cultural representation surfaces like a memory or dream from a collective unconscious; in such a dream, what is foreign becomes familiar, and the vital imperialist concepts of home and abroad are reversed, overlayed, and doubled.

Asserting the 'Cooee' and Claiming the Bard

Freud's reference to the uncanny double leads us back to the Tichborne Claimant, a supplement to any discussion of the cultural identity of the British Australian in the nineteenth century. The ideal ending from the point of view of the Claimant would have been his recognition by the Tichborne family, his incorporation into the family home, and his assumption of his inheritance. In thus attempting to act out a narrative closure, the Claimant was a paradigm of the British Australian visiting England.

Yet the Tichborne case was paradigmatic in another way. Although in court the Claimant failed to prove he was Roger Tichborne, the counter claim of his opponents was also never proved, and the Claimant went to his grave without his identity being determined. It is this undecidability of the Claimant's identity that makes him paradigmatic of a British Australian cultural identity. In the nineteenth century, cultural identity was not a question of being either Australian or British, the two were not mutually exclusive; rather, Australian visitors to England sought to find ways to maintain both identities, to assert the 'cooee' and claim the Bard. The mechanism for this was the double vision shown in Margaret Tripp's letters, a double vision that undermined even as it established recognition: 'familiar & yet strange,' 'like & not like what I had expected to find.' The Claimant's counsel had to account for the Claimant being in many ways quite unlike Roger Tichborne; yet his opponents had the equally hard task of trying to account for the uncanny fact that he was familiar to many who had known Roger Tichborne. In the end, the case of the Tichborne Claimant acted out the fears of British Australians who, despite their desire for incorporation and cultural affirmation, experienced an ambivalent identity that could be resolved only textually, in the symbolic closures they enacted in their letters and diaries.

THREE

Aborigines at the Crystal Palace: Portable Colonial Spaces

In Melbourne today one can still see examples of the portable iron housing imported during the heady days of the 1850s gold rush.[1] According to a contemporary report, between 1851 and 1852 the population of Melbourne leapt from 23,000 to 80,000.[2] The gold rush not only brought to Victoria thousands of migrants who needed housing, but also drained Melbourne of both labour and raw materials; labourers and craftsmen set off for the gold fields, wood for building became scarce, and the cost of bricks rose to three times that in England.[3] Many people lived in tents, and those like Lucy Hart who had houses, however humble, counted themselves fortunate:

> We are living in a nice house called "Devon Cottage". We pay 16 shillings per week, and that is cheap as times are here now. There are hundreds of people living in tents on the Banks of the Yarra River, and there is not houses enough for the people as they are flocking from all parts to go to the diggins and the tradesmen will not work for any money that is offered them, they are off to the diggins. I only wish my own brothers was here, they would do something for themselves. (3 May 1852)

The answer for those who could afford it was to import from Britain houses that could be quickly and relatively easily assembled. When the Government opened up South Melbourne for urban development in 1852, Robert Patterson spotted his chance and bought up a number of building lots on which he erected portable iron houses. By 1855, Patterson had a couple of rows of these houses, possibly twenty or more in total, and even had the street named after him: Patterson Place. At least one of these rows still stood a hundred years later in the 1950s, and in the early 1980s the sole remaining cottage was acquired and restored by the National Trust. Still portable today, two other iron houses from the early 1850s, one attributed to E. T. Bellhouse of Manchester, the other to Morewood & Rogers of London, have been moved to the site from elsewhere in Melbourne.[4]

Such a combination of durability and portability points to an uncertainty in the nature of portable structures. On the one hand, the houses were much like tents, only a little more sophisticated; you bought them in one place and erected them in another. When Alfred Joy arrived in Melbourne from Britain in September 1853, he brought with him both a portable iron house and a tent. He purchased some land on Courtenay (modern Courtney) Street, North Melbourne, stored his belongings in his tent, and then set about building his house, a process that took him over five months to complete. In his diary he recorded some of his disasters and triumphs:

Saturday Oct. 22nd Sunk the Piles & finished the wood foundation & had part of the iron work erected twice, but the wind blew it down each time.

Thursday Nov 24th Closed in the roof of our house, so we are now safe from the rain & shall have less trouble.

Wednesday Dec 28th Had the worst storm of wind that has been known here for years, it broke down our tent & carried away two more near us & has blown down some wooden houses about ¼ mile from us. We quite expected our own house would have been blown down & I was obliged to stand in the Passage for 2 hours holding the door to prevent it from being blown in.

Sunday March 19th Sitting room flooded by the rain coming in through the roof, & obliged to take our meals in the bedroom.

Wednesday Apl 5th Finished the ceiling of the Sitting Room, so we can now enjoy ourselves of an evening, without the risk of being smothered with dust & having the candles blown out by the wind.

Like tents, iron houses were at the mercy of the elements; they leaked in the rain, and became ovens in the sun. Iron was not the best material out of which to build a house, and life would have been uncomfortable, to say the least, for women like Henrietta, Alfred's wife, who landed in Australia carrying a newly born child. William Howitt wrote of iron houses at the time: 'They will prove admirable houses – for the doctors.'[5]

Unlike tents, on the other hand, iron houses were durable. They were prefabricated, but were not necessarily intended to be temporary, and their portability and their propensity to leak should not be seen as denying them a degree of permanence. They were not cheap, and those on sale from McLean Bros. and Rigg of Melbourne ranged from £21 for a one-roomed house (with flooring and lining) to £70 for a four-roomed house;[6] Hemming & Co. of Bristol were offering a two-roomed house such as Joy's for thirty-five guineas.[7] By comparison, Joy's tent cost him £5 in England. Additional investment was required in terms of shipping the houses from Britain, carting them to a building plot (Joy paid £12), the relatively high value of the land on which they stood, and the enhanced rateable value they could attract over wooden houses. Such an investment would have made owning an iron house beyond the pocket of most working people; Alfred Joy himself came to Victoria as a relatively affluent thirty-year-old 'gentlemen' and found employment as an auctioneer (in partnership with an acquaintance named, curiously enough, Alfred Bliss).[8] Moreover, the portable iron houses of the 1850s could be a good deal larger and more elaborate than Alfred Joy's two-roomed house; Corio Villa, manufactured by Charles Young & Co. of Edinburgh and shipped out in 1855 for Mr Gray, a Colonial Land Commissioner in Geelong, is a substantial and richly decorated building that still stands in Geelong overlooking the wharf onto which it was unloaded.[9] A comparable four-bedroomed parsonage ordered by the Bishop of Melbourne cost 250 guineas.[10]

Iron houses, therefore, were spatially ambivalent: they combined the portability of a tent with the durability of a more traditional house. They were unlike modern prefabricated structures (and the term prefabrication belongs to the twentieth century) in that they were designed to be dismantled and moved to another site as required. In this sense, they were like the migrants they housed, capable of remaining on one site or moving on as circumstances dictated. This combination of what were seen as conflicting cultural values produced an uncertain, ironic response. Alfred Joy called his iron house 'Oxford Lodge'. It is possible he was perfectly serious about this; he came from Oxford and may have wanted his house to remind him of his English home. The naming of Lucy Hart's 'Devon Cottage' has much the same purpose. Yet in Britain the term 'Lodge' could include a three-storey town house, and Joy's act of calling his two-roomed house a Lodge is either pretentious or ironic. Joy was not someone to take himself too seriously, and the day after buying the land for his house in North Melbourne, he noted in his diary:

'Shouldered my pick & shovel & turned the first sod on my estate' (19 October). In employing the discourse of landownership ironically, Joy shows himself uneasy about his own relationship to the land.

Paul Carter, in *The Lie of the Land*, has recently asked:

> *Is it not odd that ours, the most nomadic and migratory of cultures, should found its polity, its psychology, its ethics and even its poetics on the antithesis of movement: on the rhetoric of foundations, continuity, genealogy, stasis? Is it not decidedly odd that a culture intent on global colonization should persistently associate movement with the unstable, the unreliable, the wanton and the primitive?*[11]

Carter draws attention to the paradoxical connection between the mobility of Western culture and its determination to privilege dwelling over travelling: 'If we were grounded,' he says, 'the cultural opposition between movement and stasis would disappear.'[12] Carter resides predominantly in Australia and most of his work employs Australian examples; in *The Lie of the Land*, for example, Carter discusses the anthropologist, T. G. H. Strehlow, the architect of Adelaide, Colonel Light, and the Papunya Tula aboriginal painting movement. Yet Carter's primary engagement is with European thought and, unlike other postcolonial theorists from whom he pointedly distances himself, Carter uses comparisons between Europe and Australia not so much to define a colonial condition as to examine the continuity between European and colonial uncertainties.

Carter's comments about the cultural tension between movement and stasis therefore prompt us to examine colonial culture not as something distinct from the metropolitan culture, but as a culture sharing the spatial uncertainties of Britain. In a narrow sense, portable housing can be seen as a colonial phenomenon and read in terms of a distinctly colonial spatiality. Governor Phillip brought with him a house made of wood and oilcloth on the First Fleet, and from the 1820s John Manning, a London carpenter and builder, established a specialised business supplying wooden houses to intending migrants:

> *Gentlemen emigrating to the New Settlement, Swan River, on the Western Coast of Australia, will find a great advantage in having a comfortable Dwelling that can be erected in a few hours after landing, with windows, glazed doors, and locks, bolts, and the whole painted in a good and secure manner, carefully packed and delivered at the Docks, consisting of two, three, four, or more roomed Houses, made to any plan*

that may be proposed; likewise Houses of a cheaper description for labouring men, mechanics, &c. &c.[13]

From 1836, John Manning supplied houses to the new colony of South Australia (he provided both Robert Gouger and Governor Hindmarsh with houses), and Governor La Trobe's Cottage, erected in Melbourne in 1839, was also a Manning house.[14] The first authenticated example of an iron house is in Britain, a canal lock-keeper's cottage at Tipton Green, Staffordshire, erected around 1830 and demolished in 1926.[15] But iron houses, like Manning houses, were generally produced for export, in greatest number for the Californian and Victorian gold rushes. In this sense, portable houses have an association with nineteenth-century European overseas expansion and colonial settlement.

Yet a discussion of any peculiarly colonial spatiality also needs to bear in mind that the fantasy of colonial settlement, evidenced in Manning's advertisement through the establishment of 'a comfortable Dwelling that can be erected a few hours after landing, with windows, glazed doors, and locks, bolts' was a British fantasy. It was middle-class: security was needed to protect middle-class property and middle-class privacy. And it was also imperial; it regarded the spaces to be settled as homogeneous, effacing prior occupation and a diversity of climate and terrain. The fantasy of settlement was, in Carter's terms, a fantasy of grounding by which movement and the transgression of space were defined as aberrant.

Perhaps, then, it is not so much the portable houses themselves, with their unstable combination of movement and stasis, that were peculiarly colonial; iron houses were only one type of portable iron structure and although iron houses found their market primarily outside Britain, other types of portable iron structures were extensive throughout Britain in the 1840s and 1850s. Perhaps instead it is a consciousness of the tension between movement and stability that is, if not peculiarly colonial, then characteristic of the migrant. Migrants, were forced to come to terms with the fact that migration by definition located them, like the transportees before them, in the party of 'the unstable, the unreliable, the wanton and the primitive'. Certainly on the voyage out, migrants were well aware of the precarious nature of domestic space, as in Alfred Joy's description of himself and his wife, Henrietta, sitting down to dinner at sea on the *Thomas Harrison*:

Thursday Aug 25ᵗʰ A gale commenced at 9 yesterday morning which still continues. The Cabin is again swamped with water & we are obliged

to dress for meals in Indian Rubber Galoghes [sic] & water proof leggings
& if this weather continues we shall soon have to take to Oilskin[,] boots
& Sou'Westers, for during dinner today a sea broke over the Poop, dashed
in the Skylight & swamped the table, filling the plates and dishes with
salt water & drenching those sitting beneath.

The domestic space of the ship is, at this moment, in conflict with the outside space, the space though which the migrants are travelling. It is this conflict that generates the ironic tone in Joy's suggestion that soon they will have to sit down to dinner in 'Oilskin[,] boots & Sou'Westers'.

The irony in Joy's response to the land when he arrived in Australia came from a similar consciousness of a tension between movement and stability, and a consciousness that the stasis implied by 'settlement' was indeed a fantasy. Of course he was angry at the poor quality of the package he had been sold: 'The House is sent out in a most disgraceful manner & there is only sufficient lining for one room' (8 November 1853). But he was also clearly aware that the establishment of a comfortable dwelling in Australia, let alone 'a few hours after landing,' ignored factors such as the weather and the site, the rain and the dust: 'Sunk the Piles & finished the wood foundation & had part of the iron work erected twice, but the wind blew it down each time' (22 October).

Joy was also made aware of prior occupation: 'Disturbed in the night by a party of Natives who were attempting to get into the houses near us & succeded [sic] at our next door neighbours where they got rather roughly handled, however they returned about 2 in the morning & tore up and carried away the bridge over the gully in front of our house' (2 March 1854). The irony here (though, in this instance, unnoticed by Joy) is that Aboriginal people, also defined by British culture as 'unstable, unreliable, wanton and primitive,' managed by the removal of the bridge to immobilise those who claim the superiority of settlement: 'In the evening, made a bridge from the house to the street to enable Henrietta to get from one to the other' (20 March). Perhaps in her temporary incarceration, Henrietta herself came to understand the interdependence between stasis and movement.

Migrants, then, had customarily to deal with ambivalent spaces, spaces that were produced out of a continuing tension between movement and stability; such spaces gave the lie to the fantasy of settlement. In some cases, though certainly not all, migrants handled this tension by presenting their experience ironically. They were less ironic when reflecting on Britain as Home, and the representation of Britain as a stable, fixed space which the colony might try to imitative but could never recreate offered a way of maintaining the fantasy of settlement despite the contrary experience of settlement.

Yet, if we take the view that the fantasy of settlement was British, middle-class and imperial, then it is equally important to identify and examine ambivalent spaces within Britain. As Carter implies, Britain as much as Australia lacked stability; to accept the migrant view of Britain as essentially 'grounded' is to be complicit with the ideology of imperialism. And as Jane M. Jacobs has recently shown, the preservation of binary classifications such as core and periphery continues to produce ambivalent territories in a post-imperial, postcolonial London.[16] The argument that I am interested in examining, therefore, is that spatial uncertainty, produced out of a tension between such cultural opposites as movement and stasis, or portability and permanence, is not distinctly colonial, and that it is a pervasive aspect of late nineteenth-century Britain. In short, I want to try to destabilise the image of the metropolitan centre by locating within it the uncertainty migrants found in colonial space.

Paxton's Great Exhibition Building of 1851 as Panopticon

The Great Exhibition of 1851 provided a focus for portable iron houses, and for portable iron structures generally. The Great Exhibition was primarily a showcase for British industrial manufacturing, but there were also over seventy model buildings on display, among them a number of portable iron houses, such as the one exhibited by Andrew Whytock of New Oxford Street:

> *Model of emigrants' house, about one-fourth full size, made of Morewood and Rogers' patent galvanised tinned iron, corrgated.*
> *The full size weighs about half a ton, and can be packed in two cases.*
> *When once seen put together, it may be erected by two persons in as many days.*
> *Furniture of the house, made chiefly of the same material.*
> *Table and chairs with camp legs.*
> *Bath, answering the purpose of a sofa, or a bedstead, which can be solidly packed.*
> *Stove for warming and cooking.*[17]

There was even a model of one of the houses currently owned by the

National Trust of Victoria, a cast-iron house manufactured 'for emigrants' by E. T. Bellhouse & Co of Manchester. Manufacturers like Bellhouse and Charles Young & Co. were already manufacturing a range of iron buildings at the time, such as warehouses, hospitals, railway stations and schools. Bellhouse supplied the custom house at Payta, Peru, in 1854, barracks for the Crimea in the same year, and George Coppin's Olympic Theatre (known as the 'Iron Pot') in Melbourne in 1855;[18] Prince Albert was apparently such an admirer of the model iron house that Bellhouse were commissioned to erect a cast-iron ballroom at Balmoral Castle.[19] Young & Co., as well as sending out Corio Villa to Geelong, supplied the three-storey shop and dwelling erected at 43 Collins Street East, Melbourne, in 1851, barracks for the Crimea in 1854, and (after their takeover of Robertson & Lister) the cast-iron church erected in Macquarie Street, Sydney, in 1855.[20] The title of a pamphlet published by Young & Co. in the mid 1850s gives an indication of the range of structures on offer: *Illustrations of Iron Structures for Home and Abroad, Consisting of Stores, Dwelling-houses, Markets, Arcades, Railway Stations, and Roofing, &c &c.*[21]

Of course, the most celebrated portable iron structure was the 1851 Exhibition building itself, which not only won the medal for the category of Civil Engineering, Architecture and Building Contrivances, but also won the supreme prize, the Great Medal.[22] Here, the naming of the building as the Crystal Palace by Douglas Jerrold in *Punch*, even as it was under construction, ingeniously diverted attention away from the building's utility while at the same time directing attention to one of the building materials, glass. Critics, on the other hand, emphasised the functionality of the building, and John Ruskin, unable to find any moral purpose in its design, described it as 'a greenhouse larger than ever greenhouse was built before'.[23]

Joseph Paxton's Great Exhibition building quite clearly owes a great deal to the horticultural glasshouse. Paxton himself had developed many of the features of the Exhibition building at Chatsworth where he had been head gardener since 1826; in particular he developed his famous ridge-and-furrow roof design on such buildings as the Great Conservatory (1836–1840) and the lily house (1850).[24] As John Hix puts it: 'The Crystal Palace was a direct descendent of the botanical glasshouse and represented the horticultural advances of the nineteenth century in its form and function.'[25] Neither was Paxton the only person to propose a glasshouse design for the Great Exhibition. Richard Turner, an iron master from Dublin, had worked with Paxton on the Great Conservatory and had completed the Palm House at Kew in 1848.

Turner submitted a design for the Great Exhibition building that the journal *The Builder* described as 'an enormous greenhouse 1,020 feet long'.[26]

Twentieth-century cultural historians have tried to understand the social significance of this escalating use of glass in the second half of the nineteenth century, an escalation permitted by changes in glass production technology (which made available good quality sheet glass) and the abolition of the tax on glass in 1845. Tony Bennett, in *The Birth of the Museum*, places Paxton's glass exhibition building in a context of concerns about the adequate surveillance of large numbers of working people in public spaces, concerns implicit in the architectural brief for the building: internal walls were to be omitted 'allowing the eye to range at liberty, and to appreciate the extent and the vista'.[27] As McKean notes, this not only helped the visitors to view the exhibits, it helped the authorities view the visitors, a factor which may have contributed to the negligible incidence of detected crime within the exhibition building (there were twelve cases of picking pockets, and eleven of stealing goods exposed in the exhibition).[28]

Bennett lists three general principles that he argues came together in the 1851 Great Exhibition building:

> *first, the use of new materials (cast-iron and sheet glass) to permit the enclosure and illumination of large spaces; second, the clearing of exhibits to the sides and centres of display areas, thus allowing clear passageways for the transit of the public, and breaking that public up from a disaggregated mass into an orderly flow; and, third, the provision of elevated vantage points in the form of galleries which, in allowing the public to watch over itself, incorporated a principle of self-surveillance and hence self-regulation into museum architecture.*[29]

Bennett concludes:

> *In thus allowing the public to double as both the subject and object of the controlling look, the museum embodied what had been, for Bentham, a major aim of panopticism – the democratic aspiration of a society rendered transparent to its own controlling gaze.*

In stressing the opening up of the interior of the building to the regulating eye of the spectator, Bennett might have noted that on average there were also 350 to 400 police officers stationed inside the building.[30] Nonetheless, he establishes a case for self-surveillance and self-regulation, and uninhibited views of the vista were evidently part of the interior concept of the building: there were seats in the gallery overlooking the transept, and Paxton's original plan was to have optical magnifiers in the galleries.

Yet, while Bennett links glass and visibility, he does not pursue the link between iron and portability. Bennett places the exhibition building in the context of other glass and iron constructions: 'The architectural sources which fuelled the development of nineteenth-century exhibitionary institutions are many and various: shopping arcades, railway stations, conservatories, market halls and department stores to name but a few.'[31] His list is remarkably similar to the list of portable structures in Young & Co.'s catalogue of *Iron Structures for Home and Abroad*, but Bennett emphasises the size of such structures rather than their portability. A full analysis must take account of structures that can be both static and yet infinitely portable.

The 'Brompton Boilers' and the Engineer as Architect

The profits from the Great Exhibition were used by the Royal Commissioners to buy a number of estates in Kensington and to establish on them a whole array of imperial institutions dedicated to 'Science and Art'; these included the South Kensington Museum (opened 1857, and later split into the Science Museum and the Victoria and Albert Museum), the Natural History Museum (1880), and the Imperial Institute (1893). Prince Albert took a particular interest in the rehousing of the Marlborough House art collection on the Brompton Park House Estate, and Gottfried Semper, the influential young German architect, produced plans for the site, but these were rejected as too expensive. In 1855, with the need for a building urgent, the Royal Commissioners, prompted by their president, Prince Albert, turned from an architect to the engineers Charles Young & Co. As well as manufacturing portable buildings for shipment overseas, Young & Co. had, in 1853, completed the Palm House of the Belfast Botanic Gardens for Richard Turner and supplied much of the cast-ironwork for the Dublin Crystal Palace. They took just four days to produce plans for a temporary iron museum.[32]

There were several reasons for choosing a portable iron structure. Prince Albert, with his cast-iron ballroom, was clearly a champion of such structures; an iron museum could be designed and erected quickly; the Crimean War was in progress, making it difficult to justify the public

---

expense of a large stone or brick building; and, as the Commissioners pointed out to the Chancellor of the Exchequer in their application for funding, the museum was:

designed of a material which possesses a permanent pecuniary value, to which the cost of the labour employed in its construction bears only a small proportion. While, therefore, it could on the one hand be at any time taken down and re-erected, if necessary, on another site, or in another form, at a very trifling expense, it could, on the other, be re-sold.[33]

Unlike the Great Exhibition building, however, with its huge acreage of glass, the iron museum was clad in corrugated iron. The restricted glazing was an attempt (unsuccessful, as it turned out) to avoid the extremes of temperature experienced in Paxton's building, but it did not help the blank, external appearance of the structure, which was so ridiculed that it was painted like a canvas marquee in green and white stripes;[34] and, as the building had three galleries of the same span placed side by side, the journal *The Builder* soon coined the nickname, 'the Brompton Boilers'.[35]

Again, the choice of name reflects the uncertain nature of portable iron structures: both Alfred Joy, in his choice of Oxford Lodge for his house in Melbourne, and *The Builder*, in its choice of 'the Brompton Boilers' for the South Kensington Museum, undermined the pretension of such structures. The nickname 'Brompton Boilers' drew attention to what the term 'Crystal Palace' sought to avoid: portable iron buildings owed more to the engineer than the architect. As William Howitt noted of the iron houses in Melbourne: 'These . . . look like huge caravans, the roofs being arched like them; or like great steam-engine boilers, or gasometers.'[36] In Melbourne parlance, portable iron structures were termed 'iron pots'.[37] Public acceptance of corrugated iron buildings had lasted barely ten years.[38]

The large public iron buildings of the middle years of the nineteenth century were feats of industrial engineering. Paxton's 1851 Great Exhibition building was constructed by the engineering contractors, Fox, Henderson & Co, and its iron components were precision engineered in the Midlands before being brought by rail to London and riveted together in Hyde Park. As Charles Dickens put it: 'The proposed edifice could be constructed at Birmingham, at Dudley, and at Thames Bank, "brought home" to Hyde Park ready-made, and put up like a bedstead.'[39] Richard Turner, who supplied a similarly engineered proposal for the 1851 Exhibition building, built the Palm House at Kew and the Regent's Park Winter Gardens from components engineered at his Hammersmith Iron Works in Dublin.

The same engineers who built the iron buildings were building Britain's ever expanding railway network. Charles Fox was involved in constructing the 'sheds' (or roofs) of Paddington and Birmingham New Street stations, Richard Turner designed and built the sheds of Liverpool's Lime Street Station and Dublin's Broadstone Station; Young & Co.'s exhibit at the Great Exhibition was a set of four simultaneous-acting level-crossing gates, and it is likely that Young & Co. supplied some of the portable iron railway stations still standing in Brazil. Conversely, the great railway engineer, I. K. Brunel, designed a portable hospital for use in the Crimea.[40] And portable iron buildings were indirectly connected to railways through the use of the railways to transport the buildings. As Henry-Russell Hitchcock put it:

> *At the opening of Victoria's reign Railway Age and Iron Age came together to maturity. The railways, as they expanded, demanded ever more and more iron for their rails, their locomotives, and their sheds, thus continually stimulating iron production. And it was the railways that brought together the raw materials for that production, moved the semi-finished products from plant to plant, and finally distributed iron members of all sorts – including various large-scale building components – all over Britain.[41]*

Iron structures owed their portability to the development of railways and steam ships; for the 1851 Great Exhibition building, it cost more to transport the timber from the London docks than to transport the iron and glass from Birmingham.[42]

Portable iron structures can therefore be seen as just one aspect of a culture that was redefining space through industrial technology; owing more to the engineer than the architect, here were buildings that travelled. At least four million people visited the Great Exhibition,[43] an unprecedented movement of the British population, and it was fitting that the largest building in Europe should share the same technology as the trains that brought them to see it. It was fitting too that the building was designed to come down as fast as it went up, and following a vote in Parliament on 30 April 1852 ordering its removal, the building was quickly dismantled and carried away.

'No one has seen England unless he has been to the Crystal Palace'

In June 1854, the Hyde Park Crystal Palace opened as the Sydenham Crystal Palace. Paxton himself seems never to have been sure whether his 1851 building was temporary or permanent; his original brief was for a temporary structure, but in arguing for the building to be retained in Hyde Park as a winter garden, Paxton stressed that he had made it 'in every way suitable to be appropriated to a permanent use'.[44] In the event, the compromise allowed it to be both permanent and portable, and the building was shifted south-east to the top of Sydenham Hill. Unfortunately, though the chairman of the newly formed Crystal Palace Co, Samuel Laing, MP, was also chairman of the London, Brighton and South Coast Railway (the majority shareholder), there was as yet no station on Sydenham Hill, and the cost of transporting the building twenty miles by horse was one of the many construction costs that prevented the Crystal Palace Co from ever returning a profit.[45]

The Hyde Park building was modified in a number of ways to suit the new site. The ground floor area was reduced, but because of an increase in the height of the building, its actual volume was increased fifty per cent and the glass surface nearly doubled in area. This prompted Ruskin, who again failed to see any architectural merit in the building, to call it 'a cucumber frame between two chimneys'.[46] Paxton's horticultural background can certainly be seen in his landscaping of the two hundred acres that stretched away to the East. The land nearest the building was terraced in the Italian style, with symmetrical fountains and a grand central walk stretching away down the hill. Lower down, however, the English parkland style was adopted, with walks winding through groups of trees and an irregular shaped lake, dotted with islands occupied by full-size plaster models of various dinosaurs.

When Henry Incledon Pilcher visited the Crystal Palace at Sydenham on 4 August 1866, he was so impressed by what he saw that his diary entry for that day ran to seven pages of detailed description, much of it copied verbatim from Samuel Phillips' *Guide to the Crystal Palace and Park* (1854).[47] The Crystal Palace itself incorporated, so Pilcher told his diary, 'a grand central nave, two side aisles, two main galleries, three transepts and two wings'. As though there might be some doubt, he stressed that 'above the level of the floor it is constructed *entirely* of iron & glass,' and he reproduced figures from the guide book showing that by including the colonnade leading from the railway station ('720 feet in length 17 feet wide 8 feet high') there was a remarkable 'three quarters of a mile in length of ground covered with a transparent roof of glass'. Thus did the Sydenham Crystal Palace live up not only to Ruskin's evaluation but to Jane Murray Smith's description of it in 1864 as 'an enormous greenhouse' (10 April).

Once inside this splendid structure, Pilcher visited the many 'courts' or display areas dedicated to the rich architecture of earlier civilisations; here he found a Byzantine church, an Assyrian palace, and a Pompeian villa. In the South Transept, he noted the large quantity of statuary ('amongst the best in the World'), and in the Great Central Transept he praised the concert hall ('the largest & best music hall in the *World*') which contained the magnificent organ ('4,568 sounding pipes') used in the hugely popular Handel Festivals. Beyond these delights were Egyptian figures sixty-five feet high, an art gallery with 1,621 works ('all of them very choice'), an industrial museum, and schools of art, science and literature. As Pilcher concluded: 'every possible information of past ages and present times may be obtained here.'

In attempting to exhibit all human knowledge under one roof, the Crystal Palace aspired to be a living encyclopaedia, a People's Palace of enlightenment where anyone, from mill-hand to bank manager, could go for a day's entertainment and return home a wiser and better person. Here, with (according to Pilcher) its 8,000 visitors daily, was Victorian rational recreation at is best, as Pilcher himself could vouch: 'if a visitor could for a moment forget where he was, he would wonder what place of bliss he had got into. so much to please, so much to create curiosity, so much to instruct, every species of mind, excepting of course that of a fool, if a fool can be said to have one.' By experiencing the Crystal Palace exactly as the directors of the Crystal Palace Company would have wished, Henry Pilcher was the perfect visitor: he viewed the exhibits, he read his guide book, and he digested everything he saw. Indeed, he was so enthusiastic he even included descriptions of what he had not seen, such as the fountains outside ('the finest in the World') which were turned off on the day of his visit.

In its relocation from Hyde Park, the Crystal Palace at Sydenham had gained two transepts and two wings, and with its lavish gardens and greatly increased cultural content, it was no longer primarily an exhibition hall of industrial technology. The display of art and architecture that Henry Pilcher took pleasure in and which dominated at least half of the nave area was designed to provide the visitor with 'in practical fashion, an idea of the successive stages of civilisation which have from time to time arisen in the world, have changed or sunk into decadence, have been violently overthrown, or have passed away, by the aggres-

sions of barbarians, or the no less degrading agency of sensual and ener-
vating luxury'.[48] The warning against sensual luxury should perhaps be
read against the removal of the penises from the male statuary and the
riveting into place of fig leaves just one month before the opening day.
But in grander terms, the representation of previous civilisations was
integrated into a self-congratulatory narrative that seemed to lead inex-
orably from the earliest civilisations to Victorian Britain. Britain became
not just one of many civilisations, but the natural point towards which
all 'the successive stages of civilisation' pointed. At the very least, the
wealth required to mount such a display in such a building (£1,300,000)
appeared incontrovertible proof that Britain was pre-eminent among
present-day nations. The Crystal Palace therefore helped produce an
image of Britain of which the building could then become a symbol; in
this sense, the most important exhibit was the building itself, a fact
impressed on the visitors by the 1:24 scale model of the 1851 Crystal
Palace that they, like Henry Pilcher, discovered inside ('I was very much
pleased with the model'). As Pilcher implicitly admits, the Crystal
Palace had become Britain: 'No one "has seen England" unless he has
been to the Crystal Palace.'

In Harden S. Melville's painting, *The Squatters Hut: News from Home*
(1850–1851), three men in a bark and slab hut are depicted receiving mail
from Britain.[49] Watched by two caricature Aborigines, the European
men open their post, one of them leaning back in his chair to scrutinise
an illustration of the 1851 Great Exhibition Building in his copy of the
Illustrated London News. Henry Pilcher would have been 18 years old in
1851, and his identification of Britain with the Crystal Palace must have
been widespread among a whole generation of Australian-born
colonists. The irony of British culture being symbolised by a portable
iron structure, a structure much less grounded than the bark hut in the
painting, is one we can perhaps savour only by recognising that British
culture was formed out of social instability and conflict; with hindsight,
the Crystal Palace in the painting may indeed be a symbol of British
culture, but a symbol of a travelling culture, one in which the notion of
a fixed British Home was simultaneously reinforced and undermined
by the movement of people and buildings around Britain and beyond.

The Sydenham Crystal Palace as Horticultural Hothouse

In calling the Sydenham Crystal Palace 'a cucumber frame between two
chimneys,' Ruskin was correctly noting its debt to horticultural archi-

tecture, but he was wrong in at least one fundamental respect. Unlike either the Hyde Park building or a cucumber frame, the Sydenham Crystal Palace was heated, as of course a winter garden would need to be. Here Paxton again drew on his experience at Chatsworth, installing a low-pressure hot water system such as he had used for his horticultural glasshouses.[50] The Sydenham Crystal Palace, therefore, was more of a hothouse than either a greenhouse or a cucumber frame, and the creation of an artificial environment allowed Paxton to grow plants and trees inside the building as well as outside.

Paxton installed an additional boiler at the north end of the building to allow him to display hothouse exotics and, in particular, the palms that he bought in 1854 on the closure of Loddiges nursery at Hackney.[51] The Hackney Botanic Nursery was started in 1771 by the German gardener, Conrad Loddiges, and it developed into a complex of steam heated hothouses, among them a Palm House complete with artificial rain and said to have been the largest in the world.[52] Something of its effect can be gauged from an account by a German visitor published in 1829:

> *The first garden I visited was that of Messrs. Loddiges, and never shall I forget the sensation produced in me by this establishment. I cannot describe the raptures I experienced on seeing that Palm House. . . . I fancied myself in the Brazils; and especially at that moment when Mr L. had the kindness to produce. . . . a shower of artificial rain.*[53]

The development of Loddiges parallels the development of other botanic gardens, among them of course Kew, developed to contain the exotic plants being collected and sent to Britain from its growing overseas territories. During George III's reign, nearly 7,000 plant species were introduced into Britain.[54]

John Hix has argued that the engineering of an artificial climate was directly related to the nineteenth-century romanticism of the faraway place: 'it evoked the idyllic milieu of the New World and recently developed tropical lands, in contrast to the cold and unpleasant climate of northern Europe and the British Isles.'[55] Hix cites a description of Richard Turner's Regent's Park Winter Gardens (1846) given in Knight's *Cyclopaedia of London* (1851):

> *a veritable fairy land transplanted into the heart of London[,] an actual garden of delight, realising all our ideal. From the keen frosty air outside, and the floweriness aspect of universal nature, one steps into an atmos-*

phere balmy and delicious . . . . The most exquisite odours are wafted to and fro with every movement of the glass doors. Birds singing in the branches . . . make you again and again pause to ask, is this winter? Is this England?[56]

In order not to distract visitors from their romantic flights of fancy, gardeners dug tunnels to supply coal to boilers and to conduct smoke well away from such buildings; at Enville Hall in Staffordshire, for example, which Henry Pilcher visited in 1866, the smoke from the conservatory boilers issued from an 'elegant smoke tower, surrounded with Ivy, and banked up with huge banks of evergreens' concealed some distance away.[57] In some hothouses, additional features were combined with the plants: Loddiges had its artificial rain, and at Chatsworth in the 1840s, small tropical birds were introduced,[58] prompting *Punch* magazine to wax: 'The Glass Garden of Eden at Chatsworth where flourish palms without rattlesnakes, and sugar-cane with no yellow fever.'[59] In other places, brightly coloured fish floated on lily ponds or in fountains.

Unlike at Chatsworth, Paxton apparently had no real interest in having birds in his 1851 Great Exhibition building, though a group of sparrows seems to have colonised the building during construction and there was a rumour that the organisers feared resident sparrows might defile Queen Victoria herself at the official opening.[60] Some robins that made the new Sydenham building their home in 1854 were quickly eradicated,[61] but Richard Crocker visiting from Tasmania in 1859 noted 'Wattle in Blossom and young parrots' (13 August), and Henry Pilcher also found birds flying about, a feature that heightened the visitor's sense of escape to another place:

> *Different portions of the Crystal Palace abound in plants and trees brought from all parts of the World and placed in different parts of the building, in temperatures suitable for them, it has even the Australian gum growing within its walls, handsome creepers & vines are growing up the interior uprights of the building and many birds flying about loose, if a visitor could for a moment forget where he was, he would wonder what place of bliss he had got into. (4 August 1866)*

Of course, to the extent that this 'place of bliss' mimicked the faraway places of empire, it reminded Australians uncannily of their other, southern Home. The artificial climate of the hothouse, reversing outdoors and indoors, produced an exotic climate that was paradoxically familiar to the visiting Australian. If British Australians had a very fluid national identity, playing up the one side or the other as it suited them, they have been perennially never so Australian as when they were recording in their diaries and letters sights and sounds that reminded them of Australia. Eucalypts might be spotted almost anywhere: William Labett found some blue gums in Penzance in 1904; nursing sister Anne Donnell spotted 'a dear little gum tree' in a convalescent home in 1917; and in 1959 Edna Kerr came across gum trees in Stratford-on-Avon, growing in tubs on either side of a hotel entrance ('the last tree I would expect to see in a tub anywhere!').[62] When they went to the London Zoological Gardens they looked for Australian animals: Emma Walker 'Saw several Australian specimens' (5 November 1883), and Henry Pilcher spotted the carpet snake Moseley had brought over with him in their cabin: 'I saw the snake, my old bed fellow, it looks uncommonly well. Australia is well represented here, both in animals and birds' (2 September). And when Australians went to the Royal Botanic Gardens at Kew they picked out the Australian trees and plants growing in the Temperate House: 'Here I greeted the Australian plants with delight, they looked homelike and friendly. When I came to the wattles in blossom of which there was a great variety, quite a lump came into my throat' (Margaret Tripp, 23 April 1872). In escaping the climate of the colonies, the visitor from Australia suddenly felt at home in the artificial climate of the metropolitan hothouse; and had Joseph Paxton's plans for a Crystal Sanatorium ever been realised, who knows but that Pilcher, the consumptive bank manager from New South Wales, might have found himself being treated in London in an Australian climate among Australian birds and botanical specimens.

Metropolitan Aborigines

The Sydenham Crystal Palace had other exhibits to catch the Australian eye. Richard Teece, a twenty-eight year old insurance clerk from New South Wales, found Aborigines in the Crystal Palace:

*This was rather an eventful day. In the morning we visited the Horse Show at Islington where we saw a fine display of hunters. At the invitation of M*ᶜ*Laren, a friend of the General's, we accompanied him to the Crystal Palace in the afternoon. The occasion was a Flower Show, & of course there was a great display of flowers animate & inanimate. Having religiously walked ourselves tired & made several erudite comparisons of the relative merits of azaleas, rhododendrons, blue-eyed & blackeyed roses*

&c, we had dinner in the grand salon & this I may add was one of the most pleasing features of the entertainment. We were somewhat amused at seeing a number of photographs of Queensland blacks under the heading of exhibits from South Australia, & a little mortified to learn that Melbourne was the whole of Australia. A very little trouble would bring New South Wales into prominent notice, but whilst our Agent General's office remains as it appears to be a place of entertainment for billetless English swells, such a consummation is scarcely to be expected. (29 May 1875)

The photographs of Aboriginal people were most probably exhibited by Richard Daintree (1831–1878), a man who, as Agent General for Queensland from 1872 to 1876, worked tirelessly to promote Queensland as a migrant destination.[63] He was far more successful at mounting effective exhibitions than his counterparts from the other Australian colonies, even if, judging from Teece's comments, his efforts at the Crystal Palace had become appropriated by South Australia. This is one of those infrequent passages in which the diarist identifies with a specific colony rather than with a generalised Australia; yet, it mattered only to someone from New South Wales if the Aboriginal people were from Queensland or South Australia. To the British and other European visitors, what was on display here, as at Kew or in the London Zoo, were exotic specimens from some distant and less civilised place in the empire; indigenous colonial exhibits were, as Annie Coombes has pointed out, 'signifiers of British sovereignty.'[64]

For Australian visitors to the Sydenham Crystal Palace, the sense of being at home indoors must have become even more uncanny when they came to the south transept. Here was housed the Ethnological and Natural History Department and its displays brought together animals, plants, and human figures from various areas of the globe. The routes suggested by the guidebook were intended to achieve the maximum effect from this integration of different types of exhibit: 'Continuing along the path, we pass a glass-case containing a selection of North American birds, and beyond this we arrive at a group of North American Red Indians engaged in a war-dance, and surrounded by trees and shrubs indigenous to North America'.[65] In this way, the visitor could wander around the less civilised regions, marvelling at the inhabitants of the New World and the Old World before ending up, had they been following the route taken by the guidebook, in Australia. The effect of this display may be judged by Henry Pilcher's description of the Natural History Department:

it is that portion of the building which is set apart for the groupings of men animals and plants, these are so arranged, as nearly as possible, so that the men, animals, and plants, of the various climes to which they severally belong may be exhibited separately together, keeping each climate's productions separate. Life-sized plaster of Paris (or some composition perhaps wax I do not know) figures of the men[,] women & children, of the various aboriginal tribes of all new countries, are here shown, and the figures are also coloured to represent faithfully the colour of the different races, Australia has her share of representation, our natives by comparison rank very low in the scale of civilization,. [sic] the figures are all faithfully created and very life like, some are placed in the attitude of inflicting a death blow upon an enemy, and look so natural, that to come upon one of these groups suddenly is apt to startle anyone. (4 August 1866)

Like his guidebook, Henry Pilcher emphasised the novel manner in which the specimens were displayed. By grouping together humans, animals and plants, the intention was to imitate different environments, to recreate the connections between botany, zoology and ethnology that were not possible at Kew Gardens, London Zoo and the British Museum. But, of course, this way of exhibiting natural history was also intended to allow visitors to experience these environments as discrete places rather than simply as exhibits; there was a deliberate policy to eschew the glass cabinet for, according to the guide book, 'picturesque groupings.'[66] Such a division of the internal space of the building is behind Pilcher's apparent surprise at seeing aboriginal figures while wandering between the trees and the stuffed animals.

This experience was made possible by the glasshouse and the heated, artificial environment that permitted exotic plants, fish and birds to survive in Europe. Hence the clear connection between the display of enthnological figures at Sydenham and John Claudius Loudon's vision back in 1817 of the future development of the hothouse, 'when such artificial climates will not only be stocked with appropriate birds, fishes and harmless animals, but with examples of the human species from the different countries imitated, habited in their particular costumes and who may serve as gardeners or curators of the different productions.'[67] Despite its mid-Victorian intention to educate the general public, the south transept of the Sydenham Crystal Palace evokes Loudon's romantic vision, the creation in London of the authentic, inhabited tropical forest.

Of course, by the 1850s, the romanticism had waned, the image of the tropical forest had darkened, and it was now inhabited by savages who were not so benign as Loudon's indigenous curators. Indigenous peoples did not come up to British expectations, and rebellions in India in 1857 and in Jamaica in 1865 suggested to the British that their imperial subjects could only reach a certain level of civilisation.[68] In scientific terms, this was rationalised in terms of race. Indigenous peoples were no longer viewed as being variants of a common species, and the humanitarianism that had been shown in the anti-slavery movement gave way to a construction of negroes, native Americans, Maori or Aborigines as innately different, as races apart incapable of improvement to the level of the British. This racialist view gained support from a number of quarters, from the apparent decline in the number of aboriginal people, but most especially from ideas loosely defined as Social Darwinism which proposed that inferior 'races' would become extinct where unable to evolve and adapt to the pressures of a more progressive civilisation; as D. Macallister put it in the *Melbourne Review* of 1878:

> *The Australians surely demonstrate, by their evident doom, that races below the level where self-prompted progress exists are unable to adapt themselves to the conditions forced upon them by civilization, and that, therefore, they must perish when brought into contact with it. The same great fact is being exemplified in every land where savagery has been brought into sudden conflict with a high civilization.*[69]

'Self-prompted progress,' so magnificently celebrated in the Crystal Palace, would ensure that in the not too distant future Aboriginal people would only be found as exhibits in a metropolitan Natural History museum.

There was apparently nothing in Henry Pilcher's Australian way of looking at the world that made him question this. The Crystal Palace confirmed the heights that British civilisation had reached, the broadening gap between the British and the colonised of the empire, and the necessary disappearance of Aboriginal people as the lowest race on earth that such a narrative entailed. Indeed, the very notion of progress depended on the belief that some had not progressed, that there were people in the world who were backward and whose backwardness would ensure that they died out. If the Crystal Palace, that fairy palace of light, celebrated the dizzy heights that a technologically and culturally progressive civilisation could reach, the illusion was built on Aboriginality constructed as the antithesis of civilisation. Empire could be justified by theories of racial superiority, and the success of the narrative of progress that underpinned the Crystal Palace was built on the necessary construction of a racial hierarchy, at the bottom of which were those primitive and savage Aborigines that Australians saw exhibited.

Metropolitan Tropical Forests

With the sweeping away of savagery came the creation of new imperial spaces. The 'penetration' and opening up of the tropical forest was one of the major projects of British imperialism, both literally, in terms of economic exploitation, and metaphorically, in terms of christianising the Dark Continent's dark inhabitants. All was to be made transparent to 'the controlling gaze' that Bennett identified in the design of the Great Exhibition building; just as the presence of curators in museums had gradually been replaced by display cards and guidebooks, so indigenous people were no longer to be necessary to a European understanding of imperial spaces.

Even in areas where there was no tropical forest, the controlling gaze still had to be deployed if the land was to be mastered. Because of Aboriginal firing practices, the Australian bush commonly appeared to British eyes like English parkland, an open and evidently unpopulated landscape that invited settlement. Nonetheless, even in Australia, as Simon Ryan has shown, the necessity of both cartography and aesthetics as discourses of mastery over 'wild recesses' required Australian explorers to seek elevated vantage points.[70]

However, in the hothouse context, Bennett's controlling gaze does not produce 'self-surveillance and hence self-regulation'; it is not democratic in impulse and the viewer does not 'double as both the subject and object of a controlling look.' Visitors to the Great Exhibition certainly looked down onto other visitors, but the Crystal Palace gallery was also a direct descendent of the gallery in the botanical hothouse. The gallery of the Palm House at Chatsworth had a dual function: it was a watering platform and a vantage point from which to view the plants.[71] Visitors to Chatsworth were not, of course, members of the general public and so surveillance was unnecessary. The Palm House at Kew Gardens (1845–1848) also has a gallery, and though the building was built as a response to the opening of Kew Gardens to the public in 1841, the gallery does not have the primary function of self-regulation. An engraving of the Kew Palm House in the *Illustrated London News* of 1852 shows visitors 'transported into a tropical forest,' wandering along shaded walks among 'the vegetable Titans,' while above, on the gallery, others look down not on the people below but on the profusion of the forest. The text accompanying the engraving invites the visitor to enjoy a 'bird's-eye' view from the gallery, but it is a view of the gardens outside, not of other members of the general public.[72]

Anne McClintock among many has pointed out that the achievement of mastery over the new spaces of empire was cast in gendered terms; this was because much of the work was carried out by European men and because imperial ideology was patriarchal.[73] Yet this clearing away of the concealed spaces, this 'penetration' of space, required a feminine space that resisted. If, as Paul Carter argues, the cultural opposition between movement and stasis would disappear once we were grounded, then oppositions between feminine and masculine spaces, or between Aborigine and European, would also disappear once imperial ideology had completed its work. But of course imperial ideology, bound up as it was with the economic strength of an industrialised Britain, did not aim for the eradication of difference, it aimed to control faraway peoples and places. For such power to be maintained, a tension between the opposites had also to be maintained. The stability and the clearing of the ground inherent in the myth of settlement can, indeed must, never be achieved. Complete mastery would be the end of mastery.

It is in the tropical forest of the botanical hothouse that some of these tensions were articulated in the metropolis. The hothouse, in the manner of its construction, enacted a tension between mobility and stability. But it also enacted the tension between concealed and open spaces, for unlike in the self-surveying 1851 Great Exhibition building, it was possible, and perhaps desirable, for the visitor to the botanical hothouse to get a little lost among the trees. A comparison of the interiors of the Hyde Park and Sydenham Crystal Palaces shows that, although the vista remained, the Sydenham building had many areas screened by the plants, trees, creepers and vines that Henry Pilcher noted.[74] If the assertion of cultural authority depended on a landscape that resisted the all-encompassing imperial gaze, then what was being imitated in Sydenham, as in the hothouse, was a feminine Nature based on dark and wild recesses. In the same way that dinosaurs lurked among the trees of the parkland, inside among the botanical specimens were examples of human prehistory. Indigenous people were the proof of Social Darwinism, a construct of the British middle-classes; bourgeois imperial culture demanded a Nature full of concealed spaces, 'wild recesses,' in which lurked lower and historically prior forms of humanity. By inserting enthnological figures into this forest, the Sydenham Crystal Palace was merely allowing the visitor to re-enact the interplay of concealment and vision on which imperial mastery depended. Through industrial technology, it was creating in the metropolis the necessary fantasy of imperial space.

Metropolitan Degeneration

Ironically, as the British Empire rapidly expanded, the Crystal Palace, that monument to the supremacy of the British race, deteriorated. What was evidently an impressive exhibition of British technological and cultural excellence in the 1850s and 1860s was, by the 1880s, somewhat seedy and run down. Writing to her mother in 1864, Jane Murray Smith could be almost as enthusiastic about the Crystal Palace as Henry Pilcher:

> *The next day the Hunts and all of us went to the Crystal Palace. It looks at first like a fairy palace. We had only time to see the inside. It is like an enormous green house with fancy shops in it and statues etc. They have one part fitted up like an ancient Roman house, there is an Egyptian part and all different countries. It is a delightful place to go to, and would not, like everything else in England disappoint you. (10 April)*

Twenty years later, however, Emma Walker from Adelaide took the opposite view: 'Was much disappointed at the contents. Used now as a kind of bazaar, and concert hall. There were several groups of three or four races of blacks including our own. The most beautiful part, the grounds[,] I did not see, and indeed knew nothing of them till I returned' (8 November 1883). Thomas Lodge Murray-Prior from Brisbane concurred:

> *there is a sombre appearance about the place as if it was going down, did not pay, and so was more or less neglected. – among other things there are some full sized Indians &c. and Australians, the latter very unlike those I have seen, miserable looking specimens and the others gave the same feeling. Will leave any more thoughts of the locale for another visit – I was disappointed. (29 June 1882)*

The Crystal Palace at Sydenham certainly did not pay, despite attracting an average of two million people each year in its first thirty years,[75] and the cost of its upkeep gradually began to tell on the fabric of the building. Even the Aborigines seemed to have degenerated; whereas for Pilcher they were 'all faithfully created and very life like,' by the 1880s they had become so miserable as to be 'very unlike those I have seen'. In any case, by this time real humans were being exhibited to international audiences in 'native villages,' as at the 1889 Exposition Universelle in Paris.[76]

By comparison with the interior of the Crystal Palace, the extensive pleasure grounds covering some 200 acres retained their ability to impress, partly because, in an apparent contradiction to the educational thrust of the high culture exhibited within the building, they staged ever varying popular entertainments and spectacles; the Crystal Palace grounds became increasingly well-known not only for their extravagant panoramas and firework displays, but for less traditional attractions such as balloon trials and bicycle races. Even Murray-Prior, who was disappointed by his visit as a whole, was reasonably impressed by the fireworks:

a couple of Baloons [sic] with fire works in the Parachute going off at different heights was good – illuminations they had a naval fight (said.) Spanish Armada. four or five vessels. traced with fire lines. shewing Hulls and sails very effectively. and Firing at one another the masts falling sea quite green. it was intended to shew the Vefsels sinking but this did not succeed they tumbled to pieces and went out. but the illusion was very good. We did not stop to hear the Organ. as it was getting late and there was a great rush for the train. (29 June 1882)

The visual displays at the Crystal Palace were usually of a patriotic nature, and as popular opinion was mobilised in favour of empire they became increasingly jingoistic, with British military adventures in Egypt and the Sudan standard fare throughout the 1880s; the 1882 bombardment of Alexandria was enacted in fireworks and William Willis, who migrated as a child to New South Wales, saw 'a splendid panoramma [sic] of the battle of Tel el Keber' (25 May 1889). Later the Boer War provided the inspiration.

The cost of admission was used as a way of regulating the mixing of social classes at the Crystal Palace, the price on Saturday usually being raised from one shilling to two shillings and sixpence. This social segregation may be why the traditional Easter gathering of working-class Londoners at the Crystal Palace was never invested with the status of national event. Unlike the Epsom Derby, the Easter gatherings were not attended by royalty. It is true that Queen Victoria had her own apartments and was a regular visitor to the Crystal Palace, at least until the death of Prince Albert in 1861, and there is a long list of royal visitors throughout the nineteenth century, including Napoleon III (1855), Tsar Alexander II (1874), and Kaiser Wilhelm II (1899). Nevertheless, large gatherings at the Crystal Palace pleasure grounds became identified as occasions for the 'People,' though increasingly without the educational connotations of a 'People's Palace'.

Reginald Wyndham, a New South Wales pastoralist, visited the Crystal Palace a month before Murray-Prior on Saturday 20 May, a flower show making it a special five shilling day: 'Went to the Crystal Palace. saw the Flower Show very nice indeed. particularly some Australian Wild Flowers which were much finer than I ever saw in Australia. the Crystal Palace Grounds are very fine. can't say much for the old Palace' (20 May). As in Murray-Prior's description, the building disappoints. Unlike Murray-Prior, however, Wyndham found the opportunity for a second visit and this time he went on a shilling day; he wanted to go to Canterbury, but finding the train left too late, he instead joined a festive crowd of working-class Londoners enjoying the Whit Monday public holiday at the Crystal Palace:

> *Went to the Crystal Palace Grounds at five and saw a twenty mile B[ic]ycle Race. each mile on level Ground. being done on an average of four (4) minutes. there I saw a large Baloon [sic] go up with six men in it. it rapidly went out of sight. I must say I did not envy the men in it. there must have been ten thousand people* in the Grounds and it was really painful to see such a miserable degenerated lot of people. not only small. but such miserable specimens of humanity. the Girls of the lower orders here are* very ugly *remarkably* large mouths & generally a *turned up nose. (7 August 1882)*

The most interesting aspect of this visit, however, was not so much the bicycle race or the balloon ascent but the working-class crowd itself: 'it was really painful to see such a miserable degenerated lot of people. not only small. but such miserable specimens of humanity.' The description is coloured by the class viewpoint: 'the Girls of the lower orders here are *very ugly remarkably* large mouths & generally a turned up nose.' Such a description is also, of course, gendered, and male travellers often characterised specific places by the perceived beauty of working women, as in J. I. Martin's description of Belfast:

---

* *The Papers stated the number of people to be 44,760.*

It is a splendid City & much like Melbourne. Fine wide streets & foot-paths & large handsome Street Windows. We were struck with the difference in the appearance of the young Ladies: – they are by far the handsomest we have seen in any City we have visited. Even amongst the poor class, generally tripping with bare feet, you can catch glimpses of pretty fresh faces, peeping out of their shawls wrapped round their heads & shoulders. (29 June 1891)

But Wyndham constructs the crowd most especially in terms of racial degeneration. As 'miserable specimens of humanity,' Wyndham regards the working people in Social Darwinist terms much like Pilcher regarded the plaster Aborigines inside the building: 'very low in the scale of civilization.' As the guide book put it: 'The Australian men [i.e. Aboriginal men] here depicted strike us at once by their half-starved, lanky, and ill-proportioned bodies; they may be looked upon as savages, hunters, and inhabitants of forests; they possess that excessive projection of the jaw which ethnologists make one of the distinguishing traits in the most degraded forms of man.'[77] It was similarly 'ethnological' features that indicated the degeneration of the 'lower orders' in Wyndham's account: '*remarkably* large mouths & generally a turned up nose.'

This racialisation of the working classes occurred in the later part of the nineteenth century. The British middle classes, once they gained political ascendancy, were always suspicious of the growing industrial working class, and the construction of People's Palaces such as the Crystal Palace, the People's Palace in the Mile End Road, and the People's Palace in Glasgow were intended through self-education to instil civic virtues in a potentially unstable working-class population. Many of the visiting middle-class Australians seemed to see the British working classes in this light, a class viewpoint evident in Henry Pilcher's description of the crowd demonstrating in favour of Parliamentary Reform at Hyde Park in 1866:

the mob rushed the gates, broke them down, pulled up the iron palisading, attacked and sadly maltreated hundreds of policemen, tore up many young trees in the Park, very much injured the flower beds, and did all the damage it was possible for an uncontrolled ruffianly mob to perpe-trate. . . . The Inn I stopped at was close to the Park so that I had the benefit of this turbulent manifestation of English freedom commonly spoken of, as the 'Freedom of the Subject'. The object of the reform is the extension of the suffrage to which, of course, all sensible people are opposed. . . .

*Before England consents to this sort of Reform, I would say, vide,
Australian Parliaments. (23 July)*

As Catherine Hall has shown in her essay, 'Rethinking Imperial
Histories,' the debate in Britain about what it meant to be a citizen took
place within the context of changing definitions of citizenship in the
colonies. All the eastern colonies of Australia, except Tasmania, had
adopted male suffrage for their lower houses during the 1850s, an extension of voting rights bitterly opposed by men such as Robert Lowe who,
in the 1860s and now as a British MP, spoke out strongly against
extending the vote in Britain, pointing like Pilcher to the Australian
experience: 'In the colonies they have got Democratic Assemblies. And
what is the result? Why, responsible Government becomes a curse not
a blessing.'[78] He added that if rights of citizenship exist, 'they are as
much the property of the Australian savage and the Hottentot of the
Cape as of the educated and refined Englishman'. Henry Pilcher,
evidently as keen to air his views as Robert Lowe, found a like-minded
audience after tea at his hotel in the form of the Attorney General of
Nova Scotia: 'he quite coincided with me and told me that in Nova
Scotia through the instrumentality of himself & some others they
managed to abolish universal suffrage. May some patriot do the same
for Australia' (19 August 1866).

However, in the later nineteenth century this class antagonism came
to be expressed in terms of race. Industrialisation brought with it large
concentrations of urban poor, and the environment in which these
people lived and its effect on their health came to be seen as an internal
threat to the racial superiority that, as an idea, had been constructed in
the colonies. In the eighteenth century, environmental differences were
held to account for the variations in humankind to be found in the
world; it was this belief, and the possibility that a change of environment could lead to their 'improvement' that sustained humanitarian
and benevolent attitudes towards indigenous peoples. With the shift
from environment to biology as the determining factor in social development, indigenous peoples became racialised and therefore
irredeemable.

This ought to have left the British middle classes feeling fairly smug
that they were near the top in terms of racial superiority and without
any danger of sliding back down. Unfortunately, the detrimental effects
of the environment continued to lurk behind Social Darwinism,
suggesting the possibility of racial degeneration. And though it was
(hopefully) not possible for an Anglo-Saxon to degenerate into a negro

or an Aborigine, if a biological race could progress it was also possible for a biological race to regress, as J. Milner Fothergill argued in a paper given before the British Association for the Advancement of Science in 1887:

Assuming the Norse to be the highest type of mankind, we find the town dweller to be a reversion to an earlier and lowlier ethnic form. While the rustic remains an Anglo-Dane, his cousin in London is smaller and darker, showing a return to the Celto-Iberian race. . . . Nor is this reversion confined to the Celto-Iberian. In the true bred Cockney of the East End, the most degenerate cockney, we can see a return to an earlier archaic type of man. . . . In appearance, the East-ender, to the mind of the writer, bears a strong resemblance as to figure and feature, to the small and ugly Erse who are raised in the poorer districts of Ireland. . . . As towns grow larger and more numerous, the Cymri are going to have their own again – though not exactly in the manner prophesied by the old Welsh bards.[79]

The key issue here is environment. Or rather, the key issue for the racial biologists who proposed theories of racial degeneration was the environment. By the late nineteenth century, metropolitan society was an urban society, and the unprecedented size of the new industrial city brought with it a whole range of fears for the newly empowered middle classes. There was obvious urban pollution. There were problems of sanitation and water supply, the pollution of drinking water leading to outbreaks of typhoid and other bacterialogical diseases; there was obvious atmospheric pollution. There were housing problems, with jerry-built tenements quickly becoming slums. And there were social problems, such as large-scale prostitution, alcoholism, mental instability, and crime. In the late nineteenth century, the wild recesses of the city became the focus for various anxieties, and as Nancy Stepan has pointed out, racial biology was a 'science of boundaries,' employed in reaction to social mobility and class tensions: 'Racial "degeneration" became a code for other social groups whose behavior and appearance seemed sufficiently different from accepted norms as to threaten traditional social relations and the promise of "progress".'[80] Racial biology was a way of keeping people in their 'proper' places.

In a period which equated nationalism with racial type, concerns for the fitness of the working classes became concerns for the fitness of the nation, with obvious consequences for Britain's position in the world; in the same year as Henry Pilcher visited Britain, John Edward Morgan,

Physician to the Salford Hospital, published his monograph, *The Danger of Deterioration of the Race*. Many of his anxieties about public health in the cities are recognisable today, such as his concern for adequate diet, sanitation, and housing. But his remarks are framed by a more specifically late nineteenth-century concern: 'May not nations, like individuals, curtail their day of power in the world's history, by over-taxing the physical and mental energies at their disposal, thus prematurely consuming that national life-blood on which permanent greatness mainly depends?'[81] An unhealthy urban environment could undermine British industrial leadership, making Great Exhibition buildings museum exhibits in their own right. And as the empire became more important in terms of British self-confidence, so the degeneration of the urban poor came to be seen as a threat to British imperialism. Migration neatly became one way of ensuring the survival of the race, though, from Alexander Sutherland's Australian perspective in 1888, Social Darwinism necessarily entailed the extinction of Aboriginal people:

> *It was less a case of dying off than of failing to be born. The black man, indeed, paid the ordinary penalty we must all submit to; if he sadly regretted that he left none to inherit his blood we pity him, but our thoughts travel to the much harder scenes that would have been in city slums of the old world, and we are content with the balance.*[82]

It is in the context or urban degeneration that J. Milner Fothergill thought the British were degenerating into the Welsh, or worse still, the Irish:

> *A higher intellectual culture obtains in towns; there are more amuse-ments; commerce is more active. Consequently towns possess an attraction for many persons; and a steady stream of immigration sets in from the surrounding country to the central town. But in the history of the past these civilisations have not been permanent. They have become effete and disappeared under the onslaught of rude barbarians, whom, despite their civilisation, they could not cope with or resist. The old civil-isation of Egypt gave way to the Shepherd Kings; the Assyrian Empire broke to pieces; as did the Persian at a later day.*[83]

Here, then, with this mention of the Egyptian, Assyrian, and other extinct civilisations, was the connection between the various 'Courts' of the Crystal Palace with their displays of past civilisations and the

Natural History exhibits with the savages of lower races. Although the Egyptians, the Assyrians and the Persians were accorded a civilisation while Aboriginal people were not, the demise of past cultures was both a proof of Social Darwinism and a warning to the British: degenerate, as your urban working classes seem prone to do, and you will slide back down the scale towards the condition of the Aborigines. Far from being inhabitants of the imperial periphery, Aboriginal people, in the form of a racialised Aboriginality, were central both to the construction of British racial superiority and to theories of racial degeneration in the metropolis.

Boomerangs in Bethnal Green

In his speech at the fixing of the first column of the new Crystal Palace at Sydenham, the chairman of the Crystal Palace Co, Samuel Laing, MP, praised the behaviour of the working people who had visited the Great Exhibition a year earlier:

> *the experience of the Great Exhibition of 1851 had fully confuted the notion that they were unworthy of a place of amusement – that they were so immersed in the fumes of tobacco and gin that it was useless to hold out to them any temptation to better things. 6,000,000 of visitors in less than six months – (Hear, hear) – conducted themselves with a propriety which refuted that calumny, and proved that, if the palace be made worthy of the people of England, the people of England would flock in millions to it.*[84]

It is difficult to imagine today the unprecedented nature of such large numbers of working people travelling to London to view the Great Exhibition. Not only was the size of the movement unprecedented, so too was the very fact that, thanks to the railways, working people were now highly mobile. From the perspective of the middle classes, here was scope for 'wantonness' on a massive scale. That there was no attempt at revolution, and not even a riot, came as both a relief and a surprise.

Working people having apparently proved they were not 'wanton,' in Carter's sense, and could behave as responsible citizens, a number of prominent men looked at ways of sustaining the Great Exhibition's educative project not only at Sydenham but by establishing a museum for working people in the East End of London. Several schemes were discussed but nothing materialised until 1865 when it was suggested that the Brompton Boilers, due to be dismantled and removed from South Kensington, might be re-erected in the East End. A site was found in Bethnal Green on Poor Lands previously rented to butchers, and the following year, the Brompton Boilers were themselves being dismantled ready for their removal to Bethnal Green.[85]

The Bethnal Green Museum opened in 1872 with a combination of the Wallace art collection and two popular science collections: 'One was devoted to Food (explaining the chemical constituents of foodstuffs, and teaching good dietary principles), the other to Animal Products (a mix of natural history and industry, showing what useful things could be made of fur, feathers, bones etc).'[86] Both of these transferred with the museum from South Kensington, where they had been intended to educate the working classes in health and household management.[87] In fact, the Animal Products collection had previously transferred to South Kensington from the Great Exhibition, and it was displayed at Bethnal Green until the 1920s. Such are the continuities of mid-Victorian paternalism.

The museum temporarily acquired the Lane Fox collection of ethnological artefacts in the summer of 1874, the collection comprising, with the exception of a small number of skulls, mainly weaponry and miscellaneous implements. Col. Augustus Henry Lane Fox needed to find a museum to house his private collection of over 14,000 artefacts,[88] though the choice of Bethnal Green was not entirely arbitrary; Bethnal Green was an area of working-class radicalism and the exhibition was to be an experiment in the educative use of anthropology.

George Stocking has argued that the Great Exhibition stimulated new ways of thinking about human sociocultural evolution, quoting William Whewell, Master of Trinity College, Cambridge, in 1852: 'by annihilating the space which separates different nations, we produce a spectacle in which is also annihilated the time which separates one stage of a nation's progress from another.'[89] The annihilation of time and space apparent at the Great Exhibition also affected Lane Fox, and the objects in his collection were displayed sequentially and by type, so that, for example, throwing sticks and boomerangs were so arranged as to suggest an evolutionary gradation from straight to curved shapes: 'the whole of the Australian weapons can be traced by their connecting links to the simple stick, such as might have been used by an ape or an elephant before mankind appeared upon this earth, and I have arranged them so as to show this connection on the screens.'[90]

Boomerangs might instruct the working classes of Bethnal Green in three ways. First, the evolution of material culture was demonstrated to be fundamentally conservative; the arrangement of artefacts was designed to show evolution as a succession of small, slow and inevitable stages, a model that could then be used to justify the existing social order. In this model, there was no place for revolution, as Lane Fox famously put it later: 'the Law that Nature makes no jumps, can be taught by the history of mechanical contrivances, in such way as at least to make men cautious how they listen to scatter-brained revolutionary suggestions.'[91]

Second, the model of evolution suggested by the sequential arrangement of artefacts could be applied to racial as much as to social progress. In a lecture given before the Anthropological Institute at the Bethnal Green Museum in July 1874, Lane Fox pointed out that not only did the implements of 'existing savages' show no sign of having degraded from a more complex cultural form, Aboriginal wooden implements, being constructed on the grain of the wood, demonstrated that Aborigines were the 'lowest amongst the existing races of the world': 'In every instance in which I have attempted to arrange my collection in sequence, so as to trace the higher forms from natural forms, the weapons of the Australians have found their place lowest in the scale, because they assimilate most closely to the natural forms.'[92]

Lastly, the collection was designed not only to demonstrate to the working classes that evolutionary progress was essentially conservative, it was also arranged so that it could be easily comprehended by the working-class mind, a mind, as Lane Fox inferred in his lecture, not dissimilar to that of the savage; in making a distinction between the 'automaton' mind and the 'intellectual mind,' Lane Fox was also making a racialised distinction between the working classes and the educated middle classes.[93] In sum, the boomerangs in the Lane Fox collection were used simultaneously to constitute and demarcate race and class.

But visitors to Bethnal Green might have seen other boomerangs on display carrying a slightly different message. In a letter to the Colonial Secretary in Brisbane dated 13 November 1874, Richard Daintree, the Agent General for Queensland wrote: 'the complete series of photographs exhibited at Vienna [the 1873 Exhibition], has been sent to the Brisbane Museum, another is now available for the Bethnal Green Museum in the East of London, and a fair collection is already placed at the Crystal Palace.'[94] Daintree had been taking photographs of Australian scenes since his arrival on the Victorian goldfields in 1852, and his promotion of Queensland as a migrant destination depended on his imaginative and early use of photographs in the various exhibitions he mounted in the 1870s. Many of Daintree's photographs were of

geological formations and agricultural life, reflecting his earlier employment as a geologist both in Victoria and later in northern Queensland.
However, he also photographed Aboriginal people, and the
'photographs of Queensland blacks' seen by Richard Teece at
Sydenham in May 1875 were, if not Daintree's own, almost certainly
part of the collection to which Daintree refers in his letter of November
the previous year. A photograph of Daintree's Queensland annexe for
the 1872 International Exhibition at South Kensington shows two
enlarged photographic prints of Aboriginal men, holding discretely
positioned weapons in place of fig leaves, looking down on a bust of
Queen Victoria, while between the prints is a display of 'native
weapons'. The Queensland display at the 1876 Centennial Exhibition in
Philadelphia included two similar prints of Aboriginal men, in line with
the displays of the other colonies: 'the Australians considered
Aboriginal weapons and implements significant elements in the presentation.'[95] It is probable, therefore, that Daintree's Bethnal Green display
included some prints of Aboriginal people and similar Aboriginal artefacts.

Like Lane Fox's display, Daintree's photographs and artefacts were
intended to instruct. Peter Quartermaine has drawn attention to
Daintree's sense of the role of photographs and museum displays 'in a
general educational process, rather than as a political or economic end
in itself,' witness Daintree's concern to exhibit in Brisbane as well as
Bethnal Green.[96] But the immediate political and economic aim of
Daintree's work as Agent General was to promote migration to
Queensland, and in this his display at Bethnal Green differs from that
of Lane Fox. While Lane Fox intended that East Enders should remain
in their place, Daintree intended them to move, preferably to
Queensland. Indeed, as Alexander Sutherland argued in 1888, migration was a necessity for the racial health of the working-class areas of
the metropolis. The colonial context highlighted yet again a mobility
that the metropolitan context attempted to deny; less a case of demarcation than of embarkation.

The Brompton Boilers having been moved to the East End of London
so that the working classes might be kept in their place, the re-erected
iron structure was then encased in architectural brick as though it was
feared the Bethnal Green Museum might also go walkabout. The brick-
work may have been intended to give the museum extra rigidity, but it
made the building look more like a railway station than anything else.
Yet to the extent that, as Hitchcock has argued, railway stations
combined the relative permanence of masonry with the contrasting

impermanence of their iron and glass sheds,[97] the addition of a brick shell to the Brompton Boilers heightened the tension between stasis and mobility. In this sense the Museum embodies the tension between the Aboriginal displays of Lane Fox and those of Daintree, the tension between remaining in place and migration.

Even the railings outside the Bethnal Green Museum articulated opposing messages. On the one hand, they demarcated space and people, marking an inside of rational recreation opposed to the illicit pleasures of darkest London outside. On the other hand, the railings erected outside the museum were the same 'iron palisading' that Henry Pilcher recorded being uprooted in Hyde Park in 1866 only twelve days before his encounter with the Aborigines at Sydenham.[98] Both the Brompton Boilers and the Hyde Park railings were displaced in 1866, and while they have remained where they were re-erected side by side in Bethnal Green, there is a degree of situational irony in their conjunction that draws attention to the instability of boundaries in nineteenth-century Britain. And in a broader sense, like the portable iron houses owned by the National Trust in Melbourne, they are testimony to the uncertain spaces of the British Empire itself.

FOUR

Roast Beef and the Epsom Derby: Social Status and National Identity

Uncertain Departures

Reginald Wyndham was a muddled man and, somewhat perversely, his diary of his trip to Britain begins not with his own departure but with that of his wife, Julia:

> *March 8.1882. at Leconfield. I now commence to keep a Diary beginning on Saturday the 4ᵗʰ when my Wife and all our dear little Children left Sydney in the Parramatta at 6.30 A.M. Mʳˢ Champain Mʳˢ Acres & Hart also being on board. Acres & I came off in a Watermans Boat while the Parramatta was being towed out to sea. A dull morning very much like Rain. Wind unfavourable for the Parramatta. had Breakfast at the Club. then up to 12 Oclock very busy with Johnson about forming a Company to work my Coal Mine. then watched Cricket Match. England versus Australia up to 3 Oclock when heavy Rain stopped the play. Percy McDonalds Batting magnificent. Got into Newcastle at 7.30 A.M. on Sunday after rough passage. Came on here. place all right. House shut up looking very lonely & I feel very lonely. everything reminding me of my Wife and our dear little ones.*

Despite the muddle and apparent perversion of describing not his own but Julia's departure, Reginald Wyndham introduces into his very first entry the two main preoccupations of his trip to Britain: coal and cricket. The reasons for his preoccupation with coal and, in a different way, with cricket can be recovered and both relate to Wyndham's social status as a New South Wales pastoralist.

Reginald Wyndham was the twelfth of thirteen children born into what was, potentially at least, more a dynasty than a family.[1] George

---

87

Wyndham, the father, educated at Harrow and Cambridge, came to New South Wales in 1827 and established Dalwood, a large property in the Hunter Valley. During the economic depression of the early 1840s, the Wyndhams trekked north and took up properties first at Kilgra on the Richmond River and then at Bukkulla on the Macintyre; it was during these travels that Reginald was born. In 1847, they returned to Dalwood but by 1870, the year in which George died, the properties were again in serious financial difficulties and Bukkulla was foreclosed by the banks in 1875. Dalwood itself was repossessed around 1890 and the vineyards purchased by Penfolds. Although the last of the Wyndham vines was taken out in 1961, the vineyard, now owned by Orlando, continues to produce a range of wines marketed under the name of Wyndham Estate.

The failure of George Wyndham to establish a dynasty appears to have been the result of hostile economic conditions coupled with his eleven sons' uneven inheritance of their father's business acumen. Hugh Wyndham, who withdrew from the firm of Wyndham Bros. in 1874, was one of the more shrewd of the brothers, and by 1888 he was in a position to buy Bukkulla back. Reginald also withdrew just before the crash of 1875, though in his case, ironically, it was not through foresight but because he objected to measures intended to curb the spending of the more extravagant of the Wyndham brothers (including, one suspects, himself).

By the time he began his diary in 1882, Reginald owned Leconfield, part of the old Dalwood property which had been subdivided in 1870, but his financial position was again unstable and his preoccupation with coal derived from his insecure hold on Leconfield; he badly needed an alternative source of income if he was to continue the life of a gentleman pastoralist who travelled to Sydney to stay at his club and watch cricket.

In order to float his mining company, Wyndham needed to travel to London, the main source of venture capital for Australian businesses. Quite why he sent Julia and their four children on ahead by sailing ship is difficult to untangle; the *Parramatta* was a fast and reliable sailing ship with an experienced captain, but by the 1880s it was far quicker and more comfortable to travel by steamship via the Suez Canal. Possibly his financial state made him choose the cheaper option for his family, though the two women accompanying Julia, Mrs Champain and Mrs Acres, were her mother, Harriet, and her sister, Georgina; Julia therefore sailed on the *Parramatta* as part of a matriarchal group comprising herself, her mother, her sister and five children. And as Julia was also five months pregnant, there were obvious additional advantages of travelling with her mother and sister.

Although the first event in his diary is the departure of Julia to London, Wyndham actually opened his book and began writing four days later: 'March 8.1882. at Leconfield. I now commence to keep a Diary beginning on Saturday the 4ᵗʰ when my Wife and all our dear little Children left Sydney.' Possibly he began a diary because his own departure was now uppermost in his mind. Luckily, a possum fell down his chimney the day after his return to Leconfield so he had an anecdote with which to fill the pages prior to his own departure: 'disturbed by strange noise. and after getting up for the 3ʳᵈ time discover an OPossum in my Bedroom Grate. caught him by the Tail & killed him.' In the days that follow he records selling off much of his livestock, presumably to cover expenses while he is away and to provide some cash for his trip to Britain. On Thursday he takes six fat cows into Maitland: 'Cows only made 4/4/- [four guineas] per head' (9 March). The following week he is offered ten guineas a head for his 127 bulls: 'will accept offer if Cash is given.' He is allowed the weekend to consider the offer and on Monday reluctantly accepts a cheque (not cash) for £1260: 'I don't like the sale.' The following day, 21 March, he leaves Leconfield for Britain: 'feel very downhearted at leaving this pretty place which I am so fond of.'

By Thursday 23 March, he is back in Leconfield, having arrived in Sydney only to discover he had forgotten some important papers connected, doubtless, to his coal mine. The endearing aspect of this blunder is not so much that, for a man born on a journey, Wyndham is an incompetent traveller, but that once again he has to run through his sentimental repertoire for saying farewell to Leconfield: 'Saturday 25. My last day here. a lovely bright afternoon. I water Claras Pot Flowers. & Ivys little Garden. I wonder if I shall ever water these again?' (25 March). The sentimentality may have been heartfelt, but it is mercifully short-lived, and one of the more instructive aspects of Wyndham's muddled diary is the way in which his sentimentality is so obviously rhetorical. It is the product of the occasion, a fleeting impulse that, as will be seen later when used abroad, reveals contradictions in his perception of Britain.

In terms of journeys, this muddle at the beginning of the diary shows that, although we think of travel symbolically as beginning with departure and ending with arrival, in practice departure and arrival are not clearcut. Does Reginald Wyndham's departure begin with the departure of his wife and children? He clearly thinks of his diary as the diary of his travels, and he begins it with Julia leaving on the *Parramatta*. Or does his journey start with his own departure from Leconfield, his first sentimental farewell? Yet having returned to collect his papers, Wyndham notes: 'seems strange to return again. wish to be on my travels now' (23 March). He reaches Sydney once more on 26 March, dines with some friends and leaves for Melbourne by train the following day. In Melbourne he attends a dance and is kept up until 5.50 am, eventually leaving for England on the *Shannon* at 1.15 pm: 'great Crowd came to see us off' (29 March). If farewells symbolically mark departure, which farewell counts as the beginning of the journey? Journeys involve multiple departures and the muddle of Reginald Wyndham's double departure from Leconfield emphasises the way in which travel exceeds our models of the journey. Muddle is, in fact, the condition of travel.

The nature of the space left behind also questions the way in which we view journeys. Departure is conventionally seen as departure from a place, but if we consider the ways in which places are culturally constructed, we can see that departure changes the nature of the place left behind. When Julia Wyndham left Leconfield for London, she may have thought she was leaving her home behind, but homes are not fixed places, and the space she vacates changes, as Wyndham noted: 'Came on here. place all right. House shut up looking very lonely & I feel *very* lonely. everything reminding me of my Wife and our dear little ones.' The gendered, domestic space centred on his wife and children has moved off, leaving him feeling lonely, and presumably his own departure would have affected Leconfield for those he left behind. When Australians travelled to Britain, they may have thought of themselves leaving home, but the home they left behind was not there waiting for them to return. They took it with them, both as the space in which they travelled and as the Australian home in their imagination.

Indeed, if places are culturally constructed rather than physical spaces with essential characteristics, then any continuity of social identity means there can never be absolute beginnings to journeys. The problem of the final farewell is linked to the problem of delimiting social worlds. When Wyndham leaves Leconfield he goes to Sydney where he dines with friends; one of the ways in which he feels at home in Sydney is through the social practice of dining. When he leaves Sydney he goes to Melbourne and attends a dance; again, the social practice creates a familiar space. And when he leaves Melbourne, he dines and dances his way to Europe on the *Shannon*. The cultural rituals that define Wyndham's social identity stretch from Sydney to Sydenham, an homogenisation of space that defies movement and travel. Wyndham may have been a muddled man caught in a multiplicity of departures, but to the extent that he was able to retain a social identity as a gentleman landowner, he stayed in the same place.

The Social Geography of Travel

On 28 March 1882, two days before Reginald Wyndham finally boarded the *Shannon* in Melbourne, Thomas Lodge Murray-Prior left Brisbane for London on the *Almora*. Like Wyndham, Murray-Prior was a landowner and travelling first class, and in a broad sense the men were social equals, members of the pre-gold rush squattocracy, though Murray-Prior was older than Wyndham by about twenty-five years and far better connected politically; he was a Member of the Queensland Legislative Council, having been nominated in 1866, and he had served as Postmaster-General, first as a public servant and then in various ministries between 1866 and 1874.[2] As Postmaster-General, Murray-Prior had to decide along which routes the mail should be carried, a duty that required him to engage with the social politics of space, as his brief appearance in the diary of Rachel Henning makes clear:

A few days ago we had a visit from Mr Prior, the Postmaster-General, who was travelling through this district to decide on the places whence a regular mail was needed. I suppose it does not require any great talent to be a 'Postmaster-General'. I hope not, for such a goose I have seldom seen. He talked incessantly, and all his conversation consisted of pointless stories of which he himself was the hero. The witty sayings that he had said and the clever things he had done. However, we treated him very respectfully, and Biddulph [Rachel's brother] gave up his room to him, and I think he left us under the idea that a mail to Exmoor was necessary for the good of the country, and the tenders are already out for it.

So we shall probably have it at the beginning of next year, and a great benefit it will be. He was very much disgusted at the treatment he received at Fort Cooper, the next station to this. I believe it is the dirtiest station on the road, and the overseer would not lend him a horse. I do not know whether this will stop the mail from running on to Fort Cooper or not. (15 October 1863)

If journeys, like mail routes, require discrete points of arrival and departure, those points are socially constructed not only in a broad sense, but in highly specific ways: postal routes could depend on the lending of a horse.

There is no evidence that Wyndham and Murray-Prior were acquainted, and they almost certainly had no idea they were travelling to Britain at the same time, and yet the paths of the Wyndhams and Murray-Priors had crossed at least twice before. Murray-Prior had been born in the West Country, and had migrated to New South Wales in 1839 at the age of nineteen; in order to gain experience as a pastoralist, he went to Dalwood, the property established by George Wyndham, Reginald's father.[3] Even before the Dalwood connection, there was a Belgian connection; in the 1820s, Murray-Prior spent several years of his childhood in Belgium, being educated in Brussels by a private tutor, while in 1827 George Wyndham married Margaret Jay in Brussels, where her father kept a school. The economic depression of the 1840s that forced George Wyndham to take his family north from Dalwood also displaced Murray-Prior; in 1843 he met Friedrich Leichhardt (1813–48) and left Dalwood with him for Moreton Bay. While Leichhardt went on to Port Essington and fame as an explorer, Murray-Prior acquired land and went in for sheep and politics.

These travels of the Wyndhams and Murray-Priors are a reminder not only that the British in the nineteenth century were highly mobile, but that there is a social geography of travel. Belgium in the 1820s attracted the British upper classes; similarly, in the 1830s a young man in possession of moderate capital might head for New South Wales, Upper Canada, or the Cape Colony (George Wyndham himself had tried Canada before arriving in New South Wales in 1827). It is evident that over a lifetime people of similar social standing make similar journeys, and that what we call migration might be seen as part of a broader pattern of travel. Separating the migrant's 'voyage out' from other kinds of journeys to other destinations is justifiable if the object is to stress its symbolic status as a rite of passage, but it also obscures the distinctive social geography of travel and plays down the mobility of migrants, both before and after migration. In fact, we need to trace patterns of travel across generations, and Reginald Wyndham's trip to Britain in 1882 was related to that of his father, George, to New South Wales over fifty years earlier. Although he was born in New South Wales, Reginald Wyndham was, like Murray-Prior, tracing in reverse an earlier journey.

Despite differences of age and place of birth, colonial men sailing first class to Britain in the nineteenth century inhabited British culture in similar ways, sharing both a general social geography and the particularity of the journeys that constructed that geography. Passenger lists make the social inclusiveness of first-class travel obvious, and on the *Almora* Murray-Prior's fellow cabin passengers included the Hon. C. Holmes A'Court, Clerk Assistant of the Legislative Council, James Archer, brother of the Colonial Treasurer and John Sinclair, a former Mayor of Brisbane.[4] These men had probably not chosen to travel together but they would already have known each other, and in general the long voyage to Britain with its enforced social contact undoubtedly played an important role in deepening many socio-political allegiances among the wealthier colonists. Yet this should not obscure the fact that this journey was only one of number that they might have in common, and that the coming together in the cabin on ship of people with similar social statuses is part of a much wider social geography.

Quite how this worked for women is not so obvious, though the matriarchal group in which Julia Wyndham sailed suggests that the social experience of travelling women was more private than public. Certainly, Rachel Henning's view of Murray-Prior the Postmaster-General shows a more cynical attitude to public office than would have prevailed among the men on the *Almora*. Nonetheless, the reasons many women travelled and the pattern of their travelling were determined by their husbands or fathers. Jane Murray Smith, who made her first trip to Britain in 1863 with her husband, Robert, accompanied him again when he was made Victorian agent-general in 1882, the Murray Smiths embarking from Melbourne on the *Shannon*, the same ship as Reginald Wyndham. Although Jane Murray Smith's letters written on her earlier voyage have survived, there is no account of her voyage on the *Shannon* so no direct comparison can be made. Wyndham himself makes only three references to the Murray Smiths, his longest relating to Lillias, Jane's twenty-year-old daughter. The occasion is a visit to Galle (Sri Lanka):

> *the pretty Vallys [sic] & Hills meeting the Eye in every direction. with mountains the blue Sea in the distance. made the scene one I shall never forget and amply repays one for the Sea Voyage. but notwithstanding all this most charming scenery I still thought the most charming part of it was Mifs Murray-Smith (who is a pretty brunette with a nice figure and most lovely brown Eyes) in a very pretty white Drefs and large white Hat. with this Australian addition the scene was perfect. (17 April 1882)*

Such a description, like the prose in which it is written, is conventional; by placing a young women in a picturesque landscape, Wyndham is attempting both to feminise the landscape and to equate femininity with nature. The aim of such descriptions in late Victorian British culture was to construct women as objects rather than agents, to reinforce the middle-class, patriarchal doctrine of separate spheres for women and men. The practice, of course, belied such representations, as Wyndham's later diary entry in London makes clear: 'Went to 3 De Vere Gardens. Kensington. W. & Lunched with M^r & Mrs Parbury. & Mi∫s Murray Smith. there arranged preliminaries about my Coal matter with Parbury' (Sunday 23 July). The conjunction of Lillias Murray Smith and negotiations to sell a mining lease suggest that Wyndham's introduction to Parbury came from Lillias' father, Robert Murray Smith, Victorian agent-general. Doubtless Wyndham took the opportunity during the passage to Britain to outline his scheme to anyone with influence. Yet such a conjunction also demonstrates how women did not inhabit separate spheres but shared the social geography of the men, a social geography of travel in which political alliances and business deals took place. Thus it could come about that a well-connected young women from Geelong might ease the leasing of a coal mine in the Hunter Valley over lunch in a select district of London.

Uncertain Arrivals

Whilst Reginald Wyndham's diary demonstrated the difficulties of identifying where Australia ended, Thomas Lodge Murray-Prior's diary demonstrates a parallel problem of where Britain begins. In some ways Murray-Prior took the easier option, not beginning his diary until he had landed safely in Plymouth and had spent his first night in England for forty-three years:

> *Monday 22nd May 1882.*
> *Slept very little what with the strange bed and the heat and noises of Trams Carts &c. The Duke of Cornwal [sic] Hotel being just opposite the Railway. – Got up pretty early. Archer and Mr Bowen down in time for breakfast, which we enjoyed nice fresh butter. Beef Steaks and Eggs. but I cannot say there was much difference in the taste of the Beef which was excellently cooked.*

The beginning of a day, the beginning of a diary entry, and the beginning of a new diary all overlap to emphasise the break between what has come before and what is to follow. The blankness of the book is to stand in for the receptivity of the childlike mind that is ready to record first impressions of this new country. And the linearity of the diary, the way in which one page follows another, represents the linearity of time, the way in which the trip is to be seen as a narrative constructed from successive events. Thus, in the first entry, Murray-Prior travels to London and meets his sister, Louisa, whom he has not seen since his youth. The second entry takes him successively to the Bank of New South Wales in London, to lunch with his daughter, Rosa Praed, and to Hyde Park to look at the upper classes on display. On the third day he goes to Epsom Downs for the Derby, on the fourth day he is reunited with his other sister, Jemima, and on the fifth day he is shown round a South London butcher's shop.

At this point the parallel between the diary and the narrative breaks down; the sixth entry is dated Sunday 21 May, the day before the diary begins, and is an account of the *Almora*'s passage up the English Channel to Plymouth. The writing here is less dense and gaps have been left for the insertion of names, most notably the name of the hotel in Plymouth. Evidently, this entry was written before what precedes it, and it is in fact followed by a duplicated entry for Monday 22 May: 'Up early seedy and unrefreshed J. Archer and Mr Bowen came down and we had a nice breakfast punnished [*sic*] the butter and rolls then went to the Railway for 8.30 AM train.' The entry ends before the train reaches London and the next page has been left blank. The diary then resumes on Saturday 27 May, the sixth day, with Murray-Prior leaving London to stay with his daughter, Rosa.

It is not possible to recover the complete archaeology of Murray-Prior's diary, there are too many unanswerable questions, but he seems to have incurred problems similar to those that caused the muddle at the start of Wyndham's diary. While Wyndham found it difficult to identify an absolute farewell with which to begin his journey, Murray-Prior found it hard to identify an absolute arrival in England. There is a logic in beginning with the voyage up the Channel, but the fact that he left some pages blank suggests he intended filling in details of the voyage later. The problem seems to be that he lacked the time to do this, so he began again at the beginning of the book with his first night on land, omitting even the first sight of England. What we can say is that, having built up an initial and aptly termed backlog, Murray-Prior battled with his diary throughout his visit to Britain. Only a week after landing, he records: 'Intended to get up early and write up my log which I have neglected since my arrival in England and will soon forget the days: But the little boys came in and I had to tell them a storey in bed. and Rosie did not feel so well so I went in to her and had a chat with her. before Breakfast' (30 May). The question of when this entry was written further deepens the problem of recovering the relationship between the events and the writing.

Perhaps, then, it is more productive to see the issue of beginnings and endings as a matter of convention and not to expect experience to fit into a book with its clearcut linearity. Looked at this way, the question is not so much where Australia ends and Britain begins as how to construct a symbolic beginning, something that corresponds to the symbolic farewell to Australia. The difference between the two entries for 22 May gives some idea of how this might be achieved:

J. Archer and Mr Bowen came down and we had a nice breakfast punnished [sic] the butter and rolls

Archer and Mr Bowen down in time for breakfast, which we enjoyed nice fresh butter. Beef Steaks and Eggs. but I cannot say there was much difference in the taste of the Beef which was excellently cooked.

In the second version, the comparison between Australian and English beef is the first indication in the diary that we are dealing with someone who perceives he has crossed cultures, and it helps to establish the identity of the diary writer; it is evident that the second version is more artful than the first. Murray-Prior was a more than competent diary writer, he was a cultured man with a host of literary connections: his first wife, Matilda Harpur, was a daughter of the (unknown) Australian poet, Thomas Harpur;[5] his second wife, Nora Barton, was aunt of the (famous) Australian poet A. B. 'Banjo' Paterson; and his daughter, Rosa Praed, made her name in Britain as a novelist. Murray-Prior clearly knew how to select events and combine them to produce a narrative of arrival. Each is significant: the train journey to London, the recognition scenes with his sisters, Hyde Park, his trip to Epsom, his chat with the bank manager, even the inspection of the butcher's shop. Each episode serves to build up a picture of an astute and well-educated landowner being welcomed back to the land of his birth.

But an element of artifice should not be seen as invalidating the diary as evidence; it is not that the earlier version is nearer the truth, but that the second version is simply better constructed. Reginald Wyndham's diary for his first few days in Britain contains much shorter entries than Murray-Prior's and can be regarded as a continuation of his shipboard diary, when the habit of recording a few lines each day is well-established. Yet even though it is strikingly less artful, Wyndham's account follows a similar narrative pattern. Like Murray-Prior, Wyndham catches the train from Plymouth to London, taking the opportunity to describe the countryside in conventional, almost parodic terms: 'the bright Flowers everywhere nice well kept Farms and happy looking Villages. with Happy looking ruddy Faced people. besides Cattle & Sheep in every little Field in clover & gra*f*s up to their Knees made the run to London one *never* to be forgotten' (17 May). Like Murray-Prior he participates in a recognition scene; he visits Hyde Park and comments on the horses; he spends the day at the Epsom races; and he passes judgement on the roast beef: 'I certainly never tasted any Beef to equal it. and it is so very tender' (18 May).

The art of the diary, therefore, is not so much to invent a pattern, as to draw out the narrative pattern that both men were intent on performing. The similarities between the diaries, despite a clear difference in literary ability, is the result of both men performing a socially prescribed sequence of events and then selecting those things to write about. Again it is a question of a social geography. The diary colludes with the desire of the Australian pastoralist to be treated as a gentleman returning to a world which recognises his social position and his right to belong in Britain. It is the function of an account of the first few days in Britain to confirm the relationship between social identity and place.

The Roast Beef of Old England

In a letter from London dated 7 April 1829, James Macarthur recounted to his mother an incident involving roast beef and a Frenchman. Macarthur was born in New South Wales in 1798 and educated in Britain and the Continent between 1809 and 1817, his father, John Macarthur, having been effectively exiled from New South Wales for his part in the 1808 rebellion against Governor Bligh. Between 1828 and 1830, James was again in England, overseeing the sale of wool from the Macarthur estates and learning about the European wool industry. In his letter to his mother, he describes an incident in the Piazza Coffee House in London:

> *The Coffee room was undergoing some repair so we were ushered into a small room up stairs where there were only three tables one of them occupied by a Lord Hill, Sir R. Hill & another gentleman – We were soon followed by four French men, only one of them apparently spoke English – The Waiters were engaged at the moment of their entrée in setting down*

*the dinner for Lord Hill's party – utterly regardlefs of this the Frenchman
instantly bawled out 'Vetire ve vant dinnire directly – Vot ave you got
prête I mean reddie – Ave you any reddy fish'? There was no ready fish
and while the loquacious impatient Monsieur Francais was consulting
his companions the Waiter disappeared – The Poor Frenchman rang the
Bell paced up and down the room uttered some half dozen sacrés Diables
&c at last in a moment of happy inspiration he exclaimed – 'Ah I know
ve shall have se Rosbiff – Dat is always reddie – C'est une viande Anglaise
toujours prête – Vêtaire – Bring us some Rosbiff quicklee,' and so saying
he sat himself down quite happy & content without giving himself the
trouble of being satisfied whether the waiter had understood him or not
– A considerable time elapsed without any symptoms either of the waiter
or the Beef – The other French men in their turn became impatient &
asked Monsieur L'interprete whether dinner was coming – 'Oh oui,
certainement, sans doute, du Rosbiff – C'est une viande Anglaise
toujours prête.' At length the waiter came – but alas without the rosbiff
– 'Vaitere shall you bring our dinere – Ve go to de Play – de time is short
– 'What have you ordered Sir'? 'Rosbiff' – 'Roast Beef I'm very sorry Sir
but we have none to day' – 'Comment? – no rosbiff in England! den ve
shall not dine at all! &c so saying away they all walked in sad dudgeon
without their dinner – .*

In Macarthur's anecdote, the relationship between Englishness and
roast beef, and the vanquishing of the loquacious Frenchman demonstrates the superiority of the English, particularly their manners, while
reinforcing roast beef as an English dish. The roast beef confounds the
Frenchman by refusing to appear, and he departs, acknowledging that
roast beef is the quintessential English dish: 'no rosbiff in England! den
ve shall not dine at all!' Macarthur admits that, had it not been for the
Frenchman's 'noisy and intrusive demeanor' he might have helped him
procure his dinner, but he also admits that 'we laughed very heartily as
soon as they were out of hearing – Lord Hill seemed to enjoy the joke
particularly'.

The joke works, however, not only to sustain the link between roast
beef and Englishness but to establish a social rapport, as Macarthur sees
it, between himself and Lord Hill, a man well enough known at the time
to need no further introduction: Viscount Hill was a veteran of the
Peninsular war against the French and was Commander in Chief of the
British Army from 1828 to 1842; Sir Rowland Hill was his nephew and
heir. In other words, the joke should be seen in its social as well as its
national aspect, and attending to roast beef as a symbol of a generalised

Englishness is to miss its social context. Clearly Macarthur associates himself with Englishness in this encounter, but it is also an Englishness with a fairly exalted social hue, and Macarthur's patriotism, if we can call it that, should be seen in terms of his social position, something of which he is very much aware when comparing England and New South Wales later in his letter:

> *I have drawn much to cheer me in my future prospects from the experi-*
> *ence it has given me of life in England in all clafses, from the*
> *magnificence of our friend Mr Watson Taylors sphere, to the quieter*
> *circles of those who are more upon a par with ourselves. I am now*
> *convinced that many of the ills we are apt to consider as exclusively our*
> *own prevail every where – and we have many advantages which in*
> *England would be unattainable – True happinefs after all consists in*
> *useful & honorable employment with occasional recreation – All this we*
> *have within ourselves* at home *to a much greater extent than most*
> *persons in England – I do not mean to say that persons brought up here*
> *would think so, but we natives of the Woods of Australia must & ought*
> *so to consider it.*

Whether the convicts employed on the Macarthur estates would have seen it quite like this is debatable, but it is clear that James Macarthur's sense of the differences between England and New South Wales relate to the structure of society and his own place within it. In the 1820s and 1830s in New South Wales, those settlers untainted by the social stigma of transportation called themselves 'exclusives' to distinguish them-selves from the 'emancipists'; in their view, the political power of the colony should remain in the hands of those at the top of the social hier-archy. The other term used to describe this group was 'merinos' after the fine-woolled sheep pioneered in particular on the Macarthur estates. Clearly mutton, like beef, can be used as a social as well as a national symbol.

The association of beef with Englishness gained a particular nuance in the eighteenth century when, following the Act of Union of 1707 joining Scotland with England and Wales (united politically since 1536), a sense of a British national identity came into being. One of the prob-lems faced by the English both then and now has been that, because English culture is the dominant culture within Britain, the English have had problems finding an identity that was specifically English rather than British. The English derision of the diet of the Welsh, the Irish and particularly the Scots, and their praise of a wholesome and essentially

English way of cooking beef can be regarded as an attempt by the English to retain some sense of a distinct national identity. As Richard Perren points out: 'In England, and in particular London, there was a strong preference for the taste of roasted meat, but in Edinburgh and in the rest of Scotland people were very much in the habit of living on broth and boiled meat.'[6] Yet, to the degree that, as Linda Colley suggests, the sense of Britishness that came into being was influenced by an anti-French sentiment, the eighteenth-century derision of French cuisine and the use of sauces or diced meat in favour of plain roast beef can be regarded as one of the ways in which English culture came to stand for British culture.[7]

James Macarthur's use of the Englishness of roast beef could there-fore be carrying both connotations, asserting an essential Englishness and yet employing roast beef to evoke a Britishness constructed in oppo-sition to a French national cuisine and identity. Yet to concentrate on the issue of national identity is to mask the particular social contexts within which symbols of national identity operate; although a belief in the Englishness of roast beef may be shared among many people across time and across differing social groups, it is employed for different effect depending on who employs it. James Macarthur used roast beef in conjunction with a caricature portrayal of a Frenchman to define himself as English; but he also used it to associate himself with an inclusive social hierarchy.

Macarthur was writing only fourteen years after the battle of Waterloo, and his delight in the discomfiture of the Frenchman reflects the historical rivalry between the two most powerful states in Europe. A sense of that rivalry persists almost fifty years later in Mary Kater's account of her arrival in Britain from France:

> *By rail to Calais, & then across the Channel and on to London – It was so pleasant to feel oneself in an English speaking country again – We felt at home at once at the railway-station and all the officials are so much more polite than they are on the Continent – We reached the 'Great Western Hotel['] between six and seven and Harry went round to see Mrs Kater after dinner[.] We enjoyed an English Beef steak so much after the French dishes – they dont know how to cook meat in the English fashion and if you ask for Roast Beef they give you 'Fillet de Boeuf' which is meat first partially boiled, in order to extract the goodness out of it to make soup of, and just browned before the fire[.] of course it is a very econom-ical way of using the meat[.] (15 April 1875)*

Kater's sense of being at home is endorsed by eating roast beef on her first day in England, though, as in MacArthur's account, the assertion of the Englishness of roast beef masks the social context of its use, and Kater's criticism of French cooking, in displaying her knowledge of nutrition, also serves to represent her as a competent young middle-class wife and mother.

Yet the antagonism between France and England was waning (the two were allies during the Crimean War in the 1850s), and in several accounts by Australian men in the 1880s and 1890s, roast beef acted as a comparator not between France and England, but between Australia and England. William Willis, for example, on his way to the country of his birth after many years in Australia, makes no mention of the incongruity of coming across roast beef at the battlefield of Waterloo: 'We were very anxious to begin sight seeing and equally anxious for lunch. The stomach triumphed over sentiment and we were soon enjoying the best bit of roast beef, tasted since leaving home. It was cooked in real old English style' (19 May 1889). Presumably this was French beef roasted to suit the palate of English tourists, but even so his encounter with the English national dish in France provokes not Anglo-French rivalry but Anglo-Australian rivalry. Willis is writing to his wife, Alice, and his assertion of his own Englishness prompts him to remember his wife's Australianness: 'It was cooked in real old English style, or perhaps, in compliment to you, I ought to say *Australian*.' Aware that beef may now signify Australianness as well as Englishness, Willis produces the nonsense of roast beef cooked in real old Australian style. The effect of his qualification is paradoxically to undercut the Englishness of roast beef at the same time as it reinforces the Englishness of an Australian culture.

By the 1880s, beef was far more important to the Australian economy than in the 1820s and it had become, as reflected in the diaries of later Australian visitors to Britain, a measure of the success of Australian colonisation. Australian men arriving in England in the 1880s and 1890s seem to have felt obliged to try the roast beef for its quality. In 1891, J. I. Martin visited Britain as a member of the Victorian Mounted Rifles, disembarking at Gravesend and arriving at London's Waterloo Station at lunchtime: 'So we took the opportunity to get some lunch, & a very good one we got, including our first taste of the Roast Beef of Old England' (12 May). And a year later, Richard Hannan, a public service messenger who travelled to Britain with the New South Wales premier, George Dibbs, in 1892, had a 'grill steak' on his first day in London: 'but I will not say anything about [it] until I try more' (8 June 1892).

For some Australian visitors, the roast beef question is raised at the beginning of the visit and then disappears. For pastoralists like Reginald Wyndham and Thomas Lodge Murray-Prior, the quality of Australian beef was a more pervasive concern, particularly as both men came from regions which by the 1880s were predominantly cattle areas (the Hunter Valley and coastal southern Queensland). Five days after his arrival, Murray-Prior found himself passing a butcher's shop in Balham; he stopped to inspect the beef on display and found himself being shown round by the proprietor: 'I was glad to be able to compare these Animals with ours as my eye was fresh for a comparison' (26 May 1882). Both he and Wyndham commented on what caught their eye on their various train journeys, and both men visited the Royal Agricultural Society's Show at Reading in July. Wyndham's diary entry for the day is a catalogue of the livestock, and he was generally impressed by what he saw, though he was disappointed with the shorthorns: 'they were not up to what I have seen at the Sydney Show' (10 July). Australian pastoralists took particular pride in their shorthorn cattle.

When Murray-Prior visited the Reading Show two days later, he too recorded the livestock in great detail. Yet he also notes: 'The Prince of Wales came about 2.30 PM.' and 'M^r [blank] Smith asked me to remember him to Judge Harding and tell him I met him he had somehow heard I was from Queensland' (12 July). The Reading Show was open only to those who could afford the two shillings and sixpence entry fee, and its importance as a social occasion was marked by the presence of royalty. If the Reading Show was about beef, it was also about prime, socially superior beef, an indication that, for pastoralists like Wyndham and Murray-Prior, national symbols and national pride were intrinsically connected to their own social status.

The construction of beef as a symbol of Australian national identity was deep rooted. The advent of the global economic and military ascendancy of the British in the later nineteenth century was parallelled by an argument justifying imperialism in terms of race. The British assumed themselves to be superior not only in terms of technology and culture, but to be inherently superior as a race. Yet while successful colonisation seemed to support this theory, one of its concomitants, that other races were inferior because of environmental factors such as climate and food, produced an anxiety that British colonists would degenerate physically and intellectually towards the level of the indigenous inhabitants.

The quality of Australian beef intersected with this in at least three ways. First, since degeneration would occur most obviously through breeding, if cattle could breed successfully in Australia, then so could the British themselves; the quality of Australian livestock could therefore be regarded as an indicator of whether or not the British race would degenerate when transplanted overseas. Secondly, if roast beef was an indication of the kind of nourishment required by the superior race, then high quality Australian beef would support the continuance of the race in Australia. And lastly, if roast beef signified Englishness, then any superiority in the quality of Australian over English beef would indicate the national superiority of Australia. The taste of beef, like the outcome of a cricket match, could become a test of the nation's calibre. As Rolf Boldrewood put it in his essay on 'The Australian Native-Born Type' (1901), having run through the relative merits of merino sheep, race horses, and shorthorn cattle until he arrived at Australian sportsmen:

> They have abundantly demonstrated that they could 'make the pace' and yet exhibit the 'staying power,' which is the great heritage of the breed. Lofty of stature and lithe of limb as they might be – though all are not so – they have shown that they have inherited the stark sinews, the unyielding muscles, the indomitable, dogged energy of those 'terrible beef-fed islanders' from whom we are all descended. In the boat, on the cricket-field, at the rifle-targets, and in the saddle, the Australian has shown that he can hold his own with his European relatives.[8]

Or as the *Australasian* expressed it in December 1877 prior to the cricket tour of 1878: 'The visit of an Australian eleven will be productive of immense good, both to the colonies and the old country. . . . Their hitting powers will testify that the beef and mutton of the country they represent is the right sort, and their activity in the field will be the best argument that the climate is conducive to energy and muscle.'[9]

That the beef was the right sort was established decisively in 1882 when the touring Australian cricket team achieved a dramatic win over England at the Oval and returned to Australia with the 'ashes' of English cricket. In June 1882, Reginald Wyndham watched the Australians beat 'the Gentlemen of England' at the Oval by an innings and one run: 'some 20.000 people looked on. and seemed greatly surprised at the result. staring at each Australian in wonder' (24 June). And in August he watched Australia beat England, again at the Oval, by just eight runs: 'the ground was immediately rushed by some 20.000 people the excitement being immense. one man burst a blood Vessel from excitement and died immediately. this is certainly the best and most exciting Cricket Match ever played. & a glorious win for "Australia"' (29 August). As with beef, such a comparison managed to achieve what seem today to be contradictory ends: the comparison between Australian and British cricket was a measure of Australianness at the same time as it was a confirmation of a shared British culture. Wyndham had cause to celebrate the 'glorious win for Australia,' but it was nonetheless a case of beating the English at what the English could still regard as their own game, and the Ashes have remained permanently at Lord's Cricket Ground.

Many have pointed out that constructions of 'the Australian' such as Boldrewood's are gendered, but in their stress on physical prowess – 'the stark sinews, the unyielding muscles' – they also had a class aspect. In an account of his visit to Britain in 1860, Boldrewood presents himself as English by identifying with some railway navvies: 'As I noticed the broad shoulders, the vast chests, and astonishing muscular development of many a gang of navvies, I felt proud of the blood in my veins, and of my English descent.'[10] Such men, he acknowledges (and disregarding the probability that they were Irish), are 'the flower of agricultural counties of England,' but they represent the potential of all English agricultural labourers when 'fed as Australian labourers are fed, with as much beef, tea, or beer as they can consume'. His argument is therefore that the good supply of beef helps to make the average Australian labourer far above the average English agricultural labourer:

> *without the smallest desire to disparage Giles and Hodge, whose material is the best and worthiest, and, as is only the case in the nobler races, infinitely improvable, I distinctly assert that their Australian cousins, Jack Windsor and Billy Day, will meet them any day in the harvest field, and at mowing, ploughing, reaping, or haymaking will do a better day's work in considerably less time.*[11]

Boldrewood was a failed pastoralist turned successful writer, and it is instructive that as a middle-class Australian visiting Britain he should be keen to identify with the figure of a healthy, well-fed, bronzed Australian labourer. In calling upon the benefits of the Australian climate and the quality of Australian beef to counter any suggestion that Australians were racially inferior, Boldrewood turns the agricultural labourer into a representative Australian. Or to look at it another way, the labourers Jack Windsor and Billy Day become distinctively Australian as a result of a comparison between the working classes of Australia and England.

In his well-known novel, *Robbery Under Arms* (1888), Boldrewood constructs the Marston brothers as healthy, strong Australian cattlemen, sons of a selector working a small farm in New South Wales. But he also, somewhat improbably, shifts their manliness onto the hero, an upper-class Englishman turned bushranger, Captain Starlight, who is revered as much for his manners and intellect as for his horsemanship. The construction of Starlight as a character draws attention to the need to construct an Australian type who is as cultured as he is muscular; or, in terms of social status, a type who, though he may have the physical prowess of a navvy or an agricultural labourer, was nonetheless as cultivated as the English upper classes. It is therefore appropriate that the novel was dedicated to Robert Murray Smith, the Victorian agent-general who helped Wyndham lease his coal, a handsome man who was known for his learning and his chivalry.[12] While the appeal to Australian roast beef emphasised the physical aspect of an Australian national identity, those cultivated middle-class men who constructed such a type could not allow their creature to exclude them from being counted as true Australians; it could not be just a question of the quality of the beef. Nonetheless, it was with a sense of being a true Australian that Reginald Wyndham went back to his diary and, in parentheses, amended his initial impression of English roast beef: 'I certainly never tasted any Beef to equal it. and it is so very tender. (this was an exceptionally good bit of Beef)' (18 May). In its own small way, this amendment was an act of Australian patriotism.

'This being the Derby Day, we felt that we owed a duty to our country which it behoved us to discharge'

A few days after their arrival in Britain, both Reginald Wyndham and Thomas Lodge Murray-Prior travelled to Epsom Downs to watch the Derby, and their reactions, like their assessment of English beef, again demonstrate how a comparison between England and Australia could simultaneously confirm both difference and sameness, though in the case of Derby Day, the terms of the comparison could be rather more complex.

Historically, the Derby was founded by the British aristocracy, that social rank who could not only afford to stable, breed, and race animals that were of no productive use, but who could also afford the large stakes necessary to bet on the outcome of the races.[13] Horse racing developed in the eighteenth century as a rich man's pastime and, for those with little else in their aristocratic lives, considerably more than a pastime. The Epsom Derby, however, developed into something more than an occasion for aristocratic social display; it was first run in 1780 and by the early years of the nineteenth century Derby Day had been adopted as an annual festival by both the working people of London and the smaller number of travellers who ran the fair ground. The Derby's popularity with Londoners was due partly to Epsom's proximity to London (about 20 miles from central London), partly to Epsom and Walton Downs being common land and freely accessible to all, and partly to the Derby being run on a Wednesday, a good day for a festival if you were working a six-day week.[14] By the mid nineteenth century, William Frith's painting, *Derby Day* (1856–58), could portray the Epsom races as an occasion of social harmony, where the social elite could be joined by London flower sellers and fairground acrobats in the enjoyment of a national, and specifically British, occasion.

Of course, the image of social harmony should not obscure the social structure underlying it and, as with the notion of roast beef as a symbol of nationalism, in practice the Britishness of the Derby depended on a geography of social inclusion and social exclusion. Derby Day could be celebrated as an example of social cohesion because of the presence of royalty, a continuing presence at least from the later nineteenth century to the present day. But such cohesion depended on 'deference,' a key term in Walter Bagehot's analysis of the workings of the English body politic, *The English Constitution* (1867). According to Bagehot:

> *the mass of the English people. . . . defer to what we may call the* theatrical show *of society. A certain state passes before them; a certain pomp of great men; a certain spectacle of beautiful women; a wonderful scene of wealth and enjoyment, and they are coerced by it. Their imagination is bowed down; they feel they are not equal to the life which is revealed to them. Courts and aristocracies have the great quality which rules the multitude, though philosophers can see nothing in it – visibility.*[15]

Bagehot is not arguing against rule by the middle classes, rather he is observing that they coerce the lower classes using the spectacle of the monarch:

> *The apparent rulers of the English nation are like the most imposing personages of a splendid procession: it is by them that the mob are influenced; it is they whom the spectators cheer. The real rulers are secreted in second-rate carriages; no one cares for them or asks about them, but*

they are obeyed implicitly and unconsciously by reason of the splendour of those who eclipsed and preceded them.[16]

The idea of the theatrical show is instructive as it emphasises the spatial division between the workers as audience and the social elite as spectacle; with, following Bagehot's analogy, the middle classes hidden from view. Certainly, in terms of the Derby the monarch becomes visible only by spatial separation between those in the Grand Stand and those on the common land, and an acceptance of their place by the crowd. Indeed, the spatial configuration of differing social groups has remained much the same to the present day:

Broadly the classes are kept apart by the racetrack, the lower orders, the gypsies and the lesser account directors – together with bus loads of clients – are encamped in the middle of the track, on the downs. The upper orders congregate in the paddocks, enclosure, marquis [sic] and stands on the south side.[17]

As Margaret Miers makes clear, if Derby Day presented an image of the nation, it was a conservative one in which social harmony could be achieved only through the maintenance of social hierarchy and by ignoring the conflicting relations between capital and labour. Miers concludes: 'Media emphasis on the presence of the elite in the crowd, on aristocratic owners, on the unity of the Derby spectators despite diversity, and, more importantly, the emphasis on royalty, re-confirm the identity of Britain as a traditional society, united through, rather than divided by, stratification.'[18] In such a spectacle of social order there is no visible role for the industrial and commercial middle classes.

It was because of the presence of royalty and its consequent high place in the English calendar of festivities that the Derby appears yearly to have drawn to Epsom most Australians who were in London at the time; it was certainly the social event most often recorded by Australians in their diaries and letters home. In 1875, Richard Teece, a young actuary from New South Wales, took the road to Epsom, and his diary account portrays something of the carnival atmosphere of Derby Day:

Wednesday 26th May [1875]
This being the Derby Day, we felt that we owed a duty to our country which it behoved us to discharge. We had a company of 11 Australians & New Zealanders & I was deputed to mature arrangements. Consequently I procured a four-in-hand turn out, well furnished with a

hamper, the liquor not being forgotten. Thus equipped we set out a little after 9 o'clock & reached Epsom Downs in time to get a good position. The Derby being par excellence the race of the world, the scene on the occasion is one not easily forgotten. The crowds of people of all sorts, manners, creeds, nationalities, & callings are something marvellous. The Derby was won by the favourite, Galopin, but on the whole there did not appear as much enthusiasm or excitement as is occasioned by a leading Australian race nor did the display of horses impress us remarkably. The course is a severe one & not to be compared to Randwick or Melbourne. The return was the feature of the day, for the whole 22 miles the road was lined on both sides with dense masses of spectators eager on a little chaff & as far as our company was personally concerned, I think we were equal to the occasion. I have no hesitation in saying we discharged our duty with credit to ourselves & with honor to our country.

As this account makes clear, for the visiting Australian, as for the Londoners, the racing itself played only a small part in the enjoyment of the day. Most people went for the Derby Day atmosphere rather than for the race itself, and unless you could afford a seat in the Grand Stand, you were unlikely to catch more than a glimpse of the riders and probably no sight of the horses at all. Yet for Teece and his companions, this was also an occasion for the assertion of an Australian nationalism: 'we felt that we owed a duty to our country which it behoved us to discharge.' There is a self-conscious tone to this, but the grouping of Australians and New Zealanders demonstrates a sense of colonial solidarity (Teece himself was born in New Zealand), a sense of themselves as outside observers, though participating 'with honor' when required to do so. Teece and his companions were behaving like overseas tourists, and, as young men out to have a good time, they enjoyed their day at the races.

'I shall think twice as much of Australia after this'

Richard Teece's negative evaluation of the Epsom race course – 'not to be compared to Randwick or Melbourne' – was a typical Australian reaction, and it has to be admitted that, as a race course, Epsom is not particularly charming. This is not to preclude the enjoyment of people escaping from the smoke of London to a healthier rural atmosphere, but the race course cannot be portrayed as picturesque: it is not surrounded by wooded hills, it is scored by a gully running up from Langley Vale, the chalk downs make it very dry and dusty in summer, and since the spectators in the centre of the track are standing lower than the race course itself, even in practical terms it is difficult to follow the horses. The novelist Henry James seemed to miss this practical point in his account of a day at the Derby, and he was unlike Australian visitors in thinking the race course pretty, but his description does give a graphic idea of the layout of the course:

> The course at Epsom is in itself very pretty, and disposed by nature herself in sympathetic prevision of the sporting passion. It is something like the crater of a volcano without the mountain. The outer rim is the course proper; the space within it is a vast, shallow, grassy concavity in which vehicles are drawn up and beasts tethered and in which the greater part of the multitude – the mountebanks, the betting-men and the myriad hangers-on of the scene – are congregated. The outer margin of the uplifted rim in question is occupied by the grand stand, the small stands, the paddock.[19]

The most socially prestigious space, the Grand Stand, is (as would be imagined) to be found in the best position on the Downs for viewing the race.

Reginald Wyndham was even less impressed than Richard Teece:

> We went by Train which only went within one mile of the Grand Stand. We found it very dusty and were much dissapointed [sic] with the arrangements. there were 700.000 people there. an awful big crowd. Some 100 Four-in-hand Drags well appointed. the Prince of Wales, the Princefs of Wales & & were there. but I don't wish to see another Derby. our Randwick & Flemington meeting is far before it. (24 May 1882)

As an overall experience, Wyndham's day out is a disappointment, despite, and perhaps because of the sheer size of the crowd: as an indication of what confronted the visiting Australian in 1882, the crowd was about the same size as the total population of New South Wales, or ten times the size of the crowd that attended the Melbourne Cup in the same year.[20] Indeed, such was his disappointment that Wyndham became homesick and maudlin, and he ended his diary entry by asserting the superiority of Australia: 'I shall think twice as much of Australia after this. we don't know the value of it yet. I quite long to be back again.'

In this Wyndham, then, was behaving much like any overseas visitor who moved through Britain looking for ways of asserting the superiority of his or her own culture. Differences were more notable than similarities, and in their letters home travellers recorded those differences that reflected well upon their native countries. Yet unlike visitors from, say, South America or Russia, Australian visitors were also British and were therefore unable to reject British culture as such without running the risk of compromising their own cultural identity. Indeed, because they counted themselves as both British and Australian, British Australians could assert their cultural identity as much by praising Britain as by criticising it.

I am not sure when he changed his mind, but on re-reading his account of Derby Day and its sentimental praise of Australia, Reginald Wyndham, in his more down-to-earth mood, added a single word followed by two exclamation marks. In its final form, his account ends: 'I shall think twice as much of Australia after this. we don't know the value of it yet. I quite long to be back again. bosh!!'[21] There may be other readings of this, but it appears that in asserting an Australian nationalism, Wyndham perceived himself to have gone too far in his praise of Australia, praise which, if allowed to stand, would have undercut his own sense of being British; his property in the Hunter Valley, after all, shared its name with an aristocratic relative, Henry Wyndham, the second Baron Leconfield, and Reginald spent part of his time in London reading family wills (presumably in search of an inheritance). In short, although Australian-born, Wyndham was very much a British Australian, and as such it was open to him to feel as much British on one day as he felt Australian on another.

'I cannot say that I was much taken with the appearance of my country men'

Thomas Lodge Murray-Prior's response to the same Derby was more positive than Wyndham's, partly because, like Richard Teece, he travelled to the races by road rather than by rail, the road journey being, as Teece put it, 'the feature of the day'. Murray-Prior was kept waiting an hour for his coach in Balham, but he amused himself watching vehicles 'of all descriptions' heading for Epsom, though it might be noted that in his diary account his list of vehicles is organised so that it progresses from the larger and more prestigious to the smaller and more humble:

there was a constant line of vehicles of all descriptions passing by from the private drag and four horses. beautifully got up and generally driven by the Owner most probably members of the four in hand Club filled with Ladies & Gentlemen then the Huge public conveyances crammed full of all kinds of People. Aristocratic Private Carriages. containing well dreſsed people. Hackney Coaches. Handsome Phaetons – dog Carts – spring Carts. Pony Carriages. Donkey trucks, in fact every kind of conveyance, all them mixed up shouting. laughing. trying to pass one another. mixing up and getting clear most surprisingly. (24 May)

Along the way policemen made efforts to keep the traffic moving as it passed through towns and villages, and enterprising women set up stalls outside their houses selling teas and refreshments to the passing trippers. For the Australian tourist, like Murray-Prior, it was an experience not to be missed, even given the discomfort of sitting on the box seat of a Nightingale's coach: 'in places dust and grit were very unpleasant to the eyes. and I found the wind cold. but I was very glad the road had been taken instead of train for though not now like what it was before trains ran still it is a sight one can rarely see and only on such an occasion.'

Like both Teece and Wyndham, Murray-Prior thought the race course and its situation inferior to those in Australia, and he was critical of the short races, both in terms of the quality of the horses ('everything is sacrificed to speed') and in terms of what he could see even from the top of a coach: 'at ¾ of a mile very little is to be seen and unleſs the horses are known to you the whole interest is in the finish which only lasts a few seconds.' Yet, he was there for the sights not the racing and in his diary account, unlike Wyndham, he avoided being trapped into choosing between being Australian or British:

the Races were a long time between and during the intervals I walked about among the people, the Shows and tents. one thing puzzled me. men and women shouting 'accommodation' accommodation this I found was a canvas place to retire for pumping ship purposes. at 1ᵈ very needful. . . . It was a dense motley crowd to be among and I cannot say that I was much taken with the appearance of my country men they seemed to me a regular rowdy mob. here and there a few men evidently of the upper Ten thousand would be prominent among them, the scene to me was new and very amusing. (24 May 1882)

It is the combination of critical distance and identification that makes this account more successful than Wyndham's. On the one hand Murray-Prior adopts the voice of the naive overseas traveller, a persona for whom the scene was 'new and very amusing'. As was pointed out earlier, Murray-Prior was a cultured man, his daughter was the writer Rosa Praed, and his account is self-consciously literary. On the other hand, there is, I think, a less self-conscious association with 'the upper Ten thousand' in terms of social rank or class; Murray-Prior views the 'regular rowdy mob' from an assumed social superiority. The combination of the two produces a peculiar distancing in the clause: 'I cannot say that I was much taken with the appearance of my country men.' Murray-Prior was not Australian-born, he was born in Somerset and migrated as a young man when he was about twenty, but here he adopts the seemingly paradoxical stance of finding his fellow countrymen foreign. This effect is produced by an overlapping of his class viewpoint with that of the Australian outsider; the Australian views the crowd both as an overseas traveller and as one of the middle classes. It was by means of such a balancing act that Murray-Prior was able to respond to a question asked him at his hotel in London: 'An old clergyman sitting near me asked me a question – if I was a foreigner. but telling him no[,] an Australian' (14 June 1882). If he was out of place as an overseas visitor, he was nonetheless in his place as a member of the British middle classes.

This social perspective needs again to be stressed. Until the First World War, Australians visiting Britain were overwhelmingly from the middle classes and often quite well-connected in Britain. Observations of Britain were therefore as much from a class perspective as from a nationalist one, and this was especially so when Australians were commenting on crowds such as those on Derby Day. Murray-Prior's hierarchical listing of the vehicles on the road to Epsom and his criticism of the 'regular rowdy mob' must be read in this broader perspective, and alongside his observation of others on the road to Epsom: 'the last two days. Gipsies men of that kind who expected to pick up something among the crowd had been on the road, sleeping where they could on the road side. and up to any villainy.' Here he takes the same kind of attitude as that put forward in the *Times* of 1885: 'not a very orderly crowd and not one into which it is pleasant to plunge, and shut one's eyes to the fact as one may, there can be no doubt that the component parts of this crowd are, in great part taken from the very dregs of the population in London.'[22] Something of Murray-Prior's attitude to the crowds may be attributed to the very size of the gathering on the Downs; yet when he wrote of the crowds, he wrote as much as a member of the middle classes as an Australian observer, and it was a perspective that countered the conservative view of English society given voice by

Bagehot. As a member of the middle classes, Murray-Prior did not present the occasion as an example of social cohesion and harmony.

'The king & queen were there'

We can see the same social class viewpoint in a slightly later account, this time by a woman. Christobel Ballantyne Bollen was a first generation South Australian; her father was a general practitioner who had been born in the West Country, and her mother seems to have been born in Scotland. Bollen was therefore very definitely British Australian and equally definitely upper middle class. In 1913, she was a twenty-year-old socialite travelling around Europe with a female cousin and two uncles, writing home once a week to her parents with whom she had made a previous visit to Britain. In many ways she is clearly a very different person from Murray-Prior, and she travelled to Epsom by motor bus rather than on the top of a horse-drawn coach; but her description of Derby Day 1913 is similar to Murray-Prior's in its slide from a national to a class identity:

> *Derby Day is a tremendous affair, of course there are lots of smart people, but the general crowd is made up of costers & all that sort, it is the funniest thing to watch them all. The races were at Epsom, about 10 miles away, it was a lovely drive out there & back, the road was full of vehicles, just like Onkaparinga, & the women were dressed in all the commonest & brightest colours you can imagine, & their hats smothered in bright feathers, quite an Arry & Arriet day. . . . in the crowd just by us there was a photographer taking quick photographs for 6ᵈ each, Nell & I had had ours taken, I am sending mine, & I think you can see our bus in the background One man of our party got up a 1/- sweep, Nell & I each put 1/- in & got 7/- back We talked to some very funny coster women & had a most amusing half hour, one said to me, 'Show us your picture old cock,' I nearly fell down it gave me such a shock, because I hadn't seen her until that minute. The king & queen were there, we could only see them in the distance, & a suffragette tried to stop the king's horse, but she was badly kicked in the attempt & I believe is dying, it serves her right. (6 June 1913)*

It is very easy to spot the patronising attitude to 'costers & all that sort,' and the denigration of the lower-class women 'dressed in all the commonest & brightest colours you can imagine'; but it is harder to say whether the attitude is more that of the Australian outsider than that of the socially privileged young woman. As usual, Bollen prefers the Melbourne Cup race course at Flemington to the course at Epsom: 'the course isn't nearly as fine as Flemington, very badly arranged,' though she finds a similarity between the journey by road and the journey to the Onkaparinga course at Oakbank in her home state of South Australia. But if these comparisons depended on her Australian eye and enabled her to assert an Australian nationalism, by contrast it was her association with a social elite, the 'smart people' and even the king and queen, that distanced her from both the masses and the dying suffragette, Emily Davison.

It would be incorrect, then, to see these descriptions of the Derby Day crowd as peculiarly Australian; the observer's attitude to the working-class crowds is predominantly that of a member of the middle classes. I have found only one account of Derby Day by a working-class Australian, and that in an unpublished memoir of the 1840s written in 1924. By comparison with Murray-Prior and Bollen, the brief account by William Saunders is revealing in the way its author associates himself with the crowd, rather than viewing it from an assumed social superiority:

> *Born at Clapham on Jan 7ᵗʰ 1841[,] almost within the sound of Bow Bells[,] I spent nearly 11 years of my boyhood days[.] only two or three incidents stand out. One was the old schoolmaster dark sallow & crabbed with a big ruler under his arm ready to inforce discipline at the slightest provocation[.] Another was the miscellaneous crowds from London wending their way to Ep[s]om Races fours in hand, buses, donkey carts, footpaths crow[d]ed with all the rabble &c of the great city barracking, and in the best of tempers something similar to Flemington Road in later years on Cup Day.*

For Saunders, the term 'rabble' is not derogatory, the barracking is friendly, and he shows no sense that as a young child he felt threatened by the Londoners 'wending their way to Epom Races'.

Australians attending Derby Day, then, were almost all middle class, and they used social status in a complex way to negotiate an identity that was both British and Australian. They could be critical of the races, and when they compared the horses and the layout of the course with those in Australia, they were in general not much impressed by Epsom Downs. In broad terms, Australians at the Derby were most Australian when they compared the racing and the race course with Randwick or Flemington. Yet they had to be careful not to be too critical. The Derby was enjoyed by the highest in the land, and it is with these people that middle-class Australians wished to be associated. And while this gave them a position from which to criticise the working classes, any whole-sale dismissal meant rejecting the Derby as a British institution, an institution which, as British Australians, they saw as part of their own culture.

'We were amongst all the gipsies and the side shows, and everything was filthy and disgusting'

Derby Day as a great British event depended not solely on the crowds of Londoners who covered the Downs, but on a combination of the very lowest social ranks with the very highest – the monarch. As Margaret Miers puts it: 'If the Royal family, the highest in the land, are present, then the greatness of the races is reinforced, and if Royalty, as symbols of Britain[,] can be linked to the events, the centrality of the races as national events can be articulated.'[23] It was the presence of 'the highest in the land' alongside the lowest that allowed Frith to portray the Derby as an occasion of social unity. The problem with Frith's view of the Derby is that it was based more on the notion of social rank than on social class; in other words, it looked back to a pre-industrial social structure and therefore had no place in it for the new, industrial middle classes. Since the racing belonged to the upper classes, and the event to Londoners, there was no perspective that the middle classes could take that did not reflect their own distance from what they were observing. Australians rarely mention interacting with other middle-class specta-tors, preferring, as in Wyndham's account, to report either on the 'awful big crowd' or the Prince and Princess of Wales: 'an awful big crowd. Some 100 Four-in-hand Drags well appointed. the Prince of Wales, the Princefs of Wales & & were there.' As the earlier quotation from the *Guardian* pointed out, the organisation of physical space reinforced this: the aristocracy was in the enclosure, the paddocks, and the Grand Stand on the outer side of the racecourse, while the working-class crowd occu-pied the common land in the centre of the racecourse. The middle classes in their coaches and buses constituted a thin line along the edges of the racecourse. From such a position it was difficult to participate in the Derby as a demonstration of national harmony.

Australian visitors were therefore doubly displaced, doubly outsiders. As Australians, they could compare the experience with an Australian race meeting. As Australians, they could also compare the size and composition of the race-going crowds, and mingle and enjoy the fun, as in Richard Teece's account. But when they defined themselves more in terms of their social status then, unless they had a very strong sense of themselves as Australian rather than British, their alienation from the crowd made them more critical; and as they became aware of their class displacement within a massive working-class crowd so they invoked association with 'the upper ten thousand,' the smart people, those people who looked down on the racing from the Grand Stand. These were the elite of British society, their Britishness attested by the presence at Epsom of the Prince of Wales who, with Queen Victoria shunning public life after the death of Prince Albert in 1861, carried much of the prestige of the monarch. In such a way, the class identity of Australians who went to watch the Derby because it was a great British national event allowed them to be seduced into invoking their own Britishness. But if that appears to put them too much in the grip of an essential British identity, we can say that, conversely, accounts by middle-class Australians give the lie to any claim that Epsom races were occasions of British national harmony. The highest and the lowest in the land looked to their own pleasures, and those in the middle both socially and physically tried to find ways of coping with their displacement.

Here is one final example of an Australian being out of place at the Derby, this time from 1939 and therefore much later than the others, but it shows a certain continuity, despite the fact that, the Derby falling on Empire Day in 1939, the occasion was presented not only in terms of national harmony but in terms of imperial solidarity. The *Times*, noting that the King and Queen could not attend because they were on a royal visit to Canada, argued that:

> *their very absence will draw Empire Derby Day into one. Canada is just now a great deal nearer to England than it was; and even if the KING and the QUEEN should be too busy to spare a thought to the Derby, a great many people at the Derby will be wondering or settling what time it is at Winnipeg when it is three o'clock at Epsom, and how soon the KING and QUEEN in Canada will hear what has won.*[24]

Kathleen Bate was a middle-class Australian from Sydney who was on a round-the-world trip with her recently-married husband and her sister, Nancy, whose fiancé was working as an architect in London. Kathleen Bate's description of her day at the races demonstrates just how totally alienated a middle-class Australian could feel at the Derby:

The whole day was very disappointing and I think the least said about it the better. We were amongst all the gipsies and the side shows, and everything was filthy and disgusting. We couldn't see anything of the course, and we just saw a tiny flash of colour as the horses went past us in each race. We were surrounded by bookies all yelling and screaming and one really couldn't imagine anything more unpleasant. Nance and I stuck it out till the Derby was run at 3 p.m. We had had five hours of it by then, and we were nearly at screaming point ourselves. So we decided to go back by train. The Mitchells were more than fed up too so they joined us, and after being nearly trampled and jostled to death in a dirty yelling mob, we made our way to the back of the stands and found a taxi which took us to Epsom Downs station, and we luckily just caught a train and got to Victoria at 5 p.m. The Mitchells made us go back to the Cumberland with them where we all had a wash and a cup of tea and felt much better. It was a horrible day and if anyone mentions Derby to me again I'll expire. I didn't think anything so disgusting could exist in England. (24 May 1939)

Kathleen Bate's displacement here is due not so much to her Australian identity as to her class identity; she finds the gipsies, the dirt, and the noise totally alien, and it is because she is middle class that she perceived the holidaying Londoners as 'a dirty yelling mob'. The antidote to this, however, was not only 'a wash and a cup of tea,' but a dose of Britishness in the form of a socially exclusive gathering later the same evening at Grosvenor House:

The Duchess [of Kent] looked gorgeous in a sort of goldy coloured frock. The Duke looked very young and handsome. It was the Royal Empire Dinner and we had a sumptuous repast then we had speeches by the Earl of Athlone, the Duke of Kent, S. M. Bruce and other well-known men. Bruce made an excellent speech – I forgot to say that at 8 p.m. before the dinner began we heard the King's speech from Winnipeg. I wonder did you hear it in Australia too. We all stood the whole time he was speaking. (24 May 1939)

In this account, class and the British side of a British Australian identity coincide to provide the antithesis of the Derby experience. Left outside Grosvenor House are the dirt, the noise, and the working people of London; inside are to be found the smart people of the British Empire, including one of the most English of Australians, the Australian High Commissioner, S. M. Bruce. It may have been, as Bruce was reported to have said at the dinner, that the Royal Family 'was the greatest asset in the British Empire,'[25] but the space in which he comes to speak as an Australian very much depended on an exclusive and distinctively British social hierarchy.

THE ILLUSTRATED SYDNEY NEWS

AND NEW SOUTH WALES AGRICULTURIST AND GRAZIER.

No. 26—Vol. XIII.   SATURDAY, DECEMBER 22, 1877.   PRICE 1s., ANN. SUBSCRIPTION, 13s.

CONTRAST.—CHRISTMASTIDE IN ENGLAND AND IN AUSTRALIA.

'A Contrast – Christmastide in England and in Australia.' *Illustrated Sydney News*, 22 December 1877. Australia and Britain are typically represented as Antipodean opposites.

Margaret Tripp (left) with her sisters Jane (centre) and Frances. Margaret Tripp, later Principal of Toorak College, visited England in 1872 where she hoped to train as a teacher.

Portable iron houses from the 1850s, Patterson Street, South Melbourne. Such imported structures employed the same technology as the Crystal Palace.

'The Great Palm House, Kew Gardens.' *Illustrated London News*, 7 August 1852. Australians found the exotic specimens growing at Kew 'homelike and friendly'.

Interior of the Crystal Palace, Sydenham, praised by Henry Pilcher in 1866: 'No one "has seen England" unless he has been to the Crystal Palace.'

Richard Daintree's Queensland Annexe at the London International Exhibition, 1872, which displayed 'native weapons' and prints of Aboriginal men.

The South Kensington Museum, or 'Brompton Boilers'. The museum was later removed to Bethnal Green in the East End of London where it housed an exhibition of Aboriginal artefacts.

'The Mob Pulling Down the Railings in Park-Lane.' *Illustrated London News*, 4 August 1866. Henry Pilcher, a Maitland solicitor, condemned 'this turbulent manifestation of English freedom'.

Thomas Lodge Murray-Prior, Queensland squatter and politician, who visited his daughter, the novelist Rosa Praed, in England in 1882.

'Australian Nurses for the Front at the British Museum.' *British-Australasian*, 1 July 1915. Anne Donnell from South Australia is in the back row, third from the right (centre of the pillar).

SS *Almora* (built 1873) on which Thomas Lodge Murray-Prior sailed from Brisbane to Plymouth in 1882.

'Section of the Thames Embankment.'
Illustrated London News, 22 June 1867.
Australians were impressed by the scale
of the engineering.

1. The Obelisk on Sept. 11.
2. Windlass to lower the bottom end of Obelisk.
3. Obelisk descending to vertical position, Sept. 12.
4. Obelisk erect on its pedestal.

'Cleopatra's Needle, on the Victoria Thames Embankment.' *Illustrated London News*, 21 September 1878. Cleopatra's Needle quickly became a monument to imperial Britain.

Cockle Sellers at Carmarthen Market, visited by John Rae, the New South Wales Commissioner for Railways, in 1879.

SS *Arcadia* (built 1888) on which J. I. Martin sailed home from London to Melbourne in 1891.

John Duthie (built 1864) on which Henry Pilcher sailed from Sydney to London in 1866 in the company of a carpet snake.

Marion Flynn from Sydney in Athens, 1969.

AUSTRALIANS !

BOOK YOUR RETURN
PASSAGE   THROUGH

THE AUSTRALIAN TRAVEL SERVICE,
414, AUSTRALIA HOUSE

OFFICIAL AGENTS
FOR ALL STEAMSHIP LINES
(No Booking Fees)

Visitors sailing from Marseilles, Toulon,
Naples or other Continental Ports, should
consult us regarding interesting tours that
can be taken en route from London.

WE ARE SPECIALISTS
IN CONTINENTAL TRAVEL

OVAL TEST MATCH

In the event of the game being continued
beyond the fourth day, full particulars
regarding tickets for the extension can
be obtained from

THE AUSTRALIAN
TRAVEL SERVICE

An Australian Firm for Australians

Advertisement for the
Australian Travel Service.
British-Australian & New
Zealander, 21 August 1930.

Advertisement for P&O, 1935. *Home*, 1 August 1935.

FIVE

Cleopatra's Needle: Antiquity, History and Modernity in Britain and the USA

'The continuous stream of history'

One of the first places that Australians visited once they arrived in London was Westminster Abbey. Margaret Tripp, a thirty-three year old woman from Victoria, visited Westminster Abbey in 1872 and her account emphasised the way in which over the years the Abbey had accumulated diverse historical monuments:

> *Well, on Whitsunmonday, Angela, Margaret & I went to Westminster Abbey. It was very full of course, but in spite of that I thoroughly enjoyed my tour round the chapels &° the Poets' Corner and the grand tombs & historical relics. It is a wonderful place, & made me realize the life of past ages, & the continuous stream of history. (20 May 1872)*

Westminster Abbey is one of the oldest buildings in London. The earliest part of the current structure dates from the middle of the thirteenth century, predating St Paul's Cathedral, London's other major Christian temple, by over 400 years. For Anne Donnell, an Australian army nursing sister, the Abbey's age distinguished it from St Paul's:

> *The impression conveyed to me from the two Cathedrals was this – That where St Pauls was solidly grand, the Abbey was spiritually reverent, this may be on account of the age of the buildings, where St Pauls is practically modern, being completed in the early part of the 17ʰ century & the Abbey 1266 – though the oldest part dates back to 1066. (30 June 1915)*

Yet despite its obvious spiritual importance, the primary attraction of Westminster Abbey for visitors to London was as the burial place for many early English monarchs and for the more recent dead of Poets' Corner. In the first half of the eighteenth century, Westminster Abbey's 'grand tombs & historical relics' were augmented by numerous monuments to poets, scientists and public servants, and as a result the Abbey became less the domain of royalty and more the domain of a new type of public, and a new type of public figure.[1] This shift from the courtier to the commoner allowed Westminster Abbey to be projected as a national shrine, a shrine more cultural and historic than spiritual. And because of the age of its fabric, Westminster Abbey as a secular shrine gave witness to that 'continuous stream of history' which, a little paradoxically, was held to underpin the new and specifically British national identity that followed from unification with Scotland in 1707 and the accumulation of a British Empire.

Three years after Margaret Tripp in 1875, Richard Teece, a young man in his late twenties visiting London from Sydney, similarly stressed the importance of Westminster Abbey as a monument to a British national history:

> *Proceeded thence to Westminster Abbey[,] the great landmark of English history, the scene of the coronation of its Kings, the last & honored resting place assigned to its great men. 'This huge fabric, the sacred depository of fame & grandeur', bearing testimony to the events of nearly 1200 years, & recording for the example & emulation of succeeding generations the achievements of British worthies, is perhaps more worthy of study & attention than any institution in Great Britain. (8 June 1875)*

Teece correctly makes a distinction between the Abbey as a 'great landmark of English history' and its contemporary status as a British institution, but the distinction disappears in the slide between *English* kings and *British* worthies. This slippage occurs because of what is again perceived as a historical continuity; the importance of Westminster Abbey for Teece lies in its power to influence 'succeeding generations'. The fact that the Scots may have had no particular affection for Westminster Abbey as a site of early English history is overlooked, and the Abbey's 'testimony' is in support of a cohesive British national identity.

A further remark by Margaret Tripp reveals quite clearly the kind of ideological work such a national monument might carry out:

I must say I liked to see the crowds of working people, & their evident appreciation & enjoyment. And then the knowledge that the history of which this grand building is the embodiment, & the faith for which it witnesses is theirs, has of itself something to elevate & refine. (20 May 1872)

In the nineteenth century, entrance fees excluded working people from touring the Abbey until the 1840s when the Abbey, along with St Paul's and the British Museum, was opened to the general public. In Tripp's account, the Abbey is seen performing its new function as a place of rational recreation: it educates the newly enfranchised general public much as the opening of the Bethnal Green Museum in the same year was intended to do. But 1872 also saw the trial of the Tichborne Claimant come to a head, a trial that had deeply divided British society, a Republican demonstration in Trafalgar Square and strikes in London by bakers, gas-stokers and the police.[2] At a time of obvious political division, public buildings could provide a focus for an appeal for social unity through their 'embodiment' of a national history.

Descriptions of national monuments and buildings therefore reveal an unease about the state of modern society, even as those same monuments and buildings were called upon to counter a loss of social harmony. And to the extent that Tripp and Teece advocated a sense of history as a way of teaching a common set of cultural values, their unease with the present day can be seen mainly as a middle-class rather than as a specifically Australian concern. Nonetheless, when they looked at Westminster Abbey, Australians gave expression to an Australian or, perhaps more generally, a colonial attitude to historical continuity. As Tripp put it in her reflections on Westminster Abbey: 'We are rather rudely broken off as to history in Australia, & I now quite understand from my own experience the fascination everything old has for an American.' Although Westminster Abbey may have offered a comforting continuity of Britishness to which an appeal could be made in the face of social disharmony, the appeal to history also acted to remind Australians of their own apparent lack of history, a lack by which they found themselves identifying with America rather than with Britain itself.

In one sense, then, as James Hogan put it in 1889, Australians had a particular 'reverence' for the historical sites of London:

Coming from a country whose history is but of yesterday, and which on that account possesses nothing of venerable monumental interest, the

Australian feels a peculiar reverence in wandering over those scenes and structures in London that have witnessed the flight of centuries and are crowded with memories of a long-vanished past. Pre-eminent among those sacred and treasured spots is the majestic old Abbey of Westminster.[3]

Sites like Westminster Abbey, 'this History of England in stone,' as Hogan put it, appeared to offer historical foundations in the face of cultural dislocation. As London became more of a tourist destination, it seems increasingly to have been offered to its colonial visitors as 'historical London'; as the *Orient Line Guide* put it in 1890: 'There is no need to dwell any further on the advantages of a visit to the mother country. Her history is cherished by every Australian colonist as his own, and her islands are loved by many who never saw them. London, her capital, is the capital of the world.'[4] In this way, although they may have shared with Americans a sense of being cut off from history, Australians did have the advantage of being offered London as their own, an ownership that differed from the appropriation of the Abbey by American visitors such as Nathaniel Hawthorn: 'An American has a right to be proud of Westminster Abbey; for most of the men, who sleep in it, are our great men, as well as theirs.'[5] In Australian accounts, the Abbey is never considered as 'theirs'. And by the First World War, Westminster Abbey had been re-invented yet again, this time as a shrine not just to British history but to imperial history. As Corporal W. P. Sparkes put it: 'Westminster Abbey was a place that we could not but feel attracted [to]. . . . [we felt] bound to look on the famous monuments & statues[,] the tablets & memorials to the Great men of our Empire of past ages. Their [?] Souls seemed to have hallowed the fine old building & one feels as if they speak of the glory of the past & ask men to try and imitate their works' (23 June 1916).

Yet the very sites whose history was offered to the colonial visitor 'as his own,' served as witnesses to historical discontinuity. As Westminster Abbey accumulated diverse monuments, it accumulated diverse meanings. In prompting appeals to 'the life of past ages' as a way of changing the present through 'elevation and refinement,' through 'example & emulation,' or through outright 'imitation,' the historical sites of London as seen through Australian eyes bore witness not so much to a historical continuity, but to present discontinuities and to the social, cultural and, indeed, national diversity already present in any nineteenth-century Britishness.

'The only fault I have to find with London is that it looks so new'

In recent times, the removal of the two Cleopatra's Needles from Alexandria was first mooted by Dominique Vivant Denon, who had been the leader of Napoleon's team of scholars in Egypt: 'They might be conveyed to France without difficulty, and would there become a trophy of conquest, and a very characteristic one, as they are in themselves a monument, and as the hieroglyphs with which they are covered render them preferable to Pompey's pillar, which is merely a column.'[6] On the defeat of the French in Egypt, the honour of transporting the obelisks back in triumph seemed to fall to the British, and indeed the Earl of Cavan, one of the British commanders, began work on removing the pedestal of the fallen obelisk as early as 1801.

Yet the obelisks that were finally removed to France and Britain were not removed as trophies of conquest. The obelisk erected in the Place de la Concorde in 1836 was not even one of the Alexandrian obelisks. It was one of a pair still standing at Luxor, both of which had previously been promised to the British, and its removal was less the result of warfare than of diplomatic rivalry between the imperial capitals of Paris and London.[7] And though the gift of one of the Cleopatra's Needles to the British nation was repeatedly asserted by various rulers of Egypt in 1801, 1819, 1831 and around 1868, the obelisk was not finally removed until over seventy-five years after the events it ostensibly commemorates, the victories over the French by Nelson in 1798 and by Abercromby in 1801.

To a certain extent the British were forced to remove their obelisk by the threat of it being either buried or broken up for building material in the expansion and modernisation of Alexandria as a Mediterranean port; and even at the time of its removal there was no clear agreement about where in London the obelisk was to be re-erected. John Dixon, the engineer removing it, favoured a site in St Stephen's Square opposite Westminster Abbey and the Houses of Parliament, and a full-size wooden model was placed in the proposed position to gauge the effect. The journal *The Architect* supported the choice of site on architectural grounds: 'The site in Westminster partakes of the advantages of most of those in Rome. Several thoroughfares converge upon it, thus giving the obelisk a most conspicuous situation, as is the case with King Charles's statue at Charing Cross.'[8] But bringing the issue of British national history into the debate, an anonymous correspondent complained in the *Times*: 'Assuredly, to thrust this ancient obelisk brought thither from a distant part of the world, and bearing with it no connection whatever with the great events, deeds and characters of British history, on to a site and in the midst of buildings sanctified by these associations, would be a strange anomaly, partly ludicrous, partly painful.'[9] Westminster Abbey's Britishness had to be protected from contamination. However, the ultimate rejection of the site was connected less to what was above the ground than to what was below; the directors of the Metropolitan Underground Railway refused to carry the risk of 180 tons of red granite subsiding under its own weight into the Underground. The courtyard of another national building, the British Museum, was rejected due to similar fears, this time the fear of crushing gas pipes and sewers in transporting the obelisk through the streets of London.

The choice of the Thames Embankment as the site for Cleopatra's Needle placed the obelisk at the intersection of two powerful nineteenth-century forces, metropolitan improvement and imperialism. Participants in the so-called 'Battle of the Sites,' the public debate about the location of the obelisk, had drawn on both of these, as well as on the question of the sanctity of historic buildings. The historical nature of the obelisk's surroundings was not an issue on the Thames Embankment, as the Embankment itself had no historical associations. The Thames Embankment was constructed between 1864 and 1870 on thirty-seven acres of reclaimed mudflats, and was at the time probably the most ambitious engineering project ever undertaken in London. Below ground was a new trunk sewer, the Northern Low Level Intercepting Sewer. The Embankment also contained the southern stretch of the Metropolitan District Line, while above ground a curving Thames frontage, London's first public frontage onto the Thames, provided a broad highway to relieve the traffic congestion on the Strand and a faster route between Westminster and the City. Built by the Metropolitan Board of Works, the Embankment epitomised the urban improvements that, since the 1820s, had radically reshaped London.

In this sense, the Embankment was a triumph of modernity, and it was one of the many engineering schemes that Australians noted with admiration. Daniel Matthews visiting London from Victoria in 1869, for example, was impressed by the newly open Holborn Viaduct, and he noted the ease with which the Thames Tunnel, opened in 1843 and the first tunnel ever built under a navigable river,[10] was itself being replaced: 'Another tunnel is now in course of construction, under the auspices of an omnibus company, and will very shortly be opened. In this age of progress, a work that formerly took years to complete, can now be done in a few months' (7 October 1869). Electricity, another product of 'this age of progress,' was soon to appear on the streets of London, and the Embankment was chosen in 1878 for London's first large-scale experiment in electric street lighting.[11] In 1881, Martha Hudson, travelling with her parents from New South Wales, recorded its novel effect:

> *After we had had dinner Mr Alexander said he would take us and show us a little of the city, so we went in by the train, he met us at the station. We went up to Cheapside and saw St Pauls Cathedral, Charing Cross Railway station, walked some distance along the Thames embankment, and over Blackfriars Bridge, which looked very pretty lighted up by the Electric Light. (24 June 1881)*

The coming of electric streetlighting not only improved public safety, but enhanced London's newly improved metropolitan spaces, though not all Australians were in favour of it; Mary Fairfax, also writing in 1881, noted: 'We drove here by the Embankment and saw the Electric light, but I don't care for it, it is so glaring' (23 October 1881). Australians displayed a similar ambivalence towards the Underground system.

Yet the Thames Embankment was also viewed in terms of creating an imperial capital that might vie with Paris. London often made a poor impression on visiting Australians, and Martha Hudson on her first day in London in 1881 was obviously in two minds: 'Mr Alexander pointed out Paternoster Row to us. I have often seen the name of this place on books, and magazines, and thought it was a very large place, but to my surprise I found it was nothing but a lane not wider than our gate way and yet I suppose there is not more business done any where than in this narrow place' (24 June 1881). Although the narrowness of the streets of London could make the city appear more human, more manageable and, indeed, more picturesque, London's streets compared badly with Haussmann's boulevards in Paris; as Archie Barwick noted on leave at Christmas 1917: 'Paris is a lovely place & no mistake[,] easily the finest I have ever seen[,] knocks London into a cocked hat, the streets are so wide & beautiful with the trees growing along both sides & the magnificent buildings all so regular' (10 December 1917). With its broad streets and regular layout, Paris in the later nineteenth century resembled the earlier planned cities of Australia, and the preference for Paris over London was also implicitly a preference for Australia. Richard Hannan, visiting London with the New South Wales Premier, George Dibbs, in 1892, compared London's streets directly with those of Australia: 'The streets are very narrow[,] that is in comparison with what is seen in

Melbourne & Adelaide & in London they are not laid down at right Angles but seem to run at very acute angles some of them' (9 June 1892); 'The Streets are exceedingly narrow & not at all as imposing as I expected' (10 June 1892). The Thames mudflats, composed largely of sewage, might have been redeveloped because they represented a threat to public health, but in creating the Embankment the Metropolitan Board of Works also took the opportunity of providing the capital with a formal processional avenue over a mile long linking Westminster and the City and on which statues and monuments might be erected to great effect. As an imperial capital, London not only needed to demonstrate its history to its colonial visitors, it needed, like Paris, to appear modern and imposing.

During the great wave of 'metropolitan improvements' that was stimulated by the ending of the Napoleonic Wars in 1815 and which peaked in the 1830s, it was possible to see the modernisation of London and its creation as an imperial capital as two sides of the same coin. In a celebration of George IV's regency and reign, James Elmes wrote:

> *[Augustus] made it one of his proudest boasts that he found Rome of brick, and left it of marble. The reign and regency of GEORGE THE FOURTH have scarcely done less, for the vast and increasing Metropolis of the British Empire: by increasing its magnificence and comforts; by forming healthy streets and elegant buildings, instead of pestilential alleys and squalid hovels; by substituting rich and varied architecture and park-like scenery, for paltry cabins and monotonous cow-lairs.*[12]

In this account, the creation of an imperial capital is synonymous with the creation of a modern city, and an obvious consequence of this new London was the destruction of the old London: 'So rapidly indeed are these improvements taking place around us, that the absence of a few months from London produces revolutions in sites, and alterations in appearances, that are almost miraculous, and cause the denizen to feel himself a stranger in his own city.'[13] Later in the century, such optimism declined into a more utilitarian concern with public works, and while buildings continued to be torn down, roads rerouted, mudflats reclaimed, viaducts built and tunnels dug, by mid century, architectural tastes had changed and Regency architecture, when it was not condemned for being plain bad, was seen neither as modern nor as historical.[14] Not only, therefore, did the reconfiguration of London in the later nineteenth century require the destruction of many of the older spaces that might have given the imperial capital a sense of historical continuity, there was no compensating appreciation of much of the architecture of the previous century or more. Francis Smart from Melbourne, himself an architect, wrote back to Australia: 'Much of London is common place[,] and utility and a bare living is written on many of the buildings' (16 October 1900).

In an intriguing remark made in 1872, Margaret Tripp lamented London's lack of a sense of history: 'The only fault I have to find with London is that it looks so new. There is very little air of antiquity about it, not nearly so much as at Bristol, but then that is owing to the Fire. I was gratified at seeing Pudding Lane in the morning where it began' (1 June 1872). Tripp might partly have ascribed her sense of loss of what she calls 'antiquity' to the Great Fire and she is correct that the fire destroyed most of the medieval city; but her sense of the newness of London would also have been compounded by the urban redevelopment of the previous 100 years, a redevelopment that produced new streets, law courts, banks, hospitals, railway stations, schools and museums. Sir Christopher Wren's Temple Bar, marking the historic boundary between the City of Westminster and the City of London, was demolished in a road widening scheme in 1878, and in the vicinity of Westminster Abbey itself, ancient houses, almshouses and schools had been cleared in the creation of Victoria Street, a broad street running from the Palace of Westminster towards Buckingham Palace.[15]

Revisiting London from Sydney in 1871 after a gap of ten years, John Smith noted:

> the marvellous growth of London northward and westward, where stately squares and terraces have sprung up on what I remember as green fields, new streets have been opened up in the oldest parts, and a far superior (or at least showier) style of street architecture has become common. Then the Thames is scarcely to be recognized with its magnificent embankment and new bridges.[16]

It is in such a context as this that Tripp's anxieties in Westminster Abbey about a possible break in 'the continuous stream of history' should be read, anxieties that were compounded because as an Australian, 'We are rather rudely broken off as to history.' London was changing rapidly in the late nineteenth century, a transformation and a historical severance evident in exhibitions of a picturesque London past, as in 'the Old London Street' in the Colonial and Indian Exhibition of 1886.[17] The need for a sense of history drove a wedge between the modernising impulse of civic improvement and the creation of an imperial capital that could demonstrate its historical lineage.

'Historical England does not appeal to me now so much as it did before living in Egypt'

The erection of Cleopatra's Needle on the Thames Embankment in 1878 can be seen, at least in part, as an attempt to provide the sanction of antiquity to a modern imperial capital. The practice of removing Egyptian obelisks was itself antique. The removal of the two Cleopatra's Needles from Heliopolis to Alexandria in 12 BC was part of a general redistribution of Egyptian monuments by the Roman Emperor Augustus both within Egypt and beyond. The first obelisk to reach Rome was set up in 10 BC, and indeed thirteen still stand in Rome today, though repositioned to suit the demands of remodelled civic spaces.[18]

Further evidence of how Cleopatra's Needle might be used to establish London's antique lineage are the inscriptions proposed by Philip Massey, an architect in Old Bond Street, for a pedestal for the obelisk on a suggested site in St James's Park. Massey proposed that on one side would be inscribed the names of the three great monarchs in whose names the Needle changed site: Thotmes, Augustus and Victoria. Inscribed on the reverse side were to be the names of the three sites and the dates of erection: On, 2500 B.C.; Alexandria, 25 B.C.; London, A.D. 1878.[19] London's ancient genealogy was to be clearly proclaimed.

In the event, the pedestal of Cleopatra's Needle on the Embankment carried four inscriptions, three of which deal with antiquity, history and modernity. The first outlines the antiquity of the obelisk, from the Pharaoh Thotmes III, through Rameses the Great (who added his own hieroglyphs), to Augustus Caesar. The inscription on the opposite face commemorates the victories in Egypt over the French of Nelson and Abercromby, and to that extent engages with recent British history. A third inscription records the name of the engineer, John Dixon, and his patron, Erasmus Wilson, who 'through patriotic zeal' made the removal possible during the reign of Queen Victoria. Thus in the three inscriptions we have a pharaoh, an admiral and an engineer: antiquity, history and modernity.

On the fourth side are inscribed the names of the six seamen who 'perished in a bold attempt' to save the crew of the vessel bringing the obelisk to Britain. This inscription was, of course, fortuitous not only because the need to commemorate the six men could not have been foreseen, but because the death of six ordinary seamen added a popular dimension to the significance of the obelisk. Although the obelisk seems not to have had an official unveiling, the presence of a large crowd to watch it being finally swung into its vertical position on 13 September 1878 is evidence of the successful incorporation of the monument into a popular British consciousness. As the *Times* recorded it:

> *The enthusiasm of the crowd, as though the wonder they already saw before them had now for the first time struck them in all its grandeur, burst forth in ringing cheers, which were renewed from the river, road, terrace and bridge as the Union Jack was run up on the flagstaff which overtopped the pyramidion on the north side, and again the Egyptian (Turkish) flag followed on the south. These cheers for the colours were in honour of the Queen and the Khedive; but the first burst was for Dixon and his coadjutors, and in recognition of a great triumph already won.*[20]

The 'heroic' deaths of the six seamen in the Bay of Biscay had clearly increased public interest in the obelisk, and the spontaneous display of patriotism seems to have been due more to the drama of the removal of the obelisk and admiration for the engineering skills involved than to interest in the defeat of the French in Egypt nearly eighty years earlier. Indeed, an alternative popular inscription which the obelisk never had treats the antiquity of Cleopatra's Needle with a fair degree of irreverence:

> *This monument, as some supposes,*
> *Was looked upon of old by Moses.*
> *It passed in time from Greeks to Turks,*
> *And was stuck up here by the Board of Works!*[21]

The obelisk, then, as a material object seemed, like Westminster Abbey, to carry a number of meanings, though none of the successive inscriptions obscured or erased the earlier inscriptions.

The process of adding meanings to the monument did not stop with the physical act of inscription, and the inscriptions themselves were subject to later interpretation. Australians did not passively consume London's tourist spaces. Anne Donnell's description of Cleopatra's Needle in June 1915, therefore, does not merely repeat the inscriptions:

> *waiting for the bus we look at Cleopatra's Needle – twas so interesting[,]*
> *its a huge obelisk placed beside the river as a memorial of Nelson &*

Abercrombie[.] It was presented to the British Nation by the Viceroy of Egypt in 1819. It had been for centuries lying on the sands of Alexandria – And when being brought over in an iron cylinder went down during a storm in the Bay of Biscay & lay at the bottom of the sea until recovered by John Dixon in the reign of Q. Victoria 1878. (30 June 1915)

Donnell's account is taken largely from the inscriptions, but she has also added her own meanings. She omits altogether the popular, but by 1915 no longer contemporary, commemoration of the six sailors, and the statement that the obelisk 'lay at the bottom of the sea until recovered by John Dixon' is inaccurate. The inscription actually reads:

IT WAS ABANDONED DURING A STORM
IN THE BAY OF BISCAY
RECOVERED AND ERECTED
ON THIS SPOT BY
JOHN DIXON C.E.

The obelisk did not sink, nor did Dixon himself recover it. Donnell's reading of the inscription is part misinterpretation, part elaboration, a reading by a person with no memory of the events and who casts the obelisk into a stock narrative pattern. In this sense, the removal of the obelisk had itself become historical.

Donnell's reading of the inscriptions also stressed the relationship between Britain and Egypt, a reading possibly influenced by the wartime context: Donnell was an Australian army nursing sister recently arrived in London via the Suez Canal, and on her first visit to London she, along with the other nurses, spent a hectic fortnight visiting every site of national significance. Indeed, as Westminster Abbey had gained an imperial history by the First World War, so the Thames Embankment was now very much part of imperial London, judging from its place in the itineraries of Australian service men and women visiting London during the war: 'We taxied round the City visiting Westminster Abbey St Pauls Cathedral The Tower of London The Tower Bridge, the Thames Embankment &c . . . . & on the Thames Embankment we saw the celebrated Cleopatra's Needle. A huge block of granite brought over from Egypt' (W. P. Sparkes 23 June 1916). The damage caused to the obelisk's pedestal and attendant sphinxes by a bomb dropped from a German aircraft in 1917 led to a further inscription and a further dimension to the obelisk's national and imperial meanings.

The antiquities of London had one clear advantage to the visiting

Australian over the antiquities of Egypt itself: they were not in Egypt. Ada Holman, writing of her visit to Britain of 1912, noted:

> *To the child of civilisation the sacrosanct sites of the East and Italy have, to be entirely candid, a repellent as well as an alluring aspect. The dirt and disorder which are the concomitants of all the ruins I have so far had the good fortune to see, set seething in my mind notions the most iconoclastic. But the monuments of England! Piety and modernity here continue to do honour to the past, and not the most rabid antiquarian can enjoy his history less for the absence of smells.*[22]

Many Australians had, of course, travelled through the East on their journey to London and were well aware of the smell of humanity. Earlier visitors had noted much the same of London itself. But for Holman, the triumph of the Board of Works enhanced, rather than detracted from, the enjoyment of antiquity. The mud that the Thames occasionally deposits on the Embankment steps is now mercifully free of sewage.

Yet not all readings of London's antiquities flattered the imperial capital, and in their diaries and letters Australians demonstrated ways in which the Egyptian connection could be used to criticise modern London. Richard Hannan noted in 1892 how the obelisk itself had become a victim of modernity:

> *I don't know if I mentioned it yet but the Hotel Metropole overlooks Charing Cross & St Pauls Cathedral is to be seen in the distance I suppose about 1 mile away[.] About ¼ mile & in sight also on the River banks is Cleopatra's Needle which the air is destroying & it is slowly eroding away in London after resisting the air of Egypt for Centuries. (9 June 1892)*

Such a conflict between antiquity and the air pollution of a modern city meant that Egyptian antiquities could not automatically be held to validate the lineage of imperial London.

Egyptian antiquities in the British Museum could also be read critically by Australians. The museum had its own imperial significance. The British Museum acquired its first Egyptian mummy in 1756,[23] but the bulk of the Egyptian collection was based on artefacts, including the Rosetta stone, collected by the French during Napoleon's occupation of Egypt. These were acquired by the British in 1801 under the Treaty of Alexandria which allowed the French to withdraw from Egypt. Colonial visitors on official visits were routinely shown round, Australians like

Jane Murray Smith did it 'as a duty' (14 October 1864), and in 1915 Anne Donnell and the other Australian nurses had their photograph taken on its steps for the *British Australasian* newspaper. Many Australians were, of course, like Margaret Tripp in 1872, astounded by the Egyptian exhibits:

> *On Monday I finished my packing directly after breakfast & then went with Louisa to the British Museum. And certainly we acted on the principle of keeping the best till last, for few places have charmed me as did this. . . . I was ready to say with Gaudish 'the glorious hantique', 'Time would fail me to speak' of the mummies and wonderful Egyptian relics that bring the past so vividly before you. (10 June 1872).*

Nettie Higgins was similarly astounded almost forty years later in 1910: 'Went through Egyptian Galleries & Elgin Room &c. Simply thunderstruck: had to go and drink tea & be sober' (10 October 1910).

But while accepting the splendour of the exhibits, Australians who had reached London via Suez were able to assess London's antiquity through their first-hand knowledge of Egypt. William Willis in 1889, for example, thought the display of mummies in Cairo superior to that of the British Museum:

> *Here [in the British Museum] you see the form only, the bodies being entirely concealed by the wrappings in which they were originally encased.*
>
> *In the Boulak Museum at Cairo, the bodies were stripped, so we saw the Ancients themselves, being able to distinguish their features[,] color of hair &c almost as in life. (10 June 1889)*

In their assessment of the antiquity of London, Australians could be reminded that that they shared the dislocation of London's Egyptian antiquities.

Tripp's remarks about saving the best till last can therefore be seen as an implicit criticism of London, especially when read against her comment that, 'The only fault I have to find with London is that it looks so new. There is very little air of antiquity about it.' Egyptian antiquities offered reflected glory to the British Museum, but in their dislocation they challenged the presentation of London as itself an antique imperial city. Outside London, it was easier to represent England as historical, and Anne Donnell in her letters describes an Old England of the picture postcard variety: 'a favourite walk is to a little old fashioned village 4 miles away over them [the Sussex Downs] called Rottingdean. It nestles quietly between the hills by the sea – apart from the quaintness of it its chief attraction is the old old church of St Margarets' (20 January 1917). Historical England is picturesque England, an England with, as John McRae put it in 1917, 'nothing modern in it' (3 February 1917).

And yet Egypt had the power to undermine even this. Donnell, who had been so keen on London in 1915, returned from Egypt in 1917 with a completely altered outlook, and her descriptions of her walks on the Sussex Downs are prefaced by a disclaimer:

> *On my time off duty I have done a good deal of sight seeing in seeing Brighton and the interesting places around.*
>
> *Historical England does not appeal to me now so much as it did before living in Egypt. There is such a vast contrast between the two that you can't compare them, so whilst I am telling you of England and the places I see here I must put the Nile and the graceful palm trees out of my mind. (20 January 1917)*

In the way in which they reinforced and yet also were critical of London as an imperial capital, Australian visitors to London themselves displayed the same contradictions as Cleopatra's Needle. As obelisks and Egyptian antiquities were used to adorn the modern imperial capital and to give it due imperial weight, so too did the presence of visitors from around the world. They did this partly by providing an exotic presence, and though Australians were not so evidently exotic as visitors from, say, India or Africa, Australians permeated all levels of British society and the appearance of a cabbage tree hat certainly provided spectacle on the streets of London.

Australians also enhanced London as an imperial capital through their desire to authenticate London as historical London. In Westminster Abbey they may have found what they were looking for, but when the comparison switched from Australia to Egypt, London's attempt to be both modern and historical became problematic, and their very dislocation enabled Australians to distance themselves from Britain and to see Britain in terms not only of Australia but of Egypt. Rather than lend the weight of antiquity to sanction an imperial London, Egypt seen through Australian eyes offers a critique of London's modernity and hence, like the antiquity of Westminster Abbey, makes apparent in differing ways the very discontinuity it was intended to disguise.

'I could never have believed that the chief American City would have been so bad in this respect'

Although the removal of the second obelisk from Alexandria to New York in 1880/81 was surrounded by the same appeals to antiquity as were made in Britain, its removal was more obviously a project of the modern world. The United States had not had an army in Egypt at the turn of the century, and the second obelisk had been offered to the United States only relatively recently at the opening of the Suez Canal in 1869, an offer that was speedily taken up once the British started to remove theirs. A report in the *New York Times* of a talk given by Lt. Commander Gorringe, the engineer who removed the American obelisk, suggests that the United States may well have been prompted by the engineering challenge and the opportunity to rival the British and the French:

> The comparison of American with French engineering was listened to with marked interest. It required five years, and cost $500,000, to remove from Alexandria the obelisk now erected in Paris and place it in its position. Commander Gorringe was engaged at his work one year and four months, and the aggregate expenses were $105,000.[24]

The 'aggregate expenses,' though not as large as the French costs, were mostly met by a private benefactor, William H. Vanderbilt (1821–85), who had helped his father, Cornelius Vanderbilt, build up huge interests in railroads serving an ever expanding New York. The family acquired the New York Central railway company in 1867, built Grand Central Station and amassed a fortune, most of which passed to William H. on his father's death in 1877.[25] Despite the antiquity of the New York obelisk, its removal from Alexandria was cast more in terms of New World technical achievement and wealth than in terms of Old World history and imperialism.

Australians travelling through the United States on their way either to or from Europe were attracted to, and yet highly troubled by, America's obvious technological progress and its consequent wealth. The main focus of their admiration was, of course, America's entrepreneurial spirit. Richard Teece, travelling through the United States in 1875, was especially struck by Chicago, a city that had been destroyed by fire in 1871:

> We are more favourably impressed with Chicago than with any city we

have seen in America; it is in every sense a remarkable place. . . . In a little over three years the city has been almost entirely rebuilt & its magnificent streets of uniformly elegant buildings impress the beholder with a deep sense of the enterprise & public spirit of the people. (4 April 1875)

In Chicago in 1881, Martha Hudson echoed Teece's comments: 'After dinner, we had a look through the drawing rooms of the hotel which are very handsome. . . . It is wonderful when you look at this place, and think that 10 years ago, it was nothing but ashes' (15 March 1881).

And yet the same Australians who praised the United States for its enterprise were highly suspicious of the wealth that enterprise generated. Martha Hudson, for one, had been astonished by the money to be made: 'The people must make money very fast to build the places they have and are still building just as largely' (15 March 1881). In Cleveland she noted much the same: 'Altho this city is quite small compared with some of the other large cities, there seems just as great abundance of wealth' (9 April 1881).

Of all the American towns they passed through, Australians seem to have been least overawed by San Francisco, mainly, it appears, because it was a new settlement. In the early 1880s, Thomas Dow thought Melbourne had advanced more rapidly: 'Melbourne has more permanent and solidly constructed buildings, far better streets, and a larger population than San Francisco, so that it has no equal in the world among cities of nearly the same age.'[26] If some Australians recognised in San Francisco a city as young as their own, Richard Teece, from the older city of Sydney, regarded San Francisco as positively backward:

The business portion of San Francisco contains a lot of buildings, the hotels being the principal ones, but once beyond that & we have the most ephemeral & tin-pot place imaginable; wooden buildings, carved & painted to imitate stone, without foundations, & which suffer periodical removals from one place to another – we have seen several houses in the middle of the streets in transitu. (21 March 1875)

Yet if the permanence of the buildings was the prime criterion, it is not surprising that Mrs E. Barnes, a British visitor to San Francisco, should notice its similarity with the towns of Australia and New Zealand, which she had visited earlier on her world tour:

the City as I suppose they call it reminded Arthur and I strongly of Colonial Towns, you see just the same anomalies in the shape of fine and wretched buildings next to one another, the same struggling wooden houses in the suburbs, the same straight streets (though in the case of S. F filthy dirty and badly kept) that are distinguishing features of most Colonial Towns. (E. Barnes 22 June 1888)

Although Australians did not explicitly regard San Francisco as a colonial town, it appears that they either recognised the familiar newness of a colonial settlement, or they adopted a sense of superiority that was perhaps more Old World British than New World Australian. Either way, they were less in awe of San Francisco than of New York or Chicago.

If San Francisco could seem much the same as Melbourne or even Sydney, its hotels stood out as exceptional. Australians admired the scale and lavish interiors of the hotels, but they were often uneasy about the amount of money spent on the buildings, an unease that stemmed not so much from the ostentation as from what they perceived as a lack of particular cultural values. James Hogan in the late 1880s was critical of San Francisco's lack of civic amenities:

At present, the only noteworthy literary institution they possess is the Public Library – a small, stuffy, and uncomfortable place, which is far from creditable to a city of the size and importance of San Francisco. The fact is that the time, the labour, and the expense which other cities lavish on their public buildings are mainly directed in San Francisco towards the erection and adornment of monster palatial hotels.[27]

Most Australian visitors to the United States were impressed by its palaces, the 'palatial' hotels, the 'palatial' railway stations. But San Francisco's obvious modernity seemed to have resulted in the absence of comparable public buildings to house institutions, such as libraries and museums, that middle-class Australians regarded as vital to civic culture. In San Francisco, as elsewhere in the United States, Australians found a city in which the largest buildings were owned by commercial corporations.

Australians were concerned not just for the quality of America's public buildings but for the quality of civic space in general. Richard Hannan was unimpressed by New York in 1892:

It was very hot in & around the city & I was not particularly impressed with the appearance of it. I saw the overhead railway & I think that it rather disfigures the appearance of the city but there is no doubt but that it is very convenient for traffic. I have been told that in some of the narrow streets the sun never shines on account of the overhead railway blocking its rays. (84)

In Hannan's eyes, the convenience of the elevated railway did not compensate for the disfigurement of the urban landscape and the assumed threat to public health by blocking out the sun. Three years earlier, William Willis, on a world tour with his young son in 1889, was critical of New York for the same reason: 'There is an elevated railway running through some of the streets. The thoroughfares are entirely spoiled' (1 August 1889). And not content with damning the elevated railway, Willis damned New York's drains and tramways into the bargain:

We are having very bad weather. . . . This has made sight seeing rather difficult. The streets are in a shocking condition. I could never have believed that the chief American City would have been so bad in this respect.
Let me assure you that we are far in advance in many respects.
The tram arrangements in no way compare with ours. The lines are in a most disgraceful state. (1 August 1889)

Again, though, such criticisms were not based merely on aesthetics or on the convenience of the sightseer. Australians seemed to be using the condition of American cities as an index of the values of the cities' inhabitants; and Willis' description of New York leads naturally enough to an account of the manners of the people inhabiting it:

The manners of the majority are very poor. I do not say this from what is met in New York alone. It was the same wherever we met them in travelling.
There is a roughness, and carelessness of other peoples comfort, that is not the rule among the better classes of our own people.
I heard one young American lady say, that if you wanted to find a place in England people would render you every assistance, whereas among her own people, they would hardly take the trouble to give you information. An American gentleman admitted this was so. (1 August 1889)

The United States at this time was not without public buildings and public institutions, and Martha Hudson in 1881 praised the appearance of the Museum of Fine Arts in Boston: 'We had our lunch in the city and after lunch visited the Art Museum, where we saw some very ancient things. Some of the articles were used 300 and 400 years before Christ. The building from the outside has a very imposing appearance' (5 May 1881). Australians could clearly find praise for American public institutions, and the Cleopatra's Needle removed to New York was located on an impressive site that included the Metropolitan Museum of Art.

Yet even though America could boast elegant public buildings, its escalating wealth continued to trouble Australian visitors, and Elgin Munro, visiting Washington from Sydney in 1916, was suspicious that even the capital of the United States lacked solid cultural foundations:

> *Evidently the delight of the authorities of the city is to have embla-*
> *zoned on the walls of Public Buildings and particularly so in the*
> *Congressional Library, beautiful quotations which, if taken to heart and*
> *carried into the lives of the people, would release them from many asper-*
> *sions particularly in regard to their chase of the elusive yet Almighty*
> *Dollar.*[28]

Despite the construction of some imposing public buildings, it seems there was little Americans could do to alleviate the taint of the 'Almighty Dollar' that troubled many of its late nineteenth-century Australian visitors.

I want to suggest, therefore, that Australians evaluated the United States strategically, using both sides of their British Australian identities. In terms of technological progress, Australians were quite prepared to compare America with Australia. Both countries could be regarded as new worlds, and Australians felt themselves on particularly strong grounds when evaluating newer cities like San Francisco. But they were also prepared to admit the technological superiority of the United States, especially in the quality of its railways, which Australian engineers, like Martha Hudson's father, travelled to the United States precisely to study: 'We arrived in Sacramento about ½ past 2. The car, we travelled in, was a beautifully got up carriage. It took Father's attention all the morning, we certainly have not anything like it in Sydney' (4 March 1881).

Yet despite the fact that both America and Australia could be classified as new worlds, many Australians saw themselves as British when it came to cultural values. Australians throughout their travels could move between British and Australian reference points in evaluating the

United States, and they were adept at calling on their Britishness as and when it suited them. In his trip to the United States in 1875, Richard Teece had a clear idea of himself as Australian, but he was happy to align himself with Britishness when he wanted to record the strangeness of local customs. In Honolulu, for example, he was suspicious of the breakfast offered him because, as he put it, 'there are some little things which somewhat offend the Epicurean Britisher' (10 March). And in New York, he again used his Britishness as a point of comparison: 'Had a look round town, went on board "City of Richmond" where we obtained 4 halfpints of genuine British for which we paid a colonial Robert. At night we visited the fraud Opera House witnessed the representation of Ahmed a spectacular display of ballet dancers legs & tinsels' (14 April).

Teece was not so much claiming to be British as viewing America through British eyes, eyes that subscribed to British cultural values. So when he condemned San Francisco for its lack of foundations, the notion of foundation also carried with it connotations of cultural foundations. In this sense, Australian assessments of San Francisco were based, like that of the British woman, E. Barnes, on its inferiority as a 'colonial town'. And as Teece condemned the 'fraud Opera House' in New York with its 'spectacular display of ballet dancers legs & tinsels,' so the opera house in Denver failed to live up to Barnes' English standards: 'Denver is a nice town with streets lined with trees, there is nothing to do there but it is a pleasant place to break the journey at – On June 21st in the evening I went to the Opera House which is said to be the finest in the States, it is a good theatre but was poorly lighted and very draughty' (3 July 1888).

Australians were therefore prepared to be impressed by the products of modernity but not by what they considered to be its underlying values. Their Britishness came from a belief in certain civilised values, as in Willis' anecdote about the superiority of the manners of the English over the inhabitants of New York. Willis compared the New York trams with those of Melbourne: 'The tram arrangements in no way compare with ours'; but his comparison of cultural values was based on English behaviour: 'if you wanted to find a place in England people would render you every assistance.' For such commentators, the values on which they depended for their Britishness were underpinned by precisely that sense of 'continuous history' that Margaret Tripp and others eagerly sought in London. When they travelled through America, Australians carried with them not only their knowledge of Australia but a British cultural baggage that included 'the chapels &c the

Poets' Corner and the grand tombs & historical relics' of Westminster Abbey.

In these accounts, America was not seen as an alternative to Britain; indeed, America and Britain were rarely directly compared. And Australians could be as suspicious of the effects of technological progress in Britain as they were in America. But on the whole, their experience of America tended to reinforce a British identity, an identity that appeared more able to counter the raw commercialism of the United States than it did in London, where modernity was associated with the creation of an imperial capital and all the British values that entailed. Certainly Egypt could provide no handle by which to criticise modern America; in the New World, unlike in Britain, the division between antiquity and modernity was not mediated by a claim for historical continuity. And because the critique of modernity in the United States was made in terms of Britain rather than Egypt, Australians seemed more certain of their Britishness in America than in Britain.

Indeed, their sense of Britishness could be reinforced by the Americans. As today, few Americans knew much about Australia; but they knew about the Britishness of Canada, and, judging from the comment by a US customs official at Winnipeg to Richard Hannan in 1892, Americans knew on what side of the border Australians belonged:

> *I had a conversation with two men here[,] one being the custom house officer of U.S. he told me I was English decidedly English in language but after bonding my luggage through to San Francisco. he could not resist giving a dig at Queen Victoria saying 'Queen Victoria and all her colonies could not open this package or break the bond', or leaden seal which he placed upon the trunks. (88)*

In Britain, of course, Australians felt more colonial, as in Tripp's comment that, 'I now quite understand from my own experience the fascination everything old has for an American.' But in America, it seems that some Americans, at least, did not see Australians as New World cousins.

SIX

A Disgusting Climate: Being Australian in Wales, Ireland and Scotland

When Australians travelled to Britain, they mostly travelled to London. London was the seat of Empire, and if their ship docked at Liverpool or one of the South Coast ports instead of London, they were swiftly transferred to the metropolis by express train. But not all of them remained there. Wales, Scotland and Ireland were easy to reach by train from London, and the tourist routes were well travelled. For those of English descent, visiting Wales, Scotland and Ireland drew from them the ways in which they regarded themselves as English. For those of Scottish or Irish descent, Scotland and Ireland increased their awareness of being Australian. For all of them, the return to 'sunny Australia' brought with it a new sense of their Australian identity, an identity based on their experiences of having been an Australian abroad.

'a strange people speaking a language that we don't understand'

Of all the Australian visitors to Britain in the nineteenth century, John Rae may well have been the one who travelled the furthest in the shortest time. He arrived in Britain in June 1879 and after spending a month in London visiting his daughter, Amy, and other members of his family, Rae took a mere nine days to visit Doncaster, Hull, Lincoln, York, Durham, Newcastle, Sheffield, Derby, Birmingham, Stratford-on-Avon, Oxford, Cambridge, Ely, and Peterborough, before returning to London. This was, however, but a prelude. A week later he set out on an even more intensive tour, this time encompassing the West Country,

Wales, Scotland and Ireland. Despite travelling so far, Rae rarely spent more than one night in any town, and even visiting his family in Banff, in northern Scotland, detained him no longer than four nights.

John Rae had been NSW commissioner for railways between 1861 to 1878, and had overseen the expansion of the railway system within the colony. Not only was he keen to inspect Britain's widespread railway system, but his whistlestop tour was largely the result of free travel granted him by the managers of the various British regional railway companies. In this way, Rae followed an unusual and circuitous route round Britain, apparently attempting to visit as many extremities of mainland Britain as it was possible to visit by train. Having perversely travelled from London to Penzance via Ramsgate, Rae struck north-east to Cheltenham and Hereford, before zigzagging back into Wales and travelling south-west through Cardiff to Milford Haven. He caught a ferry across to Pembroke and then doubled back to Carmarthen via Tenby in order to head up to Aberystwyth and to North Wales.

In this way, Rae visited parts of Wales largely disregarded by other Australians, such as the medieval market town of Carmarthen in the west:

Had a long walk through the Town, an irregular congeries of streets & houses poverty stricken in appearance. Being Market Day I walked to the Mart where dealers most do congregate & felt at once I was in Wales, as I did not hear a word of English while I was there. It is the poorest-looking place I have seen, the people commonplace in appearance & many of the women who formed the great majority in the Market Place wearing the old Welsh habit, even to the peaked hat. The Market women all wear a common dress. With the exception of the Town Hall, some Monuments and Churches, there is nothing remarkable in the town except that we are among a strange people speaking a language that we don't understand. (23 August 1879)

For John Rae, the immediate difference between West Wales and the rest of Britain was the sound of the Welsh language: 'felt at once I was in Wales, as I did not hear a word of English while I was there.' For Australian travellers journeying through Wales, language was the primary definition of Welshness. Daniel Matthews, staying in Cardiff, travelled west for a day to just beyond Swansea: 'On reaching Swansea I was struck with the difference of the people. They seem more like Welch than those of Cardiff, both in their dress and habits' (20 September 1869). Beyond Swansea, it was the language he noted: 'Welch hats & costumes among the women amused me a little, and I heard enough of their jaw-breaking language to satisfy me for the remainder of my life.'

The relationship between language and their own cultural identity was vital to Australians. In Britain, language was only an issue when they came across the languages of Wales, Ireland and Scotland. But when travelling through Continental Europe, the main problem Australians faced was their inability to speak European languages, though they tended to see it more as the failure of Europeans to speak English. Francis Smart was more fortunate than most Australians: 'I got on well on the train, always finding someone to speak English to' (18 March 1901). Daniel Matthews was not so lucky. Two days after his trip to Wales, he crossed Europe alone by train to collect his nephew from boarding school in Cologne, and like most Australians who crossed the Channel, Matthews immediately found himself adrift in a non-English speaking culture: 'At Alost several passengers left and others came in and began to talk to me in French. My slight acquaintance with the language was of no service to me here, so I was obliged to resort to the familiar phrase '"Je ne parle pas Francais"'(27 September 1869).

After spending the night in Brussels, Matthews continued his journey towards Cologne with an increasing sense of his own cultural isolation:

A lady sat next me, whom I strongly hoped was English for I was fairly bursting for want of a talk, as I had scarcely spoken a word of English since I left the 'cotton man' [i.e. a man in the cotton trade] at Ghent. This lady looked at me several times, but I couldn't summon courage to address her. At length she spoke out a long sentence in French, that I hadn't the remotest idea of the meaning it conveyed. I replied 'je suis Anglais, madam[e], je ne vous comprends pas'. 'Do you come from London', she said[.] 'Yes, ma'am' was my answer, and it was a cheering thing for me to find there was one that could understand me. (28 September 1869)

The woman, it transpired, was a governess in a gentleman's family in Liverpool, travelling home to Aix-la-Chapelle. But though she might have been expected to understand who or what an Australian might be, especially given Liverpool's importance as a port serving Australia, Matthews identified himself as English ('je suis Anglais, madam[e]') and from London.

The following day, having reached Cologne, Matthews took a day trip up the Rhine Valley by train (he had missed the early morning steamer) to Bingen. Walking round Bingen alone, Matthews resorted to talking to himself:

A notion came into my head that I would like to recite my old piece 'Bingen on the Rhine' in the place itself, so I did as I paced down the road. The people took no more notice of me than if I had been reciting London on the Thames, or Echuca on the Murray. These Germans are a funny people. I read a word this evening on a sign-board near the railway station containing triple f. How these outlandish people sound it I don't know. (29 September 1869).

By talking to himself in English, Matthews divided himself into speaker and audience, and to that extent provided himself with the English-speaking companion he lacked. But this is actually a passage in his diary, and Matthews was more likely imagining an audience beyond himself comprising the many people to whom he might lend his diary. And that audience would be Australian. This is the reason, perhaps, that although Matthews described himself as an Englishman from London when he spoke to the governess on the train, he included in the written passage above an Australian equivalent alongside the English – 'The people took no more notice of me than if I had been reciting London on the Thames, or Echuca on the Murray.' Echuca is mentioned for the benefit of his Australian readership.

Matthews, like other Australian travellers, used his Australian identity strategically, and there were occasions to employ it when travelling in Continental Europe. But his longing to speak English on the Continent made his English identity more important, an importance it gained from being grounded in the English language: 'I got very tired of looking at the bilious faces of the Germans, and hearing the clatter of their unmusical tongues, and felt a longing to catch again the familiar sounds of my native language' (30 September 1869). National identity is here reduced to a difference in language, a language Australians were fully aware was English. And it was speaking English rather than Australian that made them at ease in Europe, witness Martha Hudson: 'We got to Calais at 2 o'clock and had some lunch in the Calais restaurant and for our first meal in the french land & among french people got on famously. Took the train again for Paris, & found the guard spoke English so we felt ourselves again' (24 October 1881). For Martha Hudson and her parents, being themselves in France was a question of speaking and hence feeling English rather than Australian.

'Such is the wretched condition of the artisan and laboring class in this land'

In his account of his visit to Carmarthen in 1879, John Rae noted not just the language of the locals but what they wore: 'It is the poorest-looking place I have seen, the people commonplace in appearance & many of the women who formed the great majority in the Market Place wearing the old Welsh habit, even to the peaked hat. The Market women all wear a common dress.' No doubt the women's costumes were a novelty, but Rae also seemed to view them as confirmation of the poverty of the place, 'an irregular congeries of streets & houses poverty stricken in appearance.' The 'common dress' of the women was also 'commonplace,' and Carmarthen's strangeness owing to its language was reinforced by an unfamiliar, but very visible, poverty.

Australians travelling in Ireland and Scotland were also struck by the visible poverty. Sir James Penn Boucaut, a former Premier of South Australia, was astonished by the poverty when he visited Dublin in 1892: 'I never saw so many poverty-stricken people together in my life as I did in that two hours – at least, apparently poverty-stricken; clothes in rags, holes, and filth, and the faces apparently as dirty as the clothes.'[1] The poverty of Edinburgh discomforted Martha Hudson: 'The first day was not very promising, for we saw such a deal of poverty and drunkeness [*sic*], it made us feel quite uncomfortable' (7 August 1881).

The geographical separation between the affluence of London's West End and the poverty of the East End seems to have shielded the majority of middle-class Australians from the unsettling poverty of London's working-class districts. The true extent of London's poverty was seen only by those who sought it, such as Daniel Matthews. In Australia, Matthews ran a mission station in Echuca, Victoria, to help displaced Aboriginal people, and he followed his missionary vocation in London by visiting working-class areas on several occasions to see for himself the conditions in which the poor survived:

Paid a visit to Tallerman's, penny dinner shop, and got two pennyworth of stew. Found it rather 'rough tack'. Eat some of it, and gave the rest to a crowd of ragged urchins who came in to get a penn'orth between them, and dont go out till they are well filled with the leavings of others.
Large numbers of people frequent the place. Among these are the filthiest and raggedest to be met with, as well as the nicely dressed city clerk. The room is small, and excessively dirty, and there is nothing attractive either

*to the person or the appetite of any one who has the slightest pretension
to respectability. (12 January 1870)*

Such a detailed first-hand description of London's poverty is extremely
rare in Australian accounts of London. Given that, like Martha Hudson,
they risked being made to feel 'quite uncomfortable' by poverty,
Australians tended to avoid the East End. The poverty was noticed now
and again from cabs, or by some of the Australian men when they
wandered off the main thoroughfares:

> *Sunday 4. Went to Church at Gordon Square at 11 A.M. Walking back I
> saw the black side of London in the back streets where the streets were full
> of men women & Children all as dirty as it was possible for them to be.
> pale Faces. all bent on Beer drinking which seems to be their one object.
> and the streets were as filthy as possible. fine (Wyndham 4 June 1882)*

Reginald Wyndham's description is a fairly predictable middle-class
reaction to working-class poverty. Poverty is first associated with dirt,
and then dirt becomes metaphorically associated with immorality
through an apparent association with beer drinking; the implicit logic
is that people living in these streets drink, the streets are filthy, so therefore the streets are filthy because the people drink. From this, it is a short
step to blaming working people for their own poverty.

Daniel Matthews' description of metropolitan poverty is therefore
exceptional not just for its detailed observation of poverty but for its lack
of moral condescension. Matthews had lived as a boy in Southwark in
south-east London in the 1840s and early 1850s, and he found the area
no better when he revisited it in 1869, the 'wretchedness, filth & poverty'
still predominating. But there is no suggestion in his accounts that
working people are poor because of an inherent immorality. In his
description of Tallerman's penny diner, Matthews is aware of the
economic causes of poverty:

> *A young man sitting opposite to me said he came home from the United
> States a few weeks ago, with £20, the savings of several months, for the
> purpose of bringing his wife back with him, but she positively refuses to
> leave England under any circumstances. He has had no employment
> since he has been home, and has no chance of getting any – he is a
> carpenter and joiner. Such is the wretched condition of the artisan and
> laboring class in this land. I recommended those around me to emigrate
> immediately an opportunity offered if they could not get employment in
> England. (12 January 1870)*

Matthews was not alone in recommending migration as a way of easing metropolitan poverty. Social reformers argued for migration to the colonies as a way of preventing social unrest among the working classes. But the reverse of this, as seen in Matthews' account, was the assumption that working-class poverty was not so serious a social problem within the colonies. Advocates of migration, at least during periods of economic growth, assumed that the metropolitan unemployed might find employment in the colonies.

In the minds of Australian travellers, if poverty was associated with an aspect of Australia it was associated not with the working classes but with indigenous Australians. For example, when confronted by scenes of poverty in Switzerland, Jane Murray Smith was reminded of Aboriginal people: 'The awful looking creatures you see in the Valleys! Our blacks really are superior, I think' (2 August 1864). Visiting Port Said on her return voyage to Australia, Emma Walker associated the smell of humanity with Aboriginal people: 'We walked to the Arab Town about half a mile out, the filth of which is almost indescribable, the perfume emitted by this race is quite as suggestive of *no baths* and as exhilirating [*sic*] upon a white person, and as much like, as that of our own aboriginal natives, as you may imagine at this stage, I began to fancy myself in Australia' (Emma Walker 28 November 1883). Once again, it is a small step between associating poverty and dirt, and equating poverty with immorality, a point made explicit in Nathan Spielvogel's account of Port Said published in 1905: 'Port Said is bad, utterly, horribly bad. Never in my maddest dreams have I imagined such a hell-on-earth as this place is – a dumping ground for all that is vicious and bad. . . . I compared the vice, the squalor, and the horrors of Port Said with the cleanliness and purity of Australia.'[2]

Richard White has noted a link in Australian accounts between London's poverty and London's weather: 'Nationalists described London's poverty against a luridly Dickensian background of fog, cold, grime and over-crowding. They felt they clinched their case once they contrasted it all with Australian sunshine.'[3] If poverty was associated with bad weather, then Australians need not admit the poverty of Australia: 'since London's fog, grime and cold did not exist in Australia, then Australia could be assumed to be a classless society.'[4] White is referring to late nineteenth-century Australian Nationalism, but the link between the climate and British working-class poverty existed much earlier in the minds of visiting Australians. Jane Murray Smith, born in Hobart but brought up in Geelong, made the connection when visiting Manchester in 1864:

> *In this country some days the smoke and steam never will rise, the atmosphere is so heavy. The houses in Manchester are all so black in the town with the smoke and no wonder, when you see hundreds of chimneys, fifty times as big as any in Geelong. The distress is very much less, but it really breaks one's heart to see women carrying about babies nearly naked in cold like this. They are not beggars, but people doing work or taking a walk.*
>
> *You can't enjoy anything very much for it is always raining or snowing. The children here don't go out for an hour during the whole week, and when they do go out they wear shetland veils and handkerchiefs tied over their mouths.* (10 March)

In Jane Murray Smith's account, air pollution, snow and poverty are linked, and she was especially concerned about the plight of the poor in the cold. Daniel Matthews voiced the same concern: 'In the afternoon I saw a poor laborer, with three little boys standing at the edge of a pavement, shivering with cold, not begging, but on the back of a shovel in the man's hand was written "out of work". This is too often the tale. I gave the poor hunger & cold nipped creatures ᵈ6' (12 January 1870).

As Nathan Spielvogel's account of Port Said demonstrates, the association between poverty and the British climate did not prevent Australians abroad acknowledging the poverty of the sunny countries through which they passed on their way to and from Europe: 'I compared the vice, the squalor, and the horrors of Port Said with the cleanliness and purity of Australia.' Yet White is clearly correct in noting the absence in Australian accounts of comparisons between the poverty they encountered on their travels abroad and working-class poverty in Australia. Daniel Matthews, the missionary from Echuca on the Murray, makes no mention of poverty in Australia, though he does make a comparison between the Welsh women of Swansea and Aboriginal women in Victoria:

> *The peculiar method the women here employ to carry their babies is worthy of notice. They wind a large shawl over the right shoulder, and under the left arm, and in the folds of the shawl suspend the infant, thus saving themselves the burden directly on the arm. The lubras of Australia carry their piccaninnies in a fold of their rug or blanket over the back. The Welsh plan is preferably I think, as it keeps the body in an upright position.* (20 September 1869)

There is perhaps an assumed correlation between the Welsh working

---

classes and Aboriginal poverty, but the comparison is disguised as an ethnological observation about gender practices. The comparison is made, but not recognised.

Jane Murray Smith's account of Manchester is unusual in apparently comparing working-class conditions with those of Geelong: 'The houses in Manchester are all so black in the town with the smoke and no wonder, when you see hundreds of chimneys, fifty times as big as any in Geelong. The distress is very much less, but it really breaks one's heart to see women carrying about babies nearly naked in cold like this.' Murray Smith appears to suggest that working-class 'distress' is less in Manchester than in Geelong, though her real focus is on the lives of women rather than on working-class conditions in general. As in Matthew's account of the women of Swansea, discussion of the lives of women emphasised gender rather than social class.

One of the main problems with admitting the existence of poverty within Australia must have been that the presentation of the Australian working man as quintessentially Australian. Working-class poverty was at variance with an image of Australia as a workingman's paradise. Yet, as White implies, any acknowledgement of Australian poverty would also have the effect of making middle-class Australians aware of their own social class: 'Real poverty, and therefore real class consciousness, could not exist in a country where the sun shone so brightly.'[5] Martha Hudson's perception of the poverty of Edinburgh in 1881 is, at least to us, plainly that of a middle-class woman: 'The first day was not very promising, for we saw such a deal of poverty and drunkeness, it made us feel quite uncomfortable.' Yet, if White is correct, then her failure to acknowledge poverty within Australia makes Hudson's comments not only middle-class but characteristically Australian. Compensation for the evident unease that middle-class Australians experienced at the sight of poverty could be found in the belief that Australia had been spared such degradation. If this is the case, then John Rae, Sir James Penn Boucaut, Martha Hudson, and even Daniel Matthews observed British poverty through eyes that were not only middle-class but distinctly Australian.

'I tried to persuade them I came of English parents & was born in an English country'

When Henry Incledon Pilcher sailed for England on the *John Duthie* in

1866, his cabin mate was Francis Moseley, a young man whose family home was Leaton Hall at Bobbington on the Staffordshire/Shropshire border. Here the Moseleys were neighbours of an even larger landowner, the Earl of Stamford and Warrington, whose seat at Enville was known for its lavish gardens, including an impressively large conservatory 160 feet long erected around 1854 at the reputed cost of £30,000.[6] Pilcher, who visited Enville while staying with Moseley, was almost as delighted with Enville's conservatory as with the Crystal Palace which he had visited only six days earlier, and he had great praise for the fountains: 'the fountains play once a week, and are considered the best in the World, excepting those at the Crystal Palace' (10 August).

Enville was not the only sight that impressed Pilcher during his brief visit to Leaton Hall, and each day presented him with fresh aspects of the English countryside, a countryside that fully matched his cultural expectations: 'the country we rode through had its fair share of the beauties, which first attract the Australian's eye, viz. calm ponds of water which in winter time are frequently skated upon, nicely trimmed hedges, composed promiscuously of Hawthorne, Mulberry, Raspberry, Holly, Hedge nuts &c, ripe corn fields, hay fields, green meadows &c' (10 August). The sights that attract 'the Australian's eye' are not only those that contrast with Australia, but also the sights that seem to confirm the image of England with which Pilcher, as a child of English migrants, had been brought up: in his Australian mind's eye the pond 'frequently skated upon' becomes an English winter's scene .

But Pilcher also looked at England from a social perspective, a perspective that favoured landed wealth. Pilcher's parents were themselves relatively affluent. Henry Incledon Pilcher (senior) and Eliza Brockley had arrived in Sydney from London in April 1830 and had taken up a 2000-acre land grant to the north of the Hunter Valley. Henry (senior) was a solicitor, and to complement his agricultural interests he set up a law practice in Maitland High Street, building a large house at 'Telarah,' a sixty-acre property in West Maitland. Henry Incledon (junior) was born in Maitland in 1833, the fourth of eleven children, and by 1865 he had become bank manager for the Bank of Australasia in East Maitland. At the time of Henry's trip to England in 1866, the Pilchers were a well established Maitland family.

In December 1865, not long after his marriage to Ann (or Anne) Borthwick, Henry Pilcher fell ill from tuberculosis and it was at the suggestion of his doctor that in April 1866 he sailed to Britain for a period of leave in the hope of regaining his health. Yet although his voyage was motivated by his state of health, Pilcher obviously regarded his trip 'home' (as he terms it) as something of a pilgrimage, dutifully recording that moment when 'I, for the first time in my life, placed my feet on English, soil' (21 July). Throughout his two months in England, Henry noted in his diary characteristics of England and the English, as when he accompanied Moseley's mother on one of her Sunday visits to the poor: 'my object was to take a peep into the English cottages of the poor[,] the cleanliness of which I have heard so much of, they quite equalled my expectations[,] the English are essentially a cleanly people' (12 August). And a week later, while travelling back to London from North Wales by train, he noted: 'there is truly very little misused or disused land here, what is not built upon is either cultivated or formed into Parks, game reserves, or Woods, containing the handsomest English trees, to say that the scenes along the line are "quite English," means all the praise which I in my poor language could express' (19 August).

Pilcher's England is defined geographically as England rather than Britain as a whole, but it was more than a purely geographic entity. In his description of the countryside, Pilcher was impressed by the productivity of the land: 'there is truly very little misused or disused land here.' To cultivate the land was to produce wealth, and this productivity lies behind his praise of the 'ripe corn fields, hay fields, green meadows &c.' Yet his greatest praise was not for productive arable land but for 'Parks, game reserves, or Woods,' that is, for uncultivated land belonging to a landed élite. Through his friendship with Francis Moseley, Pilcher had already experienced English country house living, and his observation of 'the English' was refracted through the paternalism of Moseley's mother's visit to the rural poor on the Moseley estate. Earlier still while visiting his brother in Worthing, Pilcher had made much the same link between land ownership and the beauty of the English countryside: 'Strolled about with Frank in the fields & woods, some of the gentlemen's parks are enclosed with high stone walls, here the good old English oaks abound in all their renowned glory' (26 July). There is an evident correlation between Pilcher's conservatism and his aesthetics, and his praise of the English parks and game reserves is consistent with his call for the abolition of universal suffrage in Australia: 'I . . . expressed pretty freely my opinion of universal suffrage and its injurious effects in the Colonies' (19 August).

In his sightseeing trips around Britain, Henry Pilcher behaved like a tourist, keeping his eyes open and writing down whatever struck him. But he was also endorsing a particular social structure and his own belief in that structure. Whatever pleased him, such as the neatness of the countryside or the tidiness of the cottages, may have impressed him because he was an Australian; but by increasing his admiration of English landowners, it simultaneously confirmed his view of his English cultural heritage. It is this construction of England that lies behind the valedictory address at the end of his visit: 'I have now done with old England perhaps forever, God bless her and protect her from all her enemies, my opinion of England is summed up in two words "Earthly Paradise"' (9 September).

Yet even Henry Pilcher, who identified himself so strongly as English, felt it necessary on occasion to assert an Australian identity. Shortly after arriving in Britain, he and Francis Moseley found themselves the topic of conversation in a coffee room: 'some strangers were commenting upon our appearance, and I heard one say that he was certain we were Australians. Moseley's cabbage-tree hat, and our "tout ensemble" and generally free and easy manner, must have led him to this conclusion' (21 July). Pilcher was keen to affirm the unreserved nature of the Australian, a nature that apparently extended even to Australian cattle: 'I was struck with the quietness of the English cattle, a simple rail at any opening in a hedge suffices to prevent them from going into a corn field, our Colonial cattle would break it down or jump over it, without the least demur' (25 July).

Clearly, neither their Englishness nor their social status prevented Pilcher and Moseley from regarding themselves as Australians: 'on walking about the town Moseley's cabbage tree hat attracted immense attention, every one turned round to look at it' (21 July). For the historian Russel Ward, the cabbage-tree hat came to represent an authentic and distinct Australian character because it was based on the life of the pastoral worker on the frontier; as others took it up, so an egalitarian bush ethos spread.[7] That the cabbage-tree hat was an icon of Australia is supported by Harden S. Melville's painting, *The Squatters Hut: News From Home* (1850–51), in which all three squatters possess cabbage-tree hats. And the central figure in the painting by George Bernard O'Neill, *The Return from Australia*, similarly demonstrates his Australian identity by wearing a broad-brimmed bush hat. In pictorial terms, both paintings suggest a natural association between the hat and Australian bush by including a kangaroo and a cockatoo in the composition.

Pilcher's self-consciousness of his Australianness and Moseley's cabbage-tree hat suggests the two men may been performing an egalitarian bush identity in which neither fully believed; they were privileged young men pretending to be bushmen. Yet this would be a disavowal of Pilcher's solid belief in his own social position and it may be that to assume that the cabbage-tree hat signalled an egalitarian bush ethos is to impose a nationalist history on the meaning of the hat for Pilcher and Moseley. They were, like most such visitors, attempting to negotiate and define a difference between themselves and their English observers, but their 'generally free and easy manner' was not necessarily the same thing as egalitarianism. Unlike the Akubra of today, it was possible for the cabbage-tree hat to signify Australia without carrying an association with bushworkers. Margaret Maynard has noted that: 'Cabbage-tree hats were not primarily a rural garment. They were worn in town as much as in the country, certainly in mid century, and by both sexes.'[8] Indeed, cabbage-tree hats were displayed at the 1851 Great Exhibition by Captain Webster, Governor of Darlinghurst Gaol, in order to exemplify 'the industry and discipline of the prisoners in Australian gaols,'[9] values that run counter to Ward's egalitarian bush ethos. Pilcher makes much of the 'free and easy manner' of the colonial, or what he calls elsewhere the Australian 'sang-froid' (30 July), but it is also clear that Pilcher, with his opposition to universal suffrage, did not regard the cabbage-tree hat or his general 'tout ensemble' as a declaration of a bush egalitarianism. The way in which he and Moseley dressed on their travels was primarily a display of a colonial rather than a bush identity, and like the figure in O'Neill's painting, they were Australians before anything else.

Pilcher seems to have been most conscious of being Australian on his arrival in Britain, though unpredictably he re-asserted himself as Australian when preparations for leaving England, his 'Earthly Paradise,' made him feel dejected. Having inspected his cabin, Pilcher resolved on some last minute sightseeing: 'I am determined to see some of the places of amusement, because not to have seen some, at any rate would argue that I had not seen London' (4 September). Accordingly, 'I went to the "Argyle rooms"[,] a dancing saloon, and met here with a young Yankee[,] an invalid like myself, and as we both savoured of the "Free and enlightened" we seemed to be drawn together as if by instinct.' Australian men abroad could see in American men that free and easy manner they believed also characterised themselves (and their cattle); for a moment Pilcher seemed to forget his Englishness and imagine an affinity with a Yankee.

When Pilcher and Moseley went on from Leaton Hall to Ireland, Pilcher found himself in need of an outward sign of his Englishness that corresponded to Moseley's colonial cabbage-tree hat. Travelling the tourist trail from Dublin to the Lakes of Killarney, he and Moseley were mistaken for 'Yankees' by an Irish carman ('who talked about charging us "dollars"'), a mistake Pilcher himself may have relished. But he was less content to be taken for an Irishman:

> *I have imitated the Irish so much the last few days, that I can now hardly speak plain English, consequently the boatmen & our guide will persist in calling me an Irishman much to Moseley's amusement, I tried to persuade them I came of English parents & was born in an English country, but they would not believe a word of it, so Irish I remain, in their estimation. (17 August)*

It is possible that these mistaken identities were some species of anti-English joke, of the type told to Alice Andreas by an Irish priest while crossing Lough Ree: 'An English gentleman was being driven around a town in Ireland one day; and the driver; a real old Paddy kept conversing with him in Irish; and speaking to the horse in English; and so he asked why it was, and the driver said in reply – "Sure faith English is good enough for the horse"' (24 August 1902). In Pilcher's case, the boatmen may have simply been teasing someone they thought all along to be English. Had Moseley worn his cabbage-tree hat it might have helped to confuse the Irishmen, but it would not have helped Pilcher wishing to be taken as English: 'of English parents & . . . born in an English country.'

Pilcher's wish to be taken as 'born in an English country' rather than as Irish or specifically Australian seems to have been connected to his implicit definition of the Irish as paupers and peasants. He didn't much like Dublin: 'it seems to me a dirty place, and so are the inhabitants in comparison with the citizens of English cities' (14 August). And he didn't much like what he saw of the Irish countryside: 'the hedges appeared to be all broken down[,] the ditches filled, no respectable residences, the few we met with being simply mud huts, no trees, everything looking disused and delapidated [*sic*]' (16 August). It was, in short, 'Godforgotten'. Even allowing for the effect of depopulation, it is understandable that, when mistaken for Irish, he insisted on the English side of his identity. Perhaps, too, his Englishness had already been constructed against Irishness during his growing up in Australia; Maitland had an Irish population of about fourteen percent in the 1860s.[10] And had he claimed to be Australian rather than English, he might still have been taken for an Irish-Australian.

If Pilcher's assertion of his Englishness was based on a class identity, or at least on a sympathy towards English landowners, then his antipathy towards the Irish had a similar social dimension. Pilcher seems to have associated Irishness with poverty, be it the poverty of the urban poor or the poverty of the Irish peasantry. Pilcher's attitude towards the old quarter of Edinburgh was similar to his view of Dublin: 'it is divided into the old & new town, the former is only small and consists of a number of irregular narrow & dirty streets with a mean looking population' (27 August). Fortunately, the old city 'forms only a small portion of the city as a whole,' and Pilcher was much impressed by the newer parts of Edinburgh: 'there is a neatness, an elegance[,] a cleanliness about Edinburgh which speaks volumes for the taste & wealth of its inhabitants.' Once again, as in his praise of the parkland of England, Pilcher's aesthetics have a conservative base. The irregularity of Edinburgh's streets are associated with 'a mean looking population,' whereas elegance is an indicator of the 'taste' of the wealthy. Small wonder that Pilcher was confounded by the contradictory spaces of the City of London: 'It astonishes me what narrow poking miserable looking places some of the best business streets of London are such as Mincing Lane &c' (30 August). In Pilcher's terms, this was wealth without 'taste'.

Perhaps, then, here is another reason why British Australians, when faced by scenes of poverty, were not prompted to acknowledge poverty in Australia. If their Englishness was implicitly a middle class identity, then scenes of poverty in Ireland, Scotland, Wales and even England offered them an opportunity to think of themselves as English rather than Australian. In distancing themselves from poverty, Australian visitors asserted their social superiority, respectability and taste, characteristics by which they could define themselves as English rather than as Australian. Contrary to what we might expect, for middle-class Australians, the sight of poverty in Britain could increase their sense of belonging to England.

'Everything seems so homelike now & so very different from Scotland, it is lovely to see the gum trees again'

We left today for London. The north of Ireland is a disgusting climate for an Australian who loves his blue skies & glorious sunshine. There can be no dependence placed on the weather in these latitudes. The sun may be shining brightly in the morning[,] in the afternoon rain may fall in torrents. (Martin 25 September 1891)

The summer of 1891 was in fact exceptionally wet, and J. I. Martin was unlucky in having weeks of bad weather during his visit to Ireland. Nonetheless, 'disgusting' weather was a common complaint of Australian visitors to the British Isles. Robert Murray Smith, returning to Liverpool after ten years in Victoria, was forced to admit that: 'The weather is, I must say, much as I love my native country, simply disgusting, and neither Jeanie nor I feel as if we could stand it much more' (21 December 1864).

Henry Pilcher's summer of 1866 seems to have been as unlucky as Martin's: 'before I arrived in England, they appear to have had, what people here consider a warm and dry summer, but I have as yet seen no indications of either heat, or drought, for it has rained more or less every day, and is generally cold enough for a great coat' (3 August). Unlike either Martin or Murray Smith, however, Pilcher found that the British rain cloud had a silver lining of sorts: 'there is one quality which we do not enjoy in Australia, although it rains often here, it does not rain long or hard at a time, and an umbrella is generally sufficient protection, it is the invariable accompaniment of an Englishman.' Perhaps Pilcher ought to have carried an umbrella with him in Ireland when he had difficulties proving his Englishness. But a month later, noting that heavy rain had not kept the Sunday crowds out of Regent's Park, Pilcher revised his umbrella thesis: 'English people must be amphibious' (2 September 1866).

Of course, Britain could never outshine the 'sunny land' of Australia and even when the weather in Britain was good it was regarded more as Australian than British: 'The morning opened gloriously; air clear and cool; sun bright – a perfectly Australian day' (Emma Walker 23 August 1883). As I noted earlier, this image of Australia as a 'sunny land' not only complemented the image of Britain as foggy, cold and wet, but it could be employed ideologically to disavow working-class poverty in Australia. For J. I. Martin, the 'disgusting climate' of the north of Ireland was in itself one of the material burdens of working people:

> *I would be very sorry to spend a winter in these regions, where summer is nearly as rigorous as our winter. I used to collect the lads of the village around me of an evening & tell them of the glorious climate we revelled in beyond the seas where snow was rarely seen & where the working man was better protected than in any other. It would fire their ardour for the time being, but the next day they had forgotten all about it. (25 September 1891)*

Martin was not a disinterested advocate of Irish migration as he had himself migrated from Ireland twenty years earlier when he been about ten years old. By stressing the misery of being an Irish farm labourer in a cold and wet climate, Martin hoped to persuade some of his numerous cousins to migrate to Australia rather than to America:

> *Very wet. We are staying with Aunt Deborah, my father's eldest sister. Quite a large family have lived here, numbering twelve, but four are now in America and I am trying to persuade some of my cousins to return with us to sunny Australia, where farming conditions are not so difficult as they are here, but so far I have been unsuccessful – the boys are afraid to venture so far. (11 September 1891)*
>
> *Paid a farewell visit to our Cousins, the Irvines. There is a possibility that through my representations of our sunny land Australia that M^r & Mrs Irvine & family of six may come to our land instead of to America as they have been intending. (19 September 1891)*

In fact, over the next ten years four cousins did follow him to Australia. We have no way of knowing whether the image of 'sunny Australia' was a factor, or indeed whether Martin himself believed in it; a note his daughter added when she transcribed his diary, 'heat not mentioned,' suggests he may well have understood the disadvantages of the Australian climate more than he admitted. But it is clear that Martin felt that an image of the Australian climate as the opposite of Ireland's was a key to encouraging migration.

Martin's commitment to Australia and Irish migration raises questions about the degree he thought of himself as Irish when in Ireland. His description of Pettigo, his home town, after twenty years in Australia is not flattering, especially in its comparison with Victoria:

> *We caused a great sensation as we drove up the street. It had got about that we were coming to Pettigo, & they were all on the lookout for us. The little Village presented a great contrast to our Victorian Townships. Two or three dirty streets & mostly low stone houses badly in need of whitewash & with rotting thatch roofs. We drove on, out of Pettigo, along the old familiar road, not a bit changed in the 20 years we have been away. (30 June 1891)*

Martin and his brother, Jim, were welcomed into the community and made to feel at home. Yet Martin still perceived Pettigo through the eyes of an Australian outsider. His view of Ireland with its dirty streets and run down houses echoed Pilcher's view: 'everything looking disused and delapidated.' And his condemnation of the climate was voiced by many an Australian visitor: 'The north of Ireland is a disgusting climate for an Australian who loves his blue skies & glorious sunshine.'

Nowhere in his diary does Martin refer to himself as an Irishman. In an introduction, he talks of 'going home to England,' though the notion of England in the nineteenth century could incorporate the whole of the British Isles. His primary reason for making the trip was to compete against, as he called them, 'the Britishers' in a shooting tournament as part of a contingent of the Victorian Mounted Rifles, a volunteer force. Martin was a Protestant, and he records in his diary the anniversary of 'that great victory of the Boyne to which we owe our Civil Religious Liberty we now enjoy' (12 July). He notes that the celebrations will take place 'in all parts of the United Kingdom,' a term which combined Great Britain and the whole of Ireland. Martin, therefore, seems to have had a very definite sense of himself as an Australian, as someone different from the British and those who lived in the United Kingdom as a whole. It was therefore an Australian identity that excluded being Irish. Or to put it another way, in seeing himself as an inhabitant of a sunny country, Martin conflates the distinction between being English and Irish, the English and Irish climates being equally disgusting. Returning from Ireland on the Holyhead steamer, he noted, 'The deck forward was crowded with Irishmen going to England for haymaking, each with his scythe & little bundle of clothes' (3 July). It is an observation that strangely gives no indication of Martin's own Irish background.

Daniel Matthews offers us a related example. Matthews spent his early childhood in Truro in Cornwall, migrating to Australia when he was about sixteen years old. On his visit to Britain in 1869, Matthews spent most of September touring the West Country and South Wales visiting relatives and friends. Out walking from St. Ives, Matthews found himself speaking a Cornish dialect: 'We had great trouble to get cream, as the grass is so scarce this season. We had some amusement at the various farm-houses, where we enquired. I used my Cornish dialect with great success – in fact like a native' (9 September). Yet far from representing himself as Cornish, Matthews is being ironic, mimicking the language of the locals much as Henry Pilcher mimicked an Irish accent. Two days later walking through the village of St. Erth, Matthews again distances himself from the locals:

Took the omnibus to St. Ives Road, and walked leisurely through the parish town of St Erth, a most rural looking place. A few natives juvenile and adult gazed upon us, as if they were not in the habit of seeing strangers often. One of these antiquated residents directed us to follow the path by the 'leats,' (streams of water from the mines) this we did and were soon amply repaid by seeing some fine honeysuckle hedges, fragrant & sweet. (11 September 1869)

If in one sense Matthews was himself a 'native' of Cornwall, he was also unwilling to regard himself as Cornish in Britain. This becomes even more evident when he travelled on to South Wales. In Cardiff he lodged with his uncle and aunt, and his two cousins, Jasper and Eliza:

Found Jasper as rough as he was when a boy. He just speaks out his mind in the most unadorned language. Eliza calls him 'a diamond in the rough'. He's rough enough, but very little of the diamond shows itself. He's very good hearted, and kind to his sisters and the old people; that's a good characteristic trait. They say I talk Cornish very much. I suppose I acquired it from mimicking the people in St. Ives. (19 September 1999)

Daniel Matthews, despite seeing himself as English when travelling in Europe, could only regard himself as Cornish in Britain in terms of mimicry.

The diaries of Martin and Matthews suggest that while it was open to many visitors from Australia to regard themselves as either British or Australian depending on context, when they visited their 'native home' they seem to have regarded themselves primarily as Australians. This seems at odds with the ease by which Australian visitors integrated themselves into family networks; because of close family ties, Australians quickly established a substitute home in the British Isles. And it is also at odds with the particularly strong sense of their identity that migrants from Ireland, Wales, Scotland and even Cornwall maintained in Australia.

In Australia, Ethel Rose Reid was obviously proud of her Scottish identity, and when she set off from New South Wales with her Aunt Bella and cousin Charlie, her destination was specifically Scotland rather than England or Britain:

Left Tenterfield for Sydney en route for Scotland, ever so many cousins uncles aunts etc to see us off, I think they all wished they were coming too, but there was no such luck for them or us either. We only had one lady companion[,] a Mrs Campbell from Casino. The guard said it was a real Scotch trip for him & that it was his first trip on that line for 12 *months, there were Campbells, Blighs & Reids in the sleeper. (4 April 1900)*

Though Reid herself had been born in Tenterfield in 1878, her parents had migrated from Scotland, as evidently had other family members. In 1891 there were fifty people living in Tenterfield who were Scottish-born, and though these represented only five percent of the population, they evidently made up for their small number by their clannishness.[11] Reid had been brought up in a visible Scottish community in Tenterfield, and to this extent her trip represented a journey Home to Scotland.

On arriving in Britain, Reid, like most Australians, was impressed by the English countryside. After six weeks at sea the land was 'so green & fresh looking' (25 May), though as she also pointed out, 'England was so small that it ought to look nice[,] it didn't take much to take care of it.' Having disembarked at Southampton, she, Aunt Bella and cousin Charlie caught the train to London, again passing through picturesque countryside: 'The scenery is simply beautiful from Southampton to London.' By contrast, the appearance of London was anything but beautiful: 'At last we came to dingy murky looking houses[,] thought we must be near London.' They spent only two days in London before travelling north to Glasgow, a city Reid immediately found homely: 'I felt quite at home – much more so than in London' (28 May). After two days in a hotel, Reid moved in with her relatives, the Campbells: 'I feel quite at home already – it is delightful to be in a home again after weeks on the boat & in hotels' (30 May). Reid had been swiftly and success-fully integrated into a new, yet interrelated social network.

Once again we have that combination of the familiar and the strange, the home that is and is not quite a home. In national terms, the Scottish home recreated in Tenterfield had been exchanged for the Scottish home in Glasgow. Perhaps the exchange was so successful that, like J. I. Martin and his Irish identity, Reid feels it is unnecessary to mention being Scottish in her diary; she and Martin might simply have taken their Scottish and Irish identities for granted. Yet her diary quite often notes sights and incidents which remind her of Australia: the church collec-tion for Australian missions; being lent two copies of the *Australasian* newspaper; a gum tree in the church garden.

Comments were made about her accent: 'Mrs Riddel wants to know how I pronounce "now"[,] she says I make 4 syllables out of it' (4 August). While speaking English on the Continent prompted Australians to assert an English national identity, linguistic differences within the British Isles seem to have worked quite differently, making Australians conscious of being out of place in the home country. Since the visitors spent much of their time with family members, such differences were often pointed out to them, and it was much more difficult for nineteenth-century Australians to adopt the Irish or Scottish affinities that American tourists still seem particularly keen to appropriate. Ethel Reid was teased for not being able to speak the language of her Scottish relatives: 'Murray was entertaining me[,] he is a great card, he was trying to get me to speak Scotch' (19 August). Louis Willyama Avery, visiting relatives in his home town of Dumfries, found himself out of place at church: 'Went to Church in the morning. It was Scotch & was all foreign to me' (23 December 1917). As John Rae put it in Carmarthen in 1879: 'we are among a strange people speaking a language that we don't understand.' Unlike Daniel Matthews who was made to feel English on the Continent through not speaking French, Rae's inability to understand Welsh within Britain itself may well have made him feel more Australian than British.

If Australians in Britain were on occasion made to feel they were among a strange people, they often found compensation by identifying with other colonial visitors. Reid recognised a common colonial bond with Miss Smith from Canada who also visited the Campbells in Glasgow: 'Miss Smith is same relation to the Campbells as I am only on the Mother's side' (4 June). The two spent a morning comparing notes: 'asked her to call & see us if she ever came to "Australia." She was telling me of a dreadful snow storm they had in Hamilton, Ontario[;] traffic stopped for three days' (5 June). Awareness of their colonial identities would have been sharpened by the news the same day of the occupation of Pretoria by the British forces fighting the Boers in southern Africa. And in a lightning trip to the Paris Exposition two days before sailing back to Australia, Reid noted only the colonial exhibits: 'We had such a rush there, drove to the Pont de l'Alma, saw the British Colonies – Canada & West Australia, went into the Indian palace & the Boer's Cottage – such a dirty place' (12 October).

One wonders whether Reid returned to Tenterfield as much of a Scot as she left it. She appears to have developed a sense of her own Scottishness growing up outside Scotland; yet through a similar displacement, in visiting Scotland she came to focus on her Australian identity rather than her Scottish identity. Australians abroad delighted in coming across people and objects that reminded them of Australia; and it was with the same enthusiasm for Australia that they returned home. The long period spent abroad meant that most Australians returned to Australia keen to spot familiar features, but, paradoxically, this meant they perceived Australia through the eyes of the Australian abroad. As Reid noted on her return to Adelaide: 'Everything seems so homelike now & so very different from Scotland, it is lovely to see the gum trees again' (26 November). Reid's sense of herself as an Australian was newly defined against her experience of Scotland and its absence of gum trees.

Accounts of trips to Europe typically end with the traveller leaving Europe or approaching Australia, the weather (at least to their minds) becoming characteristically Australian: 'Bright Australian day. I feel a perceptible difference in the air[,] so much lighter and more exhilarating' (Grace Marryat 23 April 1866). As with migrant accounts of the voyage out, the story is rarely continued beyond disembarkation, and descriptions of Australia are restricted to the view from on deck. Reginald Wyndham, approaching Western Australia in 1882, noted what he regarded as typically Australian features of the landscape: 'When I got up for Breakfast I was delighted to see our dear Australian Coast once more. the Sky was blue. and the Rocks stood boldly out. and to make it quite *Australian*, a Bush Fire was burning along the Coast' (5 November). Going ashore at Adelaide brought him back into contact with his countrymen: 'Adelaide seems very busy. but the people strike me now as being so *rough* so "*Colonial*". but I like to feel I am in Australia once more' (10 November). As in Reid's account of Adelaide, Australia is Australia because it is unlike Britain; it was his experience of Britain that made Adelaide strike Wyndham on his return 'as being so *rough* so "*Colonial*"'.

Australians like Reid and Wyndham, therefore, returned to Australia with a new sense of themselves as Australians. They saw Australia through the eyes of the Australian traveller abroad, a view that, as in Nathan Spielvogel's published account, could reduce Australia to as much of a stereotype as the tourist's Europe: 'London has its Abbeys and Museums; but it has its awful grinding misery. Berlin, its palaces and galleries; but it has its Militarism. Italy has its historic past; but also its filth and beggars. But here, the blue sky above, the spreading gums around, the innocence and the simple faith of my little people – all these have no "but".'[12] By defining Australia against a tourist's view of Europe, there could be no misery, militarism, filth or beggars in Australia. Such is the simplistic logic of nationalism.

Because so few accounts continue beyond arrival in Australia, it is difficult to gauge when, and in what ways, the returning travellers began again to feel Irish, Scottish or English. Did Ethel Reid reach

Tenterfield an Australian and then wake up the next morning being as Scotch as she was when she left? Put like this, the relationship between being Australian and Scottish is reduced to the simplicity of Spielvogel's post-Federation nationalism: either you are Australian or you are not. If Australians travelling to Europe did gain a new or different sense of themselves as Australians, then it was an identity that already contained within it a European identity. In this way, their sense of themselves as Australians was strongest when they imagined they were seeing Australia for the first time through the eyes of their fellow passengers. Part of Reginald Wyndham's pride in Australia comes through viewing it as though he were English: 'We got to Sydney Heads at 3. P.M. & saw our lovely Harbour and dear old Sydney in all its beauty. our English Passengers being charmed with the view' (15 November 1882). In sharing the delight of the English passengers, Wyndham views Sydney Harbour simultaneously as an Australian and as an Englishman.

For all his nationalist sentiments, Nathan Spielvogel's view of Australia is also implicated by his experiences of Europe, both of England and Germany, the country of his mother's birth. On landing at Fremantle, Spielvogel's hat causes as much comment as Moseley's cabbage-tree hat did in England:

> *The first thing I heard on landing was, 'Bli'me blokes, where did he get that hat?' referring to my German headgear. This is Australian. The Australian is a different type to the Englishman. These men at Fremantle pier were not the same as those at Southampton. The Australian is longer and thinner. His pockets were made at the same time as his hands, and he has a slouching walk. Here is the independence that is the delightful trait in the Australian. The obsequiousness of the Continental and English workmen is missing. . . . One of our first-class English passengers said, 'Take this parcel, my man!' 'Excuse me, I am not your man,' was the reply.[13]*

Spielvogel's Australia is valid to the extent that it is different from Europe. To validate it, Spielvogel first casts himself as a German, and then tests the Australian working man against one of the first-class English passengers. The result is a caricature of the Australian type, the quintessential Australian working man.

Spielvogel continues to present Australia through European eyes, this time offering to his German fellow passengers a caricature of the Australian woman:

> *Our German friends are amazed and delighted with Fremantle.*
> *'Verandahs,' said one. 'Who put these up?' 'The shopkeeper'. 'What for?'*
> *He can't understand it. And the Australian girls completely amazed*
> *them. 'Why! your housemaids and shop girls dress and behave like ladies*
> *of nobility. Look at that!' And my eyes followed a pretty little Australian*
> *draper's assistant tripping to work. She was good to look at. I felt proud*
> *of her.*[14]

Spielvogel's caricatures are, of course, intended to present Australia in a positive light when compared with their English and German counterparts. In this sense, they are written for an Australian audience. But the importance of the comparison is not that it favours either Australia or Europe, but that Australia is seen as if by Europeans. To be Australian is to be observed by a European.

Reginald Wyndham's description of his homecoming exemplifies this colonial double-vision:

> *Sunday 19. Fine. I arrived at Newcastle at 5 A.M. by the Coonanbarra.*
> *how very small she seems after the P&O Boats. got to Leaconfield at 9.30.*
> *& found the place looking very green & pretty. I must say I think it is as*
> *pretty as any place I have seen in England. that is it would be if there were*
> *no dead Trees. and if pretty green English Trees were growing in place*
> *of them. (19 November)*

Wyndham's vision may not be as flattering as Spielvogel's, with its blue sky and spreading gums, but it was a richer vision. The vision of the nationalist could admit of no 'buts,' and was therefore blind to its contrastive nature. Wyndham's vision was a more honest acceptance of the way in which his home, like Australia itself, was the product of displacement. To be Australian was to see not only the dead eucalypts, 'but' to see at the same time verdant English trees. It was this double-vision that made Wyndham truly Australian, and it had been gained from travelling abroad.

SEVEN

Australia has more of a Continental Atmosphere: Twentieth-Century Visitors to Britain

In 1902, in an essay entitled 'The Beginnings of an Australian National Character,' Percy Rowland argued that one hundred years of Australian settlement had produced a new national type: 'The Australian of to-day is an Englishman, Scot, or Irishman; but with a difference.'[1] Conceding that the influence of race remained predominant, Rowland argued, like others before him, that 'climate and other external conditions' had produced a distinctively Australian character.[2] For Rowland, therefore, Federation in 1901 marked not so much the birth of a national character as its maturity: 'The rejoicings of Federation were less of the nature of a birthday feast than of a celebration of the coming of age of the six stalwart colonies that have lived to become a nation.'[3] According to Rowland, Australian characteristics, such as a lack of subtlety, the absence of a sense of humour, a callousness towards animal suffering, though a love of horses, were the results of living in a harsh environment. Of gambling, which is still regarded as a typically Australian vice, Rowland wrote: 'The Australian is a born speculator. He is sprung from a race of speculators; for had his forbears been of the plodding type, they would not have gambled their all in coming out to dig in the Golden Continent. Plodders do not colonise.'[4]

One Australian characteristic which Rowland's essay did not mention but which it nonetheless exemplifies is the ceaseless desire to define Australian national traits. This drive for self-definition may well date from the 1820s and 1830s when Australian-born settlers started to consider themselves 'native Australians,' and it was widespread enough by 1877 for Marcus Clarke to publish a satiric treatment of the topic, 'The Future Australian Race,' in which the 'Australasian' is characterised as suffering from liver disease and premature baldness. More earnest exponents were J. A. Stanley Adam, whose essay, 'Some Australian Characteristics' (1895), viewed horse-racing and gambling as evidence of racial degeneration; and Rolf Boldrewood who argued in 'The Australian Native-Born Type' (1901) that success in the saddle demonstrated the inherited racial virtues of the Southern Briton. Russel Ward is perhaps the most celebrated dissector of the national type in the twentieth century, his *The Australian Legend* (1958) offering the 'typical Australian' as the product of 'the material conditions of outback life,' though Donald Horne's passing recognition in *The Lucky Country* (1964) of the increasingly cosmopolitan nature of contemporary Australian society was perhaps more forward looking: 'It is probably migrant talent that has leavened the lump in Australia; it is doubtful if Australia would have got as far as it has in increased sophistication without the accelerated migration of the last two decades.'[5] According to Jon Stratton, Horne's book marked 'the public beginning of the fracture in the urban middle class between those who support migration and multiculturalism and the lower middle class who reject migration and want a return to assimilation'.[6] Such a shift towards a recognition of multiculturalism ought perhaps to have resulted in a lessening of interest in national identity, but as Stratton also notes, since the 1960s the term 'national identity' has become increasingly part of everyday currency.[7] The terms of the debate may have altered since the nineteenth century, but the preoccupation with defining who or what may be Australian continues.

In the second half of the nineteenth century, catalogues of national characteristics were driven both by nationalism as an ideology and by contemporary theories of race, theories that were to persist until they were finally discredited by their justification of the Nazi death camps. In the colonial context, both nation and race were linked in terms of an evolutionary model. For Percy Rowland, Federation marked not only a stage in the development of the nation, it marked a stage in the evolution of a national type. Though this seems merely to follow common sense, the development of a national self-consciousness and the evolution of a racial type both assume that the development of a nation follows the same pattern as the development of the human individual, an assumption still being made by Geoffrey Serle in 1975 with regard to an Australian national culture:

An early period of imitation, of working in the styles of the parent civilization, is followed by a stage of national assertiveness which celebrates the local subject-matter and values of the new nation struggling to be born; then an uneasy period of clash between the nativists and those holding fast to the values of the imperial source; and finally when something like mature nationhood has been achieved, a reconciliation in which a relaxed sense of nationality is combined with openness to international influences.[8]

The problem with analysing national development in terms of the birth, childhood and maturity of the nation is that it is difficult to identify the stages by which a nation develops and those events that mark the transitions. Or to put it more simply, Australia seems perennially to be coming of age, but never getting any nearer to its mid-life crisis.

Richard White notes that while the rhetoric of the 1920s presented Australia as a child, pure, innocent and in need of protection, in the 1930s calls for a self-contained, industrial economy were parallelled by calls for a self-contained cultural maturity. White quotes the strident nationalist P. R. Stephensen from an essay published in 1936: 'It is time *now* for Young Australia to become Adult, to accept the responsibilities and duties of being Adult, of being civilized; of becoming a fully-cultured nation – self-supporting, if need be, in matters of culture.'[9] As White also points out, Stephensen's call for an independent Australian culture was echoed almost twenty years later in 1963 in the republican sentiments of Geoffrey Dutton: speaking of the way in which the English felt both affection for the colonies and contempt for the colonials, Dutton noted that 'the crowning paradox is that we accept this patronising pseudo-patronage at a time when our national identity is at last emerging in full adult strength'.[10] Dutton went on: 'The point is not to pick a quarrel with the English but to reach an adult relationship with them.' Ironically, calls for an Australian coming of age are dependent not only on the analogy between the nation and the individual but on the imperialist metaphor of the mother/child relationship between metropolitan state and its settler colonies, as in Donald Horne's comments in *The Lucky Country*, published a year after Dutton's essay:

Relations with England prickle with familial misunderstandings. It's like growing away from one's parents and seeking new patterns of identity with them, looking for common hobbies and topics of interest so that one can keep up a connexion. Relations with America are those of a young cousin to an immensely successful and older cousin, with plenty of criticism, practically no hero worship.[11]

Not surprisingly, therefore, David Solomon's model for an Australian republic, published in 1998, was called *Coming of Age: Charter for a New Australia*.[12] From Federation to the new millennium, Young Australia has remained stuck on the threshold of adulthood, unable to abandon the metaphorical ties of a colonial child to a mother country.

In Britain the growth of the heritage industry with its presentation of history as a decline from past glories has depended on the rhetoric of England or Scotland as an Old Country, and conservatives for the past century or more have been lamenting that Britain is in an irreversible state of decline. Yet as Ghassan Hage has rightly pointed out, Britain's fundamental adulthood, like that of all imperialist nations, cannot be challenged from within what he terms a discourse of maturity.[13] Only the newer postcolonial nation-states must prove their maturity. In Australia's case, the development of an economy less centred on either Britain or the USA has allowed Australia to project itself as an active economic participant in regional trade. And Australia's pursuit of a more active and independent foreign policy within the Asia-Pacific region has also provided opportunities for claims to national maturity. Hage argues that Australia's presentation of itself as a multicultural society is related to this repositioning of Australia as an Asian nation, but that claims by republicans that this demonstrates a newfound maturity give the lie to that multiculturalism. As Hage puts it:

> *If Australia has matured, even if it has matured 'because' of multiculturalism, an essential continuity between the immature and the mature Australia has to exist as a necessary condition of possibility of any utterance concerning national maturation. This continuity cannot be other than that of an Anglo-Celtic White Australia.*[14]

For Hage, republicanism with its talk of a 'break' with the monarchy wrongly assumes the centrality of the relationship with the Queen as mother-figure in the lives of non-White Australians. For such Australians, the discourse of maturity has little meaning.

The advent of multiculturalism, then, even among left-wing intellectuals, has not diminished this 'discourse of maturity,' and in *The Oxford Book of Australian Travel Writing*, as I noted in Chapter 1, the historians Ros Pesman, David Walker and Richard White perpetuate the nationalist view of history that nineteenth-century Australians were not yet fully Australian:

> *Throughout the nineteenth century, most Australians overseas saw*

*themselves simply as British travellers, making no great distinction
between their reactions and what they imagined were those of the British
abroad. If they did think of themselves as diverging from the norm, it was
in being a colonial variant rather than being distinctively Australian.*[15]

Although neither Pesman, Walker nor White would argue that with
Federation Australia suddenly stopped being British, this passage
assumes the kind of imperialist mother/child metaphor Horne
employed: the 'distinctive Australian' develops though maturing away
from the parent culture.

One way of testing the proposition that the non-indigenous inhabi-
tants of Australia have become more authentically Australian since
Federation is to examine the diaries and letters of Australians visiting
Britain. Assuming twentieth-century Australians gained a newfound
Australianness, the trip to Britain offered Australian visitors plenty of
opportunity to assert it.

In 1928, Mabel Dowding spent two months in Britain prior to visiting
her brother's grave in France. Sailing into Southampton, Mabel was
every bit as enthusiastic about arriving in Britain as her nineteenth-
century counterpart: 'And so we have our first glimpse of England as
the boat makes its way to its moorings. One couldnt help the thrill as we
saw the old Mother Country we know so well from reading & hearsay.
"So this is England", but I'm afraid lots of us cant realise it' (18 May
1928). The train journey from Southampton to London provided a fuller
opportunity to admire England: 'Never shall any of us forget our first
sight of rural England & the Countryside of Devonshire. The trees were
simply glorious, like nothing we had seen before for growth & color &
the hillsides all dotted with tiny daisies. First from one & then another
"Oh isn't it beautiful" "Look at those trees!!" It was a chorus of "Oh's"
& "Looks"' (18 May 1928). In her anticipation of 'the Old Mother
Country' and her delight in the English countryside, Dowding in 1928
seems as much of a colonial as any nineteenth-century Australian visitor
to Britain.

Dowding also shared the nineteenth-century traveller's disappointment with the 'dingy look' of London:

*St Pauls is a wonderful old building but really it seemed to depress us. It
looked dusty & gloomy & we could hardly hear anything that was said.
So far many of the buildings have had a depressing effect on both of us,
Parliament House, Westminster Abbey, St Pauls & others that have got
the black of ages all over them, streaked with lighter shades where the rain*

has beaten on & washed it cleaner. Some folks say 'there lies their beauty & charm', not so with us anyway & in the rain it looks most gloomy. Perhaps it won't be quite so bad when fine weather comes. I feel somehow as tho' those who have been here on a visit before should have prepared us, we were struck so forcibly with the dingy look. (20 May 1928)

As an Australian, Dowding preferred a brighter and sunnier environment: 'We're getting quite used to this wet weather, but dear me we would like to see some of our good old blue skies about' (9 June).

Dowding was more impressed by Glasgow, though mainly because the city looked similar to Sydney: 'Glasgow has reminded us most of our home town so far, its narrow streets, & bustling people. Edinburgh doesn't bustle, neither does London, the shops too to some extent made us think of some of ours. Being the 2nd city of the Empire naturally thered be more folk than Edinburgh' (30 May). Dowding's visit to Glasgow gave her a number of opportunities for reflecting on herself as an Australian. She and her travelling companions were given free tram tickets: 'Similar happenings have come our way on other occasions because we are Aus*trel*ians (as they call us) How will we manage when we are mere Aussies when we get home!!!' (31 May). A few days later on a boat trip down the Clyde, Dowding found an opportunity for more actively asserting herself as an Australian: 'We saw the yard where the great Warship "Hood" was built & then again the latest addition to the Australian Navy nearing completion the "Canberra". Cheers & coo-ees were sent across the water to the men working on her & they were acknowledged by waving &c. from the men' (5 June).

Because she was travelling with a delegation of Australians, Dowding may have been encouraged to exaggerate her Australian identity, but feeling self-consciously Australian and even a little homesick did not prevent her from being reluctant to leave Britain:

Off to do some shopping first thing after breakfast & then to Australia House to collect our mail. Had a good old read up. What a long long way Aussie seems to us. It must be that the only news we get is in our letters, the papers here have nothing. Next off to the Bank & to pay our final account re passage across Canada & home by 'Niagara'. Dear me how the time has flown to think we are to say 'Goodbye' to this wonderful old 'old world' on 21st August! And such lots of things we've to work in yet. (24 July)

Overall, there is not much in Dowding's diary that demonstrates what Pesman, Walker and White suggested, that the twentieth-century saw a move away from a British colonial identity. Dowding's love and admiration of Britain was the love and admiration of the Old Country. Neither, almost thirty years after Federation, were there are any new markers of Australianness in her account; coo-ees and a longing for a blue sky were just as Australian in the nineteenth century.

What is different, though, is that she visited Britain on a conducted tour and therefore she spent most of her time as a sightseer. Not all of it was sightseeing, she unexpectedly discovered relatives in Inverness and she made a special trip to the West of England to meet cousins:

> *We were at last to see our Cousins we have communicated with all the years. Cousins Lav & Alice were to meet us at Bristol. The 'identification badge' was to be a bright scarf worn by Lav. She told us she was a 'small person' & we had seen photos of her some years ago. . . . Arrived at Bristol & had no difficulty in picking out our Cousins. It really seemed unreal that we were at last meeting face to face after all these years of corresponding, since schooldays. (2 July 1928)*

Dowding's delight in Britain owed much to the influence of her father who had been brought up in Chipping Sodbury and no doubt encouraged Mabel to correspond with her British cousins from an early age. Yet there was clearly a fundamental conflict between the manner of her visit to Britain, the conducted tour, and her desire to visit relatives; the conducted tour has a fixed itinerary which is unlikely, except by luck, to take the tourist near to living relatives or even the graves of grandparents, and though Dowding's cousins in Inverness were an unexpected encounter on the tour, the two trips she made to stay with her relatives in Chipping Sodbury were made as independent excursions.

The cheap tour of Britain developed in the interwar years and it brought to Britain an increasing number of Australians travelling third class. Often they wore the kangaroo badge of the Australian Travel Service whose brochure in 1930 offered:

> *a PERSONALLY CONDUCTED TRIP to ENGLAND at the MOST MODERATE COST, within the means of the great majority. PARTICULARS OF THIS TRIP ARE DETAILED IN THE FOLLOWING PAGES, and a glance will show what a wonderfully comprehensive and cheap trip it is. EVEN THE MOST TIMID PERSON CAN WITH EVERY CONFIDENCE JOIN THIS PARTY.*

For £200, the trip included fourteen days in London and a tour of Belgium, Germany, Switzerland, Italy, France, and the Great War battle-fields. Britain became part of a European itinerary, presented, like France and Germany, through the eyes of the tourist. Australian visitors continued to feel British, indeed the travel companies utilised the pull of the Old Country and a British history with which Australians could feel associated, but the absence of a prolonged stay in the home of a close relative meant that these Australian visitors were no longer integrated into British society to the same extent as those who had the time and the money to remain in Britain for a number of months. The conducted tour offered visiting Australians a guidebook Britain, as Mabel Dowding admits in her description of a boat trip along the Thames from Hampton Court: 'All along the banks were dainty little cottages like dolls' houses some of them looked so neat & trim & gardens like pictures. In fact it was as tho' we were turning the pages of some picture book, delight-fully colored, such bright splashes of color all along the way' (1 July 1928). Such were the descriptions Australians recorded in the 1930s in their Collins' Trip Books.

Nancy Newell must have been one of the last Australian tourists to visit Britain in the interwar years. She arrived in Southampton from NSW in April 1939, only six months before the declaration of war restricted travel between Australia and Britain. It was possible that Nancy knew what to expect of Britain from reading the diary of her mother, Ethel Reid, who visited relatives in Scotland in 1900. In 1900, Reid like most nineteenth-century visitors had been charmed by the British countryside: 'The scenery is simply beautiful from Southampton to London, we went by the L & S. W. Railway. Lovely big trees, green fields, hedges, lanes[,] pretty houses[,] it was all delightful' (25 May 1900). The journey from Southampton of her daughter, Nancy Newell, in 1939 was as charming as Reid's had been: 'The train left at 2.50 p.m. and the trip was a very beautiful one through some of the loveliest country I have ever seen. Primroses were growing wild on the hillsides close to the train and all the trees were just blossoming. It was a wonderful sight. It was a quick trip up, arrived at Waterloo Station at 4.40 p.m.' (19 April 1939). After two days sightseeing in London, Newell was driven out to Windsor by her financé, Robert Cranna, who was already in Britain training as an architect: 'It was a lovely drive to Windsor, everything about England is beautiful, even the tumble down houses and sheds. . . . it was a thrill to be actually there where the King and Queen were' (22 April 1939). Almost forty years after Federation, visitors to Britain appeared as British as they had ever been.

Yet unlike Ethel Reid, who had spent four months in Scotland living with relatives, Reid's daughter, Nancy, spent just eight days north of the border, touring Scotland as part of an extensive tour of the whole of Britain with her sister, Kathleen Bate. The sisters came to Britain as independent travellers, their first-class passage paid for by their father, and although they were not on a conducted tour they nonetheless experienced Scotland as tourists. They followed an itinerary prepared by the Automobile Association which took them from London through Stratford-on-Avon, North Wales, the Lake District, Glasgow, Aberdeen and Edinburgh, spending only one night in the home of a relative, Mr Campbell of Catrine, the owner of two Rolls Royces (a sedan and a tourer) and an Armstrong Siddeley roadster. After a two-day excursion into Northern Ireland to see cousins on their father's side, they returned to their London hotel via Birmingham and Cambridge, having covered, so Kathleen's diary proudly records, 3,246 miles in three weeks.

Britain in these interwar diaries is less a substitute home and more a country to be toured; it is experienced less as a series of extended visits to relatives than as a series of historical sites on an itinerary. The Australian Travel Service provided itineraries not only for those on its conducted tours but also for independent travellers like Nancy Newell who called into its offices in Australia House when she wanted to tour the West Country. The diaries that resulted from this type of travel were largely catalogues of places visited, such as the diary of Harriet Grover Roberts, who toured Britain and Europe sporting her ATS kangaroo badge in a motor coach in 1937:

> *We left Torquay via Newton Abbott for Exeter, lunch at Great Western Hotel. After lunch we left for Bournemouth, via Honiton famous for its lace. Axminster of Carpet fame (County of Dorset[)], Charmouth[,] Bridport, Wareham, Poole (County of Hampshire[)] to Bournemouth. One of the most popular South coast holiday resorts of England. The streets are rather straggling. Woolworths here as everywhere in England. The road to the seashore is called a chine. A very lengthy beach, open air entertainment – little rooms built all along promenade, which can be hired for day or week. (31 May 1937)*

Such accounts were predominantly a collation of received information: Honiton's reputation for lace, Axminster's reputation for carpet, and the popularity of Bournemouth. There is little here that is specific to Roberts' own trip, except perhaps her observation of the ubiquity of Woolworth's, though this is more a general remark than a record of an event particular to 31 May 1937. Nineteenth-century travellers followed itineraries, of course, and the indefatigable railway traveller, John Rae, rarely stopped for more than one night in the same town. But between the wars the proportion of the visit spent sightseeing appears to have increased. This is not to say that Australians did not still think and speak about Britain as Home, and they used London as a home-base from which to explore Britain and Europe; but the homeliness of Britain seemed to reside less in the presence of relatives than in its hotels and the familiarity of its tourist sites. For Marjorie Shields in 1930, calling on friends of the family was seen as something of a chore: 'In Birmingham I 'phoned the family Auntie Flo asked me to look up. Mrs Heaton answered the phone but she had just lost her husband & last year her only child died, she seemed in great distress so I stayed away, did not feel like intruding there. The Beesley people were away so I reckon I did my duty, don't you?' (3 September 1930). The familiarity of London seemed to Shields more important than human contact: 'From the [Tate] Gallery we walked along the Embankment to Whitehall. It was a lovely gray [?] day, & the little boats were hurrying along up & down the River, it reminded me of the pictures I had seen in my "young days". I'm always thrilled when [I] see the Thames' (14 July 1930). Overall, the diaries and letters suggest that more Australians visited Britain as transient observers and that relatively less came as temporary inhabitants. They came, in this sense, like the Americans, as pilgrims claiming a British heritage but regarding themselves as significantly 'other'.

Yet put like this, and from a British perspective, it was a question not so much of Australians becoming more 'distinctively Australian' than of them becoming less British. It is true that Australians were aware of the differences between Britain and Australia; Ida Haysom, for example, in 1936 made a list at the back of her diary of 'Oddities we notice. London'. Top of her list was 'Peas & beans 2/- lb'. It went on:

No blinds on windows
No 3^d pieces
No showers
No set shop hours – some open till 9 & after Saturday night.
No Chinese laundries
No hot meals at Y[WCA] till 7 pm.
No telegraph or electric wires
No horn blowing even in heavy traffic

Apart from what was not present, Haysom noted:

Taxis everywhere
Hundreds of statues and monuments.
Forty minutes in the tram for 2ᵈ – special cheap rates for certain hours of
the day.
Tips given in even ordinary cafes.

There are a few observations here that might be thought distinctively Australian, such as the high price of fruit and vegetables and a dislike of tipping. Marjory Casson, a postwar visitor to Britain, also included the price of fruit on her list of what struck her as an Australian: '*London Impressions* Beards. Less make up than in Australia More freedom & less freedom And (as at Bournemouth) a great mass of dead inert life. Asparagus 5/- per bundle. Grapes 2/6 per lb.' (10 May 1949). As might be inferred from this, Casson had taken a particular dislike to Bournemouth, a retirement resort on the English south coast, which she had visited two months earlier: 'Bus, & walk through gardens to Front. Tame dull sea. Deck chairs 3ᴰ. Enormous pressure of elderliness. Reserved! – May be more alive than they look? Pop: abt 145,000. Feel v. Australian – with thankfulness' (17 March 1949).

Yet how far do such tourist notes reflect a more mature Australian national identity than existed in the nineteenth century? When Casson noted, 'Feel v. Australian,' did she feel more Australian than a colonial visitor? The widespread English habit of tipping was noted by a number of nineteenth-century visiting Australians, among them Daniel Matthews, though in Matthews' case his temperance principles left him equally critical of Australia:

The railway porters, and in fact all government, and private servants, expect as their customary right a penny or two pence. This may be an evil, and certainly is not permitted in the colonies. But by placing it against the abominable practice we have of drinking 'nobblers' with every one we come in contact with (I speak of colonists) the badness of the habit is greatly modified. (13 August 1869)

In addition to complaints about the price of fruit, tipping, the bad weather and so on, the twentieth century produced some new complaints. The rise of surf bathing at the beginning of the twentieth century and the gradual association of Australia with a beach culture meant that British beaches came in for much criticism:

Minehead is a nice town and quite large with wide streets and lovely trees but its beach is pebbly and uninteresting like all others we have seen in England. (Kathleen Bate 5 May 1939)

We left the country of Devon and arrived in Cornwall, where we stayed the night at Bude. It is a large holiday resort, but from our point of view there seemed little to attract anyone. There is very little beach and only partly sandy. (Edna Kerr 21 June 1959)

The beach [Brighton], of course, consisting almost entirely of large round pebbles, strange to Australian eyes. (Donald Balfour 10 March 1963)

These are distinctively twentieth-century 'Australian eyes,' as are those of Mary James who, in a letter of 1953, compared Britain and Australia in terms of 'mod-cons' and domestic hygiene:

Much as we both like England, Australia is far ahead of her in many ways – I have not seen a decent kitchen in England yet – our housewives just would not put up with them, but then on the whole I don't think much of the English housewives & they are very ordinary cooks. Of course to be fair to them they have had a very lean time ever since the war with rationing & I think a lot of them have lost interest & don't care. Now that things are fairly plentiful again they can't be bothered.

Having lived among them for some months now & kept house here I feel I do know what I am talking about. Of course there are exceptions, they are not all alike, but they do have mucky untidy kitchens, even the best of them. We have been more than lucky having this cottage, it is fairly up to date as far as mod-cons go & has got a decent kitchen & bath room – the latter is a rare commodity in many places. (10 November 1953)

Yet despite the modern nature of Mary James' concerns, it is not easy to see how James is more Australian than, say, Mary Kater who, some eighty years earlier, also commented on British domestic arrangements:

We went to 'Heavy tea' at the Brocklehursts at 7.30 – 'Heavy tea' is a sort of tea-dinner which people ask you to, when they wish to ask you to something less formal than dinner – in fact it is just the same kind of meal as we have often had at The Brush after a croquet party when people have stayed for the evening – In the country here when people give a croquet-party, and wish people to remain the evening they ask them to croquet and 'Heavy tea' as then they can remain in their croquet dresses, whereas if asked to dinner they must appear in evening costume[.] (15 May 1875)

Mary Kater's interest in croquet and social etiquette may show her to be higher up the social scale than Mary James, but the human development model would require us to believe that James was more 'distinctively Australian' than Kater. Even if she was more Australian, James was as reluctant to leave Britain as any colonial visitor: 'Well packing up is on in earnest now, & we leave here next Friday week Jan 15th, horrible thought, I hate leaving this lovely England, but one has to come down to earth some time & we have had a marvellous trip' (4 January 1954).

Perhaps it is overly reductionist to reduce national identity to a comparison of bathrooms and beaches, yet accounts by twentieth-century visitors demonstrate a continuity that is largely ignored by those who seek to show that colonial Australians were not real Australians. Australian visitors to Britain continued to regard themselves as British for most of the twentieth century. In his guide to Britain, *Australians, Go Home!* (1958), Stuart Gore describes how watching the Changing of the Guard outside Buckingham Palace, 'I no longer cared whether we were Australians, New Zealanders or even Colonials. British, I felt, was sufficient.'[16] When Edna Kerr arrived back in Melbourne after five months touring Europe in 1959, she was quite clear what it meant to be Australian: 'It was a great relief to pass the Customs Officer; he was a perfect example of a casual Australian, and I thought how wonderful it was to be amongst Australians again! We really are an entirely different people to those of any other country' (168). Yet Kerr was nonetheless happy to be regarded as British in Europe, partly because Australians travelled on a British Australian passport until the mid 1960s, as Kerr herself recorded on her way to France: 'Before you reach Dover you see the chalky whiteness in the hills and then you arrive in the thickly populated town and the train takes you to the pier. We joined the queue for British passengers and had our passports checked' (14 July 1959). And in common with other Australians, Kerr identified herself as British when travelling in Continental Europe: 'When we arrived at Amsterdam we had a taxi driver who wasn't at all congenial to us – in some places you don't know if it's because you're British or because they have a bad liver; *he* obviously wasn't at all inspired by our appearance anyway' (23 July 1959). Kerr apparently had no objection to the taxi driver assuming she was British.

If the Continentals were suspicious of Australians, Australian travellers who ventured across the English Channel were equally suspicious of Continental culture. In 1959, Edna Kerr found café life completely outside her experience: 'We stayed our last night in France at Boulogne – eventually finding somewhere to stay at 10.15 p.m! After dinner we had our coffee at the street tables outside the hotel – and tried to imagine doing the same thing at home at that time of night! We couldn't!' (77). Like her nineteenth-century counterparts, Kerr found the familiarity of British culture a welcome relief after her experience of Europe: 'We had left England on April 16th, crossing from Newcastle to Stavanger (Norway), and now it was June 14th and we were back "home", where we could read everything we saw, and understand the same language!' (77). Apart from language, there was that other major marker of cultural identity, food: 'When we left England I hoped that I had had my last British Breakfast (Bacon, eggs and toast) for quite a while, but believe me, I never want to see another Continental Breakfast of Rolls and Coffee as long as I live! I now consider the B.B. a most wonderful meal!' (79). If Kerr did not totally identify with the British, she nonetheless found herself at home in the culture of Britain.

Yet Australia itself was changing. As the British Empire dissolved, so too did the loyalty of Australians to Britain. And by the 1950s and 1960s, Australians no longer had to travel to Europe to experience European culture. Continental Europe had come to Australia in the form of postwar migration. Large scale migration from Eastern and Southern Europe transformed urban Australian culture, a transformation which, potentially at least, enabled Australians of British descent to feel slightly more at home touring Continental Europe. And more Australians than ever were travelling to Europe. In 1959, Edna Kerr sailed to Britain on the *Orion*, but she flew back to Melbourne via Amsterdam, Vancouver, Honolulu, Fiji, Auckland and Sydney. Australians had been flying to Europe since the mid 1930s, but numbers rose with the development of longhaul air travel in the 1950s and 1960s, and by the time the ocean liner finally gave way to the 747 in the early 1970s, an even larger portion of the 'great majority,' as the ATS termed them in 1930, was making the trip to Europe.

Ironically, it was precisely at the time when travelling to Britain came within reach of the majority of Australians that Australians came to feel much less British. Ros Pesman summarises the change:

As the sun set on the British Empire in the 1960s and 1970s, the Australian map of the world shifted and London's place as the magnetic centre waned. Britain began to look 'foreign' and not 'home' when Australians lost their automatic right on entry to a job, a vote, free dental care, and a social security card. They were confronted with visible signals of their foreignness the moment they set foot on 'England's green and pleasant land'; while Germans strolled through the gates marked 'British and EEC', Australian queued with the rest of the world beneath the sign 'Aliens'. Australia itself became 'foreign' under the impact of the postwar European and then Middle Eastern and Asian migration; the ancestral homes and family burial grounds of Australians now lie anywhere and everywhere.[17]

As I have tried to show, the development of the cheap conducted tour in the interwar years turned Britain into more of a tourist destination than a northern British home into which visiting Australians might be socially integrated. Nonetheless, postwar visitors retained a strong sense of their British identity, especially when travelling in Europe. But it is clear that by the late 1960s and early 1970s, as Pesman notes, Australians were coming to feel less at home in Britain. And as travel to Europe became more democratic, so more Australians were going to be disappointed; with knowledge of Britain no longer in the guardianship of the social elite, there was little hope that the image of Britain circulating within Australia itself might remain pristine.

We can gauge something of this accelerated process of becoming less British by comparing Edna Kerr's 1959 account with that of a young woman from a working-class background, Marion Flynn, who sailed from Sydney on the *Fairstar* in January 1968 and returned by plane in 1972. Flynn, Australian-born, single and in her mid twenties, travelled to Britain like many other young Australians both before and since to work for a few years and see something of Europe. It took her two days to find a flat-share in Chelsea, and only two further days to find employment as a temporary typist at St Thomas' Hospital, where a forthcoming visit by the Queen prompted Flynn to some verbal flag-waving: 'Tomorrow the Queen is coming to open a new wing so I am thinking of waving a few flags and a banner marked "Australian" so maybe she'll think I am one of her loyal colonial subjects and talk to me' (27 February 1968). While still acknowledging the subject relationship of Flynn, and therefore Australia, to the Queen, the phrase 'one of her loyal colonial subjects' would seem to mock more typical Australian declarations of loyalty. This is a long way from Nancy Newell's sentiments on her visit to Windsor Castle in 1939: 'it was a thrill to be actually there where the King and Queen were.' In writing to her mother and sister about the Queen's visit, Flynn is probably unconsciously wanting to impress and doubtless it would have been a thrill to meet the Queen, but the irony qualifies any suggestion that Australians are either colonial or subservient.

Partly as a consequence of her refusal to defer to the English, in the following months Flynn discovered that integrating into British society was now far more difficult than it had been for previous generations of Australians: 'Sometimes it is hard being a foreigner in a strange country 12,000 miles from your family and friends' (16 April 1968). As a young and self-confident Australian, Flynn accounted for her alienation by the failure of the British to adjust their own national identity to suit the diminished imperial fortunes of Britain:

> *I'm thinking of leaving the flat when I get back [from the Continent]. I suppose it was expecting too much to plonk myself into a flat full of English girls & have them accept me as one of them. There always seems to be an air of resentment about & I'm sure it's just because I'm Australian & they are envious. That's the trouble with a lot of Poms. They still think they are the king-pins & are living on their laurels. (25 April 1968)*

Flynn's background gave her an affection for a working-class Englishness, an image of 'old England' which she appeared to accept despite the fact that she herself failed to conform to a stereotyped Australian identity, 'the inevitable Waltzing Matilda':

> *That Saturday night we had dinner at a fish place called the Contented Sole. The food was good (I had scampi for the first time) but not spectacular. However, the atmosphere was unbelievably fantastic – a funny little man was playing on one of those old fashioned pianos songs like 'There'll always be an England' etc. and everybody was joining in at the tops of their voices – completely uninhibited and all bawdy and smoky. They found out I was Australian and along came the inevitable Waltzing Matilda – I can never remember the words of that crazy song. The waitresses wore long black skirt, black stockings, white frilly blouses and straw boaters with ribbons dangling down the back. One was Australian so we greeted each other like old friends and had a good chat. But it was truly a little bit of old England and I shall never forget it. (6 March 1968)*

Flynn also fell for the charm of the English countryside: 'I can't understand why but I seem to have developed a passion for the country. It never used to worry me living in the big city of Sydney but now I love getting out of London for even just a day. I must admit I like the English countryside much more than in Australia – it's so pretty here and everything is green & gentle' (30 July 1968). Nevertheless, her admiration for England and the English remained conditional, and she showed no deference to Westminster Abbey as a commemoration of a great British history: 'Went to Westminster Abbey. Horrible. Just like a graveyard with stone tombs and crypts, etc. all over the place' (20 June 1968).

The most striking difference between Marion Flynn's experience and that of Edna Kerr who visited Europe less than ten years before was Flynn's experience of Germany: 'Perhaps I'm a little more used to Europe now but in many ways I feel less of a foreigner here than in London. Although London is so much closer to the continent I have always felt Australia has more of a continental atmosphere as we have so many immigrants from Germany Italy etc. & they have all left their mark on the country' (5 September 1968). Flynn was working in Germany whereas Kerr had been on a conducted tour, but despite this Flynn's attitudes towards European cultures was far less exclusive. And while Kerr like most Australians before her had been pleased to cross back over the Channel to Britain and British food, Flynn surprised herself by discovering she preferred Continental to Australian cooking:

> *I have developed a sudden passion for cooking. For the last year or so I have been collecting recipes from German magazines and have been quite pleased with the results of some of my cooking. I now know much more about cooking with spices and herbs and am able to improvise much more. I find continental cooking much better than English (including Australian) as it's so much more interesting and varied. (29 July 1970)*

Here then, in becoming more European, is another way in which Australians became less British rather than more Australian. And as Ros Pesman points out with reference to her own daughter, for Australians the globe has continued to shrink:

> *My daughter lives in Paris, works for a French organisation, has a French partner. . . . Identity is not a problem for my daughter. She has two family hearths, two passports, and moves with ease between them. Her sense of double identity separates her from my generation, but links her to her nineteenth-century immigrant and second-generation Scots and Irish maternal forebears who also saw themselves as possessing two homes.*[18]

Despite unimaginable differences in communication and transport, Pesman suggests an affiliation between the more inclusive cultural identities of her daughter and her daughter's colonial ancestors.

Flynn's observations and Pesman's comments make it clear that the existence of multiple national loyalties is a common feature of both colonial and modern Australia. Even Marion Flynn in the 1970s was able to feel at home in both Britain and Germany in addition to Australia. And yet it is precisely an unease about this that prompts the assertion that Australians have become more 'distinctively Australian' in the twentieth century. In advertising a discussion chaired by Barry Jones between Miriam Dixson, David Williamson and Peter Botsman as part of the 1999 Brisbane Writers Festival, the programme posed the question: 'As Australia moves towards political and cultural maturity, how will we balance our search for unity in diversity with our desire for a cohesive national identity?' This question is the source of the apparent contradiction in the argument that Australia has become more multicultural and more Australian, and it is hard to see how any attempt to reconcile two differing models of the nation-state, the one based on citizenship and the other based on cultural homogeneity, is not fundamentally flawed. However, such a question is in turn subsumed under the discussion's proclaimed theme: 'Coming of age in a new millennium.' Australia, so we are variously told, will come of age when it becomes a republic, with the advent of the new millennium and at the centenary of Federation. At the end of the twentieth century, we return to the analogy that has dominated nationalist thinking in Australia for its entire history, the analogy between the development of the human individual and the development of nationhood.

There are two sides to this in terms of the historical and cultural links between Britain and Australia. The first is that the notion of adulthood and maturity suggests a cutting of ties and the development of an independent identity. In Australia's case, the 1950s would seem to offer an image of what that identity might be. Opponents of governmental multiculturalism, to use Jon Stratton's term, have looked back, somewhat nostalgically perhaps, to the 1950s as a period of a coherent and distinctive Australian nationalism.[19] Yet that nationalism was not at the expense of a rejection of Australia's historical and cultural links with Britain, and Australians abroad continued to find Britain familiar, while nonetheless asserting their own difference. This combination of familiarity and difference defined Australian culture even in the 1950s as a culture of displacement, and it continued to prompt calls for Australia to grow up. Any denial that Australia and Britain share a common heritage represents a dangerous narrowing of our concept of the nation.

On the other hand, if we follow Ghassan Hage, any claim that Australia is 'coming of age' makes sense only for those Australians who are in a position to recognise something of their own family history in Australia's supposed 'infancy'; becoming adult presupposes a degree of continuity with being a child, a continuity with a British heritage. However, unlike Hage, I think this paradox in the idea of maturity can be employed on behalf of multiculturalism. If the notion of maturity acknowledges continuities with other national loyalties, to be a 'mainstream' Australian is once again to be the product of displacement, with the multiple loyalties that displacement entails. Or to turn the analogy between the nation and the individual back on itself, as we grow older all of us who knew our parents discover in what we thought was our unique identity traces of our mothers and fathers.

There are, then, ways of accommodating the rhetoric of a 'coming of age' or of a national 'maturity' with a more inclusive sense of cultural identity by demonstrating that such a rhetoric contains within it continuity and a recognition of multiple loyalties. My own view, however, is that a more radical approach is required, and that the whole rhetoric of a 'coming of age' or of a national 'maturity' must be abandoned if Australia is to move beyond a narrow vision of its nationhood. Paradoxically, this may best be achieved not through abandoning a sense of history but through acknowledging the continuity between Australia's colonial past and its postcolonial present. As Peter Cochrane has put it, 'Some say the British inheritance in Australia is the set of institutions and the field of relationships that made multiculturalism possible. Others insist it is a remnant, distinguished by supremacism and intolerance. The debate forges on with just one certainty – that a clearer understanding of our British past will mean a better grasp of our multicultural present.'[20]

To argue that Australia must accept rather than reject continuities with its colonial past is not to argue that Australia must somehow rediscover a filial relationship to Britain. For many, if not most Australians, modern Britain is rightly an irrelevance, and apart from when the issue of the monarchy is raised, Australia is no longer defined against Britain, as it was for Australian nationalists well into the 1980s. But it is to argue that Britain and Australia have a shared history, and that both have been formed by their experience of empire. The British Empire produced a global displacement of peoples and their cultures, and it is in the wake of that displacement that Australia and Britain must find ways of creating cohesive societies out of cultural diversity.

The abandonment of the rhetoric of national maturity means that we must reappraise Australia's past. To continue to regard the nineteenth century as Australia's childhood is to continue to invest in an imperial geography which organises the world into centres (the mothers and fathers) and peripheries (the children). If Australia is to avoid either forever looking back to a period when Australians were true Australians or forever looking forward to the point at which Australia will attain maturity, then national identity must be related to cultural displacement rather than be seen as trending to or from a purer form. To help with this shift of perception, historians in both Britain and Australia must move beyond seeking to explain cultural identity in terms of national histories. In the globalised world of the 1990s, it is not coincidental that the discipline of Geography, untroubled by political boundaries, has shown itself better placed to investigate national identity than the discipline of History, locked, as it so often is, into narratives of the nation. To question the imagined geography of centre and periphery is not to deny the inequality of power between colonial Australia and imperial Britain, but it is to recognise that, as modern states, Britain and Australia are equally products of a human displacement that cannot adequately be explained by national histories.

Part of this reappraisal must be a reappraisal of those Australians condemned to a colonial inauthenticity. In 1828, Australian-born James Macarthur (1798–1867) wrote to his mother from London where he had recently arrived from New South Wales: 'Dr Cook was so exceedingly kind & attentive to me on the Voyage home (to England I mean not *home*) that I hope you will make his stay as agreeable as you can in the Colony' (10 November 1828). Macarthur was writing only forty years after the arrival of the First Fleet but already his cultural displacement, his sense of having two homes, meant that he saw Britain from a distinctively non-British perspective. In his journey back to London from Devon by coach, his view of Britain was refracted through images of Australia:

> *Talk of Australian rains – Tropical thunder storms or Monsoons – I will back this Devonshire downfall against the rains of the whole world. At Exeter, we changed our Clothes, & we aſsured our places also – Mr Jones left me at Andover, and the next morning at daylight I found we were on the Eastern edge of Salisbury Plain which reminded me a little of Goulburn Downs – Some part of the Vale of Berks which we paſsed over later in the day is very like Bathurst. (7 April 1829)*

Australians have become less British than Macarthur, less likely to call England Home, but it is debatable, I would think, whether Australians visiting Britain today have a keener sense of themselves as Australians. Despite being a mere colonial, Macarthur deserves recognition as one of the first to perceive Britain through distinctively Australian eyes.

Biographical Sketches

Richard Hannan was born on 9 April 1858 in Castlemaine, Victoria, though he lived most of his life in NSW. He was of Irish Catholic descent, his father, John, an Irish seaman. Richard's mother was Julia Simmons (or Symes, Sims, Symms or Simms), and she had five children with John: Richard (b. 1858); Mary Hannah (b. 1860); John Thomas (b. 1862); Francis Joseph (b. 1869); and David Frederick (b. 1872).

In May 1892, Richard Hannan accompanied Sir George Dibbs, the Premier of NSW, to London on the *Orotava* as a Messenger, his chief duties being delivering letters and purchasing odd items, duties which gave him plenty of opportunities for sightseeing. The NSW Blue Book gives the date of his first appointment as 1 November 1891, though he was officially appointed Temporary Messenger on 16 September 1892, the time of his arrival back in NSW via Canada and the USA. Perhaps he was taken abroad as a form of probation. In any case, Richard Hannan appears to have acquitted himself well enough in London to be confirmed in his post.

Richard married Ellen M. Sheedy (b. 1864 or 1865) from Tipperary in

I am indebted to the *Australian Dictionary of Biography* for information on Henry Hudson, Thomas Lodge Murray-Prior, Charles Edward Pilcher, Rosa Praed, Richard Teece and George Wyndham; Dr Chris Tiffin (University of Queensland) patiently answered queries about Thomas Lodge Murray-Prior; Mrs Ann Ashby generously shared information about her relative, Henry Pilcher; and Ros Shennan (Monash University) disappeared into the archives on a regular basis and always emerged triumphant with information on everyone and everything. Additional material on Richard Teece was obtained from R. A. Littlejohn, *Richard Teece: A Biographical Note* (Australian Mutual Provident Society, 1979); additional material on Margaret Tripp was obtained from Jeffrey Robinson, *The Echoes Fade Not: A History of Toorak College* (Toorak College, 1987); additional material on Dalwood and the Wyndham family came from Hugh Leslie Wyndham, *Bukkulla Station* (1957) and Alward Wyndham and Frances McInherny, ed., *The Diary of George Wyndham of Dalwood, 1830–1840* (Dalwood Restoration Association, 1987).

Sydney on 6 February 1894, and together they had three children: John T. (b. 1895); Richard F. (b. 1897); and Mary E. (b. 1899). Their marriage certificate gives the occupation of Ellen's father as blacksmith, and her own as domestic servant. In 1894, Richard was earning £120 per year, a salary equivalent to a junior clerk; in 1920, Richard was Chief Messenger in the same office with an annual salary of £252. Four days before his sixty-fifth birthday in 1923, Richard became Emergency Chief Messenger. Richard appears not to have been an ambitious man and, the date of his death proving elusive, one hopes he had a long and content retirement.

Martha E. Hudson was the daughter of Henry Hudson (1836–1907), a NSW engineering contractor and manufacturer, for whom Henry Lawson once worked. Hudson had migrated with his parents from England at an early age, and had married Mary Ann Turner on 17 July 1858 in Redfern. Between 1859 and 1879 they had ten or eleven children, of whom Martha (b. 1861) was the second.

Martha Hudson visited Britain with her parents in 1881 as part of her father's business trip to the USA, Britain and Continental Europe. As a consequence of her father's business interests, the family spent four months travelling extensively in England and Scotland, with Martha, as a young woman of about twenty, occupied for much of her time as a companion to her mother.

Martha married James C. Alexander by whom she had at least three children: the twins, Vida E. and Enid E. (b. 1891), and Jean W. (b. 1895).

Thomas Lodge Murray-Prior is remembered today as the father of the novelist, Rosa Praed (1851–1935). He was born in Somerset on 13 November 1819, the son of Elizabeth Skynner and Colonel Thomas Murray Prior, and migrated to NSW as a young man in 1839. On 3 September 1846 he married his first wife, Matilda Harpur, by whom he had twelve children, including Rosa Caroline in 1851. Thomas became a successful Queensland squatter and was a nominated member of the Legislative Council, holding office on and off as Postmaster General from 1866 to 1874.

His first wife died in 1868, and on 18 December 1872, Thomas married his second wife, Nora Clarissa Barton, whose sister, Rose, was the mother of the poet, A. B. (Banjo) Paterson. With Nora, who was almost thirty years younger than himself, he was to have a further eight children.

Thomas sailed to Britain on the *Almora* in 1882, partly to visit Rosa and two of his sisters, Louisa and Jemima, and partly to try to solve the disappearance of some funds which had caused Henry Martin, the husband of his wife's sister, Georgie, to resign from his post with the Queensland Public Service and go to live in England. Thomas spent three months in southern England before leaving for home via the Continent.

Thomas died on 31 December 1892 at the age of eighty-three.

Henry Pilcher was born into a relatively affluent NSW family. Henry Incledon Pilcher (senior) and Eliza Brockley had arrived in Sydney from London in April 1830 and had taken up a 2000 acre land grant to the north of the Hunter Valley. Henry (senior) was a solicitor, and to complement his agricultural interests he set up a law practice in Maitland High Street, building a large house at 'Telarah,' a 60 acre property in West Maitland. Henry Incledon (junior) was born in Maitland on 21 January 1833, the fourth of eleven children.

At the time of Henry's trip to England in 1866, the Pilchers were a well established Maitland family, and Henry's younger brother, Charles Edward, later became a leading NSW barrister. Henry married Ann (or Anne) Borthwick in Sydney in 1865, by which time he was bank manager for the Bank of Australasia in East Maitland, and they had one child, Florence Incledon, who was born in Maitland in 1867.

In April 1866 and on the advice of his doctor, Henry took six months leave of absence from the bank and travelled to Britain. He visited his brother Francis, a Church of England curate at Broadwater, near Worthing, whom he had not seen for nine years, and he went on excursions to Ireland and Scotland. He spent two months in Britain before returning to Sydney on the *John Duthie*, the same ship as he had travelled out on.

Henry died of tuberculosis on 27 December 1868 at the age of thirty-five, two years after his return to Australia, and he was buried in the Church of England burial ground in East Maitland.

Richard Teece was born in New Zealand on 29 April 1847 of a Welsh-born father, William Teece, and an Irish mother, Catherine Hassatt (or Hassett) from Limerick. His father, a shoemaker by trade, brought his family to NSW in 1853 or 1854, settling in Goulburn where Richard attended the Grammar School before studying at the University of Sydney. Richard joined the Australian Mutual Provident Society at the age of nineteen, and remained with the Society until his retirement in

1917, becoming Actuary and General Manager in 1890. On 10 February 1876, Richard married Helena Palmer, London-born daughter of Benjamin Palmer, hotel owner and mayor of Sydney (1875–76), with whom he was to have eight children.

At the beginning of his diary, Richard gives three motives for travelling to Britain in 1875: 'To recruit my energies which had been somewhat shattered by the arduous labours of an Investigation; To improve my knowledge of my profession by examining the systems of conducting business in the colossal institutions of a kindred character in America & England; To gratify a desire for travel before settling down in life.' To this end, he took nine months leave of absence and set out for Britain via North America with his 'chum,' Sam Beard.

Richard was to return to Britain a number of times: in 1893, in 1904 (during which trip Henry Pilcher's brother, Charles, spoke at a luncheon given in London for Richard), and in 1906, each time travelling via North America and each time travelling on business, though he was twice accompanied by his wife, Helena, with whom he understandably went sightseeing. Helena died in 1914. On 13 December 1928 and at the age of eighty-one, Richard shot himself, apparently while temporarily deranged as a result of Parkinson's disease.

Margaret Oliver Tripp was the fourth of six children born to William Upton Tripp (1804–1873), a solicitor, and Elizabeth Leigh (1809?–1899). She was born on 28 December 1838 in Beggearn Huish in Somerset, but moved to Melbourne with her parents at an early age in 1849 on the *Samuel Boddington*. In the 1850s, her parents became increasingly estranged and in 1859 her mother, Elizabeth, established a school in Melbourne in order to provide for herself and her three unmarried daughters. In 1861 the school moved from South Yarra to East Leigh in Prahran where it quickly developed into a prominent ladies school.

As is often the case with European travel in the nineteenth century, there seem to have been several reason's behind Margaret's arrival in Britain in February 1872. Partly she went to visit relatives, and both her father and mother had brothers and sisters still living in the West Country. Her older sister, Florence, who, like Margaret, remained unmarried, had made the trip before her in 1870 and sending unmarried daughters to Britain may have been a common practice; Emma Walker was sent at roughly the same age, and perhaps Elizabeth thought her daughters might find husbands in England. While in Britain, Margaret wrote home asking to be allowed to study at Newnham Hall, Cambridge, and qualify as a teacher, but in this she was disappointed. However, though she had planned to return to Melbourne in November 1872, she spent the early part of 1873 in Paris studying at Madame Bouten's school before being recalled by her mother. Her father died later the same year.

Elizabeth Tripp invested wisely, and in 1880 she was able to retire from managing East Leigh and take Florence and Margaret with her on a visit to Britain. In 1892, Margaret Tripp established her own private school at Rewe in Toorak, moving it to the Toorak College buildings in 1895. Her mother died in September 1899, and with herself and Florence in poor health, Margaret gave up control of Toorak College, though she continued working as a governess, one of her charges being Joan Lindsay, author of *Picnic at Hanging Rock*. Florence died in February 1901, and Margaret died the following year on 6 July 1902 at the age of sixty-three.

Like Margaret Tripp, **Emma Walker** was a teacher for most of her life, though unlike Tripp, Emma Walker was Australian born. Her parents, Thomas Moody Walker (1800–1878) and Mary Ann Lamb (1813–1900), came from Lincolnshire; they married in 1830 and migrated with their first three children to South Australia in 1838 on the *Lord Goderich*. Thomas became a successful soap manufacturer and Mary gave birth to six more children, among them Emma and her twin sister, Eliza, who were born in Adelaide on 6 June 1850.

Emma Walker was therefore thirty-two, a comparable age to Margaret Tripp, when she sailed from Adelaide on the *Hesperus* in January 1883. After a short and at times lonely stay in London, she went to stay with her father's brother, 'Uncle Ben,' in Frampton in Lincolnshire. Emma passed some time mounting emu eggs on white leather, but she spent most of her time sightseeing, visiting Yorkshire for its history and the Midlands for its manufacturing. As a single women she remained dependent on her circle of friends and family and never went beyond eastern England during her six months in Britain. She returned on the *Potosi* in November.

Emma remained unmarried. Her twin sister died in 1937 and Emma herself died on 10 December 1944 at the age of ninety-four.

William Samuel Willis was another of those Australians who migrated with parents at an early age. He was born in London on 27 March 1846 to William Organ Willis, a whitesmith, and Jane Dixon, and had migrated to NSW with his mother and father in 1852, the family moving on to Victoria in 1854, a move presumably related to the gold rush.

Perhaps, as a whitesmith, his father made a fortune dealing in gold, but by 1889 William Samuel could afford to take his young son, William Organ, on a world tour lasting eight months and covering the Middle East, Europe, Britain and North America.

William married Alice Holland Robarts, a native of Liverpool, England, in Melbourne on 29 March 1872, and they had six children, the last being born in 1888. Whether out of choice or necessity, when William sailed for Europe with his son on the *Oroya* in January 1889, Alice was left behind in Melbourne to look after the house and the remaining children. William, of course, had close relatives in England and he was no doubt proud to be able to show off young Willie to his aunts, uncles and cousins. But he spent only two months in Britain and, though he had a desire to show his eleven year old son something of the wider world, he was clearly an enthusiastic traveller himself; he charged Alice, to whom the letters were nominally written, to retain them for him as a record of his tour. The letters contain detailed instructions regarding when and to what address Alice should reply, and one can only admire William's meticulous planning and detailed knowledge of the mail steamers which allowed him to coordinate an exchange of letters while touring a world without planes and telephones.

William did not live to enjoy rereading his account in old age. He died of acute pneumonia at the age of forty-five on 14 July 1891, less than two years after his return to Victoria. Though he was described as an engraver on his marriage certificate, the registration of his death gives his 'Rank or Profession' as 'gentleman'. Alice, his wife, died in 1917.

Reginald Wyndham was the twelfth of thirteen children born into what was, potentially at least, more a dynasty than a family. George Wyndham (1801–1870), the father, educated at Harrow and Cambridge, migrated to New South Wales in 1827 and established Dalwood, a large property in the Hunter Valley. During the economic depression of the early 1840s, the Wyndhams trekked north and took up properties first at Kilgra on the Richmond River and then at Bukkulla on the Macintyre; it was in 1845, during these travels, that Reginald was born. In 1847, they returned to Dalwood but by 1870, the year in which George died, the properties were again in serious financial difficulties and Bukkulla was foreclosed by the banks in 1875. Dalwood itself was repossessed around 1890 and the vineyards purchased by Penfolds. Although the last of the Wyndham vines was taken out in 1961, the vineyard, now owned by Orlando, continues to produce a range of wines marketed under the name of Wyndham Estate.

The failure of George Wyndham to establish a dynasty appears to have been the result of hostile economic conditions coupled with his eleven sons' uneven inheritance of their father's business acumen. Reginald withdrew from the firm just before the crash of 1875, though ironically it was not through foresight but because he objected to measures intended to curb the spending of the more extravagant of the Wyndham brothers (including, one suspects, himself). By the time he began his diary in 1882, Reginald owned Leconfield, part of the old Dalwood property which had been subdivided in 1870, but his financial position was again unstable and he badly needed an alternative source of income if he was to continue the life of a gentleman pastoralist who travelled to Sydney to stay at his club and watch cricket.

Reginald Wyndham married Julia Bateman Champain (1844–1888) in 1867. By March 1882 and their trip to Britain, they had one son and three daughters, with Julia carrying a fourth daughter who was to be born in July in London. They travelled separately to London, Julia and the children by the *Parramatta*, a sailing ship, while Wyndham took the P&O steamer, the *Shannon*. Quite why Reginald sent Julia and their four children on ahead by sailing ship is difficult to untangle; possibly his financial state made him choose the cheaper option for his family, though she was accompanied by her mother, Harriet Champain, and her sister, Georgina Acres, an obvious advantage to a woman five months pregnant with four children.

Because of his insecure hold on Leconfield, Reginald was keen to exploit the coal on his land, and in order to float a mining company, he needed to travel to London, the main source of venture capital for Australian businesses. He spent some time negotiating a financial arrangement, but he also indulged in his passion for cricket and horses by watching the touring Australian cricket team and spending a day at the Epsom Derby. He passed most of his time in London, with the occasional excursion into southern England, though he did manage two days sightseeing in Paris at the end of his trip. Leaving his family behind, Reginald sailed from London on the *Peshawar* in September 1882, after spending four months in Britain.

Reginald's attempt to save Leconfield only postponed the inevitable; the wharfies strike of 1890 killed the coal trade and forced the sale of Leconfield. Following Julia's death in 1888, Reginald married Kathleen Osborne, by whom he had a further six children. He died in 1913.

Notes

Introduction

1 Woollacott, '"All This is the Empire, I Told Myself"', p. 1016. See also Woollacott's full-length study, *White Colonials, Modernity and the Metropolis: Australian Women in London 1870–1940* (forthcoming).
2 Mulvey, *Anglo-American Landscapes*, p. xi.
3 Burton, *At the Heart of the Empire*, p. 1.
4 Burton, *At the Heart of the Empire*, pp. 19–20.

Chapter one *Neither English nor Foreign: Australian Colonial Identity*

1 Colley, *Britons*, p. 5.
2 Colley, *Britons*, pp. 5–6.
3 Colley, *Britons*, p. 6.
4 Marshall, *The Cambridge History of the British Empire*, p. 319.
5 Marshall, *The Cambridge History of the British Empire*, p. 320.
6 Jupp, *The Australian People*, p. 63.
7 Rowland, 'The Beginnings of an Australian National Character', p. 401.
8 *The Illustrated London News*, 7 August 1886, p. 157.
9 Knox, *The Races of Men*; quoted in Horsman, 'Origins of Racial Anglo-Saxonism in Great Britain before 1850', p. 407.
10 Ryan, 'Chinese Australian History', p. 71. See also Ryan, *Ancestors: Chinese in Colonial Australia*.
11 Hall, 'Rethinking Imperial Histories'; Hall, 'Histories, Empires and the Post-Colonial Moment.
12 See Driver and Gilbert, ed., *Imperial Cities*.
13 Burton, *At the Heart of the Empire*, p. 13.
14 Hall, 'Imperial Man'.
15 Hall, 'Rethinking Imperial Histories', p. 16.
16 Pratt, *Imperial Eyes*, p. 6.
17 Whitlock, 'A "White-Souled State"'.
18 MacKenzie, *Orientalism*, p. xiv.
19 Inglis, 'Going Home', p. 106.
20 White, 'The Soldier as Tourist', p. 65.

21 Pesman, *Duty Free*, p. 3.
22 Pesman, Walker and White, *The Oxford Book of Australian Travel Writing*, p. xi.
23 Pesman, *Duty Free*, p. 17.
24 Pesman, Walker and White, *The Oxford Book of Australian Travel Writing*, p. 2.
25 Stoler and Cooper, 'Between Metropole and Colony', p. 34.
26 Hall, 'Histories, Empires and the Post-Colonial Moment', pp. 66–7.

Chapter two *Familiar and Yet Strange: First Experiences of Britain*

1 See Woodruff, *The Tichborne Claimant*.
2 *Times*, 18 May 1871.
3 I am grateful to the English Folk Dance and Song Society for the following version of the chorus from the traditional North Country ballad, 'The Oak and the Ash':
    It's home, boys, home, oh, it's home I want to be,
    Home far away in my own counterie
    Where the oak and the ash and the bonny ivy tree
    Are all a-growing green in the North Counterie.
4 Stratton, *Writing Sites*, p. 85.
5 Simpson, *Wake Up in Europe*, p. 279.
6 J., 'Australian Song Birds'.
7 Boucaut, *Letters to My Boys*, p. 71.
8 Carter, 'Spirits of the Dead', p. 29.
9 Kröller, *Canadian Travellers in Europe*, p. 91.
10 Kröller, *Canadian Travellers in Europe*, p. 92.
11 *Illustrated Guide*, p. 86.
12 Stratton, *Writing Sites*, p. 80.
13 Freud, 'The Uncanny', p. 226.
14 Freud, 'The Uncanny', p. 241.
15 Gelder and Jacobs, *Uncanny Australia*, p. 23.

Chapter three *Aborgines at the Crystal Palace: Portable Colonial Spaces*

1 In 1853, 6,369 packages of iron houses valued at £111,380 were imported into Victoria ('Portable Houses', p. 12); in the same year, 15,960 packages of wooden houses valued at £246,371 were also imported (Lewis, 'The Portable House', p. 278).
2 Howitt, *Land, Labour and Gold*, p. 157.
3 Howitt, *Land, Labour and Gold*, p. 159.
4 Lewis, 'The Diagnosis of Prefabricated Buildings, pp. 61–2.
5 Howitt, *Land, Labour and Gold*, p. 159.
6 McLean's advertisement appears in Archer, *The Great Australian Dream*, p. 61.
7 *Illustrated London News*, 30 April 1853; quoted in Robertson, 'The Australian

Verandah', p. 243.

8 I am grateful to Ros Shennan for details of Alfred Joy's background and subsequent life in Victoria.

9 Herbert, 'A Cast-Iron Solution'.

10 *Illustrated London News*, 30 April 1853; quoted in Robertson, 'The Australian Verandah', p. 243.

11 Carter, *Lie of the Land*, pp. 2–3.

12 Carter, *Lie of the Land*, p. 3.

13 Archer, *The Great Australian Dream*, pp. 47–50.

14 Archer, *The Great Australian Dream*, p. 25, pp. 46–50; 'Portable Houses', p. 12.

15 White, *Prefabrication*, p. 12.

16 Jacobs, *Edge of Empire: Postcolonialism and the City*.

17 *Great Exhibition Catalogue* Vol. I, p. 326.

18 Herbert, 'A Cast-Iron Solution', p. 373.

19 *Illustrated London News*, 20 September 1851, p. 363; 22 November 1851, p. 613.

20 Herbert, 'A Cast-Iron Solution'; Lewis, 'The Diagnosis of Prefabricated Buildings'; the Macquarie Street church was moved to the Rosewood Asylum, Lidcombe, in 1899 and was finally demolished in 1958.

21 Herbert, 'A Cast-Iron Solution', p. 373.

22 McKean, *Crystal Palace*, p. 41.

23 Ruskin, *Stones of Venice*, p. 361.

24 McKean, *Crystal Palace*, p. 15.

25 Hix, *The Glasshouse*, p. 175.

26 McKean, *Crystal Palace*, p. 9.

27 McKean, *Crystal Palace*, p. 12.

28 *Great Exhibition Catalogue*, Vol. I, p. 125.

29 Bennett, *The Birth of the Museum*, p. 101

30 *Great Exhibition Catalogue*, Vol. I, p. xiv.

31 Bennett, *The Birth of the Museum*, p. 101.

32 This paragraph draws on several sources: Physick, *The Victoria & Albert Museum*, pp. 19–24; *The Museums Area of South Kensington*, Vol. 38, pp. 98–9; Hix, *The Glasshouse*, pp. 138–9; and Herbert, 'A Cast-Iron Solution', p. 378; the building may have been designed by the civil engineer, William Dredge (*The Museums Area of South Kensington*, p. 98).

33 Quoted in Physick, *The Victoria & Albert Museum*, p. 24.

34 *The Museums Area of South Kensington*, p. 98.

35 Physick, *The Victoria & Albert Museum*, p. 25.

36 Howitt, *Land, Labour and Gold*, pp. 158–9.

37 Freeland, *Architecture in Australia*, p. 113.

38 Lewis, 'The Corrugated Iron Aesthetic', p. 52.

39 Dickens, 'The Private History of the Palace of Glass', p. 386.

40 White, *Prefabrication*, p. 16.

41 Hitchcock, *Early Victorian Architecture*, Vol. 1, p. 495.
42 Bird, *Paxton's Palace*, p. 127.
43 McKean, *Crystal Palace*, p. 60.
44 *Times*, 15 July 1851.
45 Bird, *Paxton's Palace*, pp. 126–8.
46 McKean, *Crystal Palace*, p. 49.
47 The diary of Henry Pilcher was found by a vigilant refuse collector who showed it to his cousin Sharon Bakewell; she arranged for it to be copied onto microfiche and traced Ann Ashby, the great-great-granddaughter of Henry Incledon Pilcher (senior), to whom I am also indebted.
48 Quoted in Beaver, *The Crystal Palace*, p. 84.
49 For full details of the painting, see Bonyhardy, *Australian Colonial Paintings*, pp. 144–9.
50 Chadwick, *The Works of Paxton*, p. 148.
51 Chadwick, *The Works of Paxton*, p. 148; the north transept was destroyed by fire on 30 December 1866.
52 Hix, *The Glasshouse*, pp. 36–7.
53 *Gardener's Magazine*, 5 (1829), p. 379; quoted in Preston, "*The Scenery of the Torrid Zone,*" p. 15.
54 Hix, *The Glasshouse*, p. 27.
55 Hix, *The Glasshouse*, p. 42.
56 Hix, *The Glasshouse*, p. 141.
57 Fish, 'Enville Hall', p. 376.
58 Hix, *The Glasshouse*, p. 88.
59 McKean, *Crystal Palace*, pp. 28–9.
60 McKean, *Crystal Palace*, p. 29.
61 Carter, *The Victorian Garden*, p. 134.
62 4 September 1904; 12 April 1917; 4 July 1959.
63 Quartermaine, 'International Exhibitions'.
64 Coombes, 'Museums and the Formation of National and Cultural Identities', p. 61.
65 Phillips, *Guide to the Crystal Palace*, p. 105.
66 Phillips, *Guide to the Crystal Palace*, p. 16.
67 Hix, *The Glasshouse*, p. 42–4.
68 See Catherine Hall's 'Imperial Man' for the change in attitude towards indigenous peoples by one particular colonial administrator, Edward Eyre.
69 Reynolds, *Dispossession*, pp. 114–5.
70 Ryan, *The Cartographic Eye*, p. 97.
71 Hix, *The Glasshouse*, p. 88.
72 *Illustrated London News*, 7 August 1852, pp. 97–8.
73 McClintock, *Imperial Leather*.
74 Compare, for example, the illustration in McKean, *Crystal Palace*, p. 31, with the photograph reproduced in Hitchcock, *Early Victorian Architecture*, XVI p. 26.

75 Beaver, *The Crystal Palace*, p. 105.
76 Greenhalgh, *Ephemeral Vistas*, p. 87.
77 Phillips, *Guide to the Crystal Palace*, p. 114.
78 Hall, 'Rethinking Imperial Histories', p. 16.
79 Fothergill, 'The Town Dweller', pp. 112–14.
80 Stepan, 'Biological Degeneration', p. 98.
81 Morgan, *The Danger of Deterioration of Race*, p. 4.
82 Alexander Sutherland, *Victoria and its Metropolis* (Melbourne, 1888); quoted in Reynolds, *Dispossession*, p. 11.
83 Fothergill, 'The Town Dweller', p. 2.
84 *Illustrated London News*, 14 August 1852, p. 113.
85 The establishment of the Bethnal Green Museum is dealt with in Physick, *The Victoria & Albert Museum*, pp. 144–5.
86 *Bethnal Green Museum of Childhood*, p. 44.
87 *The Museums Area of South Kensington*, p. 99.
88 Chapman, 'Arranging Ethnology', p. 29, pp. 33–4.
89 Stocking, *Victorian Anthropology*, p. 6.
90 Lane Fox, 'On the Principles of Classification', p. 303.
91 Pitt-Rivers, 'Typological Museums', p. 116.
92 Lane Fox, 'On the Principles of Classification', p. 301.
93 Bennett, *The Birth of the Museum*, p. 201.
94 Quoted in Quartermaine, 'International Exhibitions', p. 50; I depend on this excellent article for much of my information regarding Daintree as a photographer.
95 Rothenburg, 'Australia at the 1876 Exhibition', p. 58.
96 Quartermaine, 'International Exhibitions', p. 46.
97 Hitchcock, *Early Victorian Architecture*, Vol. 1, p. 493.
98 Physick, *The Victoria & Albert Museum*, p. 146.

Chapter four   *Roast Beef and the Epsom Derby: Social Status and National Identity*

1 Details of Dalwood and the Wyndham family come from *The Australian Dictionary of Biography*; Wyndham, 'Bukkulla Station'; and the research of Ros Shennan.
2 Details of Murray-Prior's background come from his Memorandum Book and from *The Australian Dictionary of Biography*.
3 'Pioneers of the "Thirties"'.
4 *Brisbane Courier*, 29 March 1882; information kindly supplied by Ros Shennan.
5 Clarke, 'The *Other* Harpur'.
6 Perren, *The Meat Trade in Britain 1840–1914*, p. 26.
7 The anti-French thesis comes from Linda Colley, *Britons*; I am indebted to my colleague, Peter Miles, for pointing out to me how this was voiced in terms of the opposition to French cuisine.

8 Boldrewood, 'The Australian Native-Born Type', p. 355.
9 Quoted in Mandell, p. 236.
10 Boldrewood, 'England, Home and Country', p. 16.
11 Boldrewood, 'England, Home and Country', p. 17.
12 *Australian Dictionary of Biography*.
13 My rehearsal of the historical background of the Derby is drawn from Miers, 'The Derby'.
14 Restrictions of use were introduced on Epsom Downs in the 1980s to protect the training gallops (Miers, 'The Derby', p. 63); since 1995, the Derby has been run on a Saturday.
15 Bagehot, *English Constitution*, p. 267.
16 Bagehot, *English Constitution*, p. 268.
17 *Guardian*, 2 June 1988, p. 1; quoted in Miers, 'The Derby', p. 234.
18 Miers, 'The Derby', p. 447.
19 James, 'Two Excursions', p. 174.
20 The 1881 census gives NSW a total population of 749,825; the Victoria Racing Club estimates the size of the 1882 Melbourne Cup crowd as 70,000. I am grateful to Ros Shennan for supplying me with both figures.
21 'Bosh' means 'nonsense'; the word entered the English language from Turkish through its frequent use in *Ayesha* (1834), a novel by James Justinian Morier (1780?–1849) who was born at Smyrna and served as a British diplomat in Persia.
22 *Times*, 4 June 1885: 10; quoted.in Miers, 'The Derby', p. 74.
23 Miers, 'The Derby', p. 98.
24 *Times*, 24 May 1939, p. 17.
25 *Times*, 25 May 1939, p. 18.

Chapter five *Cleopatra's Needle: Antiquity, History and Modernity in Britain and the USA*

1 Bindman, *Roubiliac and the Eighteenth-Century Monument*, chapter 2, 'Public Space and Public Sphere'.
2 de Maré, *The London Doré Saw*, p. 211.
3 Hogan, *The Australian in London and America*, p. 141.
4 *Orient Line Guide*, p. 30.
5 Quoted in Mulvey, *Anglo-American Landscapes*, p. 96.
6 Quoted in Clayton, *The Rediscovery of Ancient Egypt*, p. 41.
7 Habachi, *The Obelisks of Egypt*, pp. 152–64.
8 *The Architect*, 18 August 1877; quoted in Noakes, *Cleopatra's Needles*, p. 64.
9 Quoted in Noakes, *Cleopatra's Needles*, pp. 67–8.
10 Barker, *London*, p. 276.
11 Barker, *London*, p. 328.
12 James Elmes, *Metropolitan Improvements* (1829); quoted in Tyack, *Sir James Pennethorne and the Making of Victorian London*, p. 16.
13 James Elmes, *Metropolitan Improvements* (1829); quoted in Tyack, *Sir James*

Pennethorne and the Making of Victorian London, p. 16.

14 Summerson, *Georgian London*, pp. 288–9.
15 Metcalf, *Victorian London*, p. 22.
16 Smith, *Wayfaring Notes (Second Series)*, p. 218.
17 Burton, *At the Heart of the Empire*, p. 141.
18 Clayton, *The Rediscovery of Ancient Egypt*, p. 9.
19 Noakes, *Cleopatra's Needles*, pp. 29–30.
20 *Times*; quoted in Habachi, *The Obelisks of Egypt*, p. 175.
21 Barker, *London*, p. 321.
22 Holman, *My Wander Year*, p. 24.
23 Caygill, *Sir James Pennethorne and the Making of Victorian London*, p. 14.
24 *New York Times*, 16 March 1881, p. 2.
25 Hoyt, *The Vanderbilts and their Fortunes*.
26 Dow, *A Tour of America*, p. 29.
27 Hogan, *The Australian in London and America*, p. 39.
28 Munro, 'Sketch of Journey in United States Canada and the British Isles', p. 23.

Chapter six A Disgusting Climate: Being Australian in Wales, Ireland and Scotland

1 Boucaut, *Letters to My Boys*, p. 96.
2 Spielvogel, *A Gumsucker on the Tramp*, p. 77.
3 White, 'Bluebells and Fogtown', p. 54.
4 White, p. 55.
5 White, 'Bluebells and Fogtown', p. 55.
6 Fish, 'Enville Hall', p. 375.
7 Ward, *The Australian Legend*, pp. 12–13.
8 Maynard, *Fashioned from Penury*, p. 170.
9 *Great Exhibition Catalogue*, Vol. II, p. 990.
10 I am grateful to Ros Shennan for the figure of the Irish population of Maitland.
11 In 1891, 3.25 percent of the population of NSW was Scottish-born. Of the 2477 Scottish-born inhabitants of Tenterfield, 50 (2%) were Scottish-born (34 males and 16 females). I am grateful to Ros Shennan for these figures, taken from the 1891 NSW census (Australian Bureau of Statistics).
12 Spielvogel, *A Gumsucker on the Tramp*, p. 107.
13 Spielvogel, *A Gumsucker on the Tramp*, pp. 105–6.
14 Spielvogel, p. 106.

Chapter seven Australia has more of a Continental Atmosphere: Twentieth-Century Visitors to Britain

1 Rowland, 'The Beginnings of an Australian National Character', p. 401.
2 For an account of the debate about the effects of climate, see Tiffin,

'Imagining Countries, Imagining People'.
3 Rowland, 'The Beginnings of an Australian National Character', p. 402.
4 Rowland, 'The Beginnings of an Australian National Character', p. 407.
5 Ward, *The Australian Legend*, p. 76.
6 Stratton, *Race Daze*, p. 94.
7 Stratton, *Race Daze*, p. 116.
8 Serle, *From Deserts the Prophets Come*, p. 229.
9 White, *Inventing Australia*, p. 140.
10 Dutton, 'British Subject', p. 15.
11 Horne, *The Lucky Country*, pp. 93–4.
12 Solomon, *Coming of Age*.
13 Hage, *White Nation*, p. 143.
14 Hage, *White Nation*, p. 146.
15 Pesman, Walker and White, *The Oxford Book of Australian Travel Writing*, p. 2.
16 Gore, *Australians, Go Home!*, p. 31.
17 Pesman, *Duty Free*, p. 220.
18 Pesman, *Duty Free*, p. 221.
19 Shoemaker, '"Don't Cry for Me, Diamantina": An Alternative Reading of Pauline Hanson.'
20 Cochrane, 'Britishness in Australia', p. 73.

Bibliography

Personal Accounts

Aldridge, Henry. Memoir 1883–1886. Private collection.

Anderson, Joan. Diary 1851. La Trobe Collection, State Library of Victoria MS 9413.

Anderson, Thomas. Diaries 1850–1854. La Trobe Collection, State Library of Victoria MS 9413.

Andreas, Alice May. Diary 1902. Private collection.

Anonymous. 'Hints and Suggestions for a Friend on a Voyage to England by the P&O SS. *Parramatta*'. State Library of NSW B805.

Anonymous. Diary 1937–1938. State Library of NSW ML MSS 2494.

Argall, John H. Letters 1914–1916. State Library of South Australia D6431(L).

Atkinson, Thomas. Diaries 1866–1869. State Library of NSW ML MSS 2730.

Avenall, Edith. Letters 1915–1917. La Trobe Collection, State Library of Victoria MS 12567.

Avery, Louis Willyama. Diary 1915–1918. State Library of South Australia PRG 500/1–7.

Avery, William E. Diaries 1897. State Library of South Australia D6220(L).

Balfour, Donald. Diary 1963. National Library of Australia MS 1010.

Balfour, Donald. Diary 1967–1968. National Library of Australia MS 1010.

Barnes, E. Letters 1888. National Library of Australia MS 4022.

Barwick, Archibald. Diaries 1914–1919. State Library of NSW ML MSS 1493/1–3.

Bate, Kathleen. Diary 1939. Private collection.

Baxter, Annie Maria. Diaries 1851. State Library of NSW DL MSQ 181–183.

Bedford, Randolph. *Explorations in Civilization*. Sydney: n.p., n.d.

Bennett, R. Diary 1859. National Library of Australia MS 8225.

Blaikie, Flora Josephine. Diary 1903. State Library of NSW ML MSS 4376.

Blake, Irene. Diary 1915–1919. State Library of South Australia D7620(L).

Blannin, A. *Hasty Notes of a Flying Trip with the Victorian Rifle Team to England and America in 1876*. Melbourne: Published for the author, 1877.

Boldrewood, Rolf. 'England, Home and Country'. *Australians Abroad: An*

Anthology. Ed. Charles Higham and Michael Wilding. Melbourne: Chesire, 1967. 12–19.

Bollen, Christobel Ballantyne. Diary 1913. State Library of South Australia PRG 278/2.

Bond, Florence. Diary 1925–1926. State Library of NSW ML MSS 9196.

Bond, Florence. Diary 1927. State Library of NSW ML MSS 9196.

Bond, Florence. Diary 1939. State Library of NSW ML MSS 9196.

Boucaut, James Penn. *Letters to my Boys: An Australian Judge and Ex-Premier on his Travels in Europe.* London: Gay and Bird, 1906.

Boyce, Francis. Diary 1889. State Library of NSW B1179.

Brewer, Hector. Diaries 1915–1919. State Library of NSW ML MSS 1300.

Brown, Amelia Harriet. Diary 1912. State Library of South Australia PRG 373/13d/6.

Brown, Kathleen Mary. Diary 1912. State Library of South Australia PRG 373/13g/3.

Brown, Victor Voules. Letters c1860. State Library of South Australia PRG 373/8a/1.

Brown, Victor Voules (jnr.). Letters 1916–1918. State Library of South Australia PRG 373/13e/2.

Casson, Marjory. Diaries 1949–1950. State Library of South Australia PRG 28/1/1–2.

Clayton, R. B. B. Memoir 1871. National Library of Australia MS1470.

Cleland, John Burton. Diaries 1903–1905. State Library of South Australia PRG 5/40.

Cohen, Alan Jack. Diary 1938. State Library of NSW ML MSS 6032.

Corsellis, Esther. Diaries and Letters 1953–1954. State Library of NSW ML MSS 6555/1–2.

Corsellis, Esther. Diaries and Letters 1975. State Library of NSW ML MSS 6555/1–2.

Corsellis, Esther. Diary 1986. State Library of NSW ML MSS 6555/1.

Crocker, Richard. Diary 1859. Private collection.

Cunliffe, T. J. J. Diary 1941–1944. Private collection.

Curtis, Daisy Rose. Diaries 1927–1928. State Library of South Australia D6842(L).

Davidson, Hugh Laidlaw. Diary 1911. State Library of South Australia D6762(L).

Deakin, Stella. Letters 1909. National Library of Australia MS 9056.

Donnell, Anne. Circular Letters 1915–1918. State Library of NSW ML MSS 1022/1.

Donnell, Anne. *Letters of an Australian Army Sister.* Sydney: Angus & Robertson, 1920.

Douglas, Edward M. Letters 1940–1942. State Library of South Australia PRG 488/6–25.

Dow, Thomas Kirkland. *A Tour of America.* Melbourne: *The Australasian*, 1884.

Bibliography

Dowding, Mabel. Diary 1928. State Library of NSW ML MSS 4249/1.

Dowding, Mabel. Diary 1956. State Library of NSW ML MSS 4249/2.

Duckles, George William. Diary 1950–1951. National Library of Australia MS 8546.

Fairfax, Mary. Diary 1881. State Library of NSW ML MSS 459.

Falkiner, Una Caroline. Diary 1929. State Library of NSW ML MSS 423.

Falkiner, Una Caroline. Diary 1938. State Library of NSW ML MSS 423.

Fergie, Henry Penketh. Diary 1887. La Trobe Collection, State Library of Victoria MS 12791.

Fitchett, William Henry. Diary letter 1911. La Trobe Collection, State Library of Victoria MS11621.

Flynn, Marion. Letters 1968–1972. Private collection.

Foote, Joseph. Diary 1897. Australian National Maritime Museum MS IND.

Gordon, Annie Grace. Diary 1909. La Trobe Collection, State Library of Victoria MS 9484.

Gore, Stuart. *Australians, Go Home!* London: Hale, 1958.

Graham, Minnie. Diary 1873. La Trobe Collection, State Library of Victoria MS 10986.

Hall, Dora. Diary 1885. La Trobe Collection, State Library of Victoria MS 12843.

Hall, Dora. Diary 1889. La Trobe Collection, State Library of Victoria MS 12843.

Hannan, Richard. Diary 1892. State Library of NSW, ML MSS 2638.

Hart, Lucy. Letter 1852. La Trobe Collection, State Library of Victoria MS 8838.

Haslett, Samuel Torrens. Diary 1852. National Library of Australia MS 7385.

Haysom, Ida. Diaries 1936–1937. La Trobe Collection, State Library of Victoria MS 10015.

Hayward, Johnson Frederick. Diairies 1858–1859. State Library of South Australia PRG 395/2/1–2; PRG 395/3/1–3.

Henning, Rachel. *The Letters of Rachel Henning.* Sydney: Angus & Robertson, 1986.

Higgins, Nettie. Diary 1910–1911. National Library of Australia MS1174/16/1.

Hitchcock, George M. Diary 1860–1861. La Trobe Collection, State Library of Victoria MS 8505.

Hitchcock, George M. Diary 1888–1889. La Trobe Collection, State Library of Victoria MS 8934.

Hingston, James. 'The Australian Abroad' (1882). National Library of Australia MS 7470.

Hogan, James Francis. *The Australian in London and America.* London: Ward, 1889.

Holman, Ada A. *My Wander Year: Some Jottings in a Year's Travel.* Sydney: William Brooks & Co., [1914].

Hudson, Martha. Diary 1881. State Library of NSW ML MSS 1948.

James, A. H. Clement, and Helena Glazebrook T. ('Tib') James. Letters 1930. State Library of NSW ML MSS 4834.

James, Henry. 'Two Excursions'. *English Hours.* London: Heinemann, 1905.

James, Mary. Diary 1953–1954. La Trobe Collection, State Library of Victoria MS 12558.

Jennings, Henrietta. Diary 1887. La Trobe Collection, State Library of Victoria MS 9432.

Jennings, Sophia. Diary 1887. La Trobe Collection, State Library of Victoria MS 9432.

Joy, Alfred. Diary 1853. Australia National Maritime Museum.

Kater, Mary Eliza. Diary 1875. National Library of Australia MS 2243/1/3.

Kerr, Edna. Letters 1959. La Trobe Collection, State Library of Victoria MS 12101.

Klauer, Augustus. Diary 1875. State Library of South Australia D5883(L).

Labett, William. Diary 1904. La Trobe Collection, State Library of Victoria MS 11808.

Lloyd, Thomas. Diary 1883. State Library of South Australia D5251/1(L).

Lilley, Ena. *A Possum Abroad*. Brisbane: Hews, 1901.

Macarthur, James. Letters 1828–1829. State Library of NSW ML MSS A2931.

Mack, Louise. *An Australian Girl in London*. London: Fisher Unwin, 1902.

Maddon, Henry. Letters 1891. La Trobe Collection, State Library of Victoria MS 13055.

Maddon, Lily. Letters 1891. La Trobe Collection, State Library of Victoria MS 13055.

Marryat, Charles. Diary 1865–1866. State Library of South Australia D3076/4(L).

Marryat, Grace. Diary 1865–1866. State Library of South Australia D3077/10(L).

Martin, J. I. Diary 1891. La Trobe Collection, State Library of Victoria MS 11125.

Martin, Jennie. Letters 1926. La Trobe Collection, State Library of Victoria MS 11125.

Matthews, Daniel. Diary 1869–1870. National Library of Australia MS 2195/1–3.

Maughan, James. Diary 1869–1870. State Library of South Australia PRG 197/1.

Mayo, Helen. Letters 1904–1906. State Library of South Australia PRG 127/2.

McRae, John Duncan. Diary 1916–1917. State Library of NSW Z ML MSS 1031.

Mease, Mary. Diary 1851. State Library of South Australia D4006(L).

Morey, Alfred Ernest. Letters 1916–1917. National Library of Australia MS 6048.

Mukasa, Ham. *Sir Apolo Kagwa Discovers Britain*. Ed. Taban lo Liyong. London: Heinemann, 1975.

Munro, Elgin. 'Sketch of Journey in United States Canada and the British Isles (1916)'. National Library of Australia MS 3483.

Munro, Lawrence. Diary 1869–1872. La Trobe Collection, State Library of Victoria MS 13079.

Murray-Prior, Thomas Lodge. Diary 1882. State Library of NSW ML MSS 3117/6.

Murray Smith, Jane. Letters 1863–1865. La Trobe Collection, State Library of Victoria MF57.

Murray Smith, Robert. Letters 1864–1865. La Trobe Collection, State Library of Victoria MF57.

Newell, Nancy. 'Diary of an Overseas Trip' (1939). State Library of NSW ML MSS 5148.

Newland, Henry Simpson. Letters 1901. State Library of South Australia PRG 288/25.

Newland, Henry Simpson. Letters 1914–1919. State Library of South Australia PRG 288/28–29.

Newland, Henry Simpson. Letters 1932. State Library of South Australia PRG 288/54.

Nichols, William. Diary 1849. National Library of Australia MS 8166.

Nitschke, R. H. Diary 1935. State Library of South Australia D6788(L).

Padman, Thomas. Diary 1863. State Library of South Australia D5039A(L).

Parkhouse, Devon. Diary 1917. State Library of South Australia PRG 300/B1–B8.

Peach, William E. Letters 1915–1916. National Library of Australia MS 929.

Phillips, Philip David. Diary 1889. La Trobe Collection, State Library of Victoria MS 12491.

Pilcher, Henry Incledon. Diary 1866. Australian National Maritime Museum.

Pinnock, Dorothy Ilma. Diaries 1938–1939. La Trobe Collection, State Library of Victoria MS 11536.

Pinnock, Dorothy Ilma. Diaries 1948–1949. La Trobe Collection, State Library of Victoria MS 11536.

Postlethwaite, William. Diary 1846–1847. La Trobe Collection, State Library of Victoria MS 10948.

Rae, John. Diary 1879. State Library of NSW ML MSS 4472.

Reibey, Mary. Diary 1820–1821. State Library of NSW Z ML MSS 2132.

Reid, Ethel Rose. Diary 1900. State Library of NSW ML MSS 6565.

Roberts, Harriet Grover. Diaries 1937. State Library of NSW ML MSS 2602.

Rowcroft, Oscar G. Letters 1941–1942. La Trobe Collection, State Library of Victoria MS 11826.

Russell, Annie. Diary 1851. La Trobe Collection, State Library of Victoria MS 11984.

Saunders, William. Memoirs. La Trobe Collection, State Library of Victoria MS 12752.

Sayer, Will. *The Diary of Will Sayer*. [Diary on *Samuel Plimsoll*, London to Sydney, 1876.] Parks, NSW: Parks & District Historical Society, 1989.

Shields, Marjorie Josephine. Letters 1930. State Library of South Australia MS D6951(L).

Simpson, Colin. *Wake Up in Europe: A Book of Travel for Australians and New Zealanders*. Sydney: Angus & Robertson, n.d.

Smart, Francis Joseph. Letters 1900–1901. La Trobe Collection, State Library of Victoria MS 12360.

Smith, John. *Wayfaring Notes (Second Series): A Holiday Tour Round the World*. Aberdeen: Brown, 1876.

Smith, John. *Wayfaring Notes: Sydney to Southampton by Way of Egypt and Palastine*. Sydney: Sheriff & Downing, 1865.

Sparkes, W. P. Diary 1916. State Library of NSW ML MSS 3047.

Spence, Catherine Helen. 'An Australian's Impressions of England'. *Cornhill*

Magazine, 13 (January–June 1866): 110–20.

Spielvogel, Nathan. *A Gumsucker on the Tramp*. 2nd ed. Melbourne: Robertson, 1905.

Stewart, William. Diary 1866–1867. La Trobe Collection, State Library of Victoria MS 10555.

Street, Sir Philip, and Belinda Maud Street. Letters 1929. State Library of NSW ML MSS 1933.

Sutton, J. W. Diary 1875. La Trobe Collection, State Library of Victoria MS 12390.

Suttor, George. Diary 1844. State Library of NSW ML MSS 2417/2.

Teece, Richard. Diary 1875. National Library of Australia MS 5354.

Teece, Richard. Diary 1893. National Library of Australia MS 5354.

Teece, Richard. Diary 1904. National Library of Australia MS 5354.

Teece, Richard. Diary 1906. National Library of Australia MS 5354.

Timewell, Louisa. Diary 1852. La Trobe Collection, State Library of Victoria MS 12353.

Tripp, Margaret. Letters 1872–1873. La Trobe Collection, State Library of Victoria MS 11539.

Twigg, Anne Beatrice. Diary 1968. State Library of NSW ML MSS 4015.

Valentine, Charles Jonas. Diary 1885. State Library of South Australia MS D6335(L).

Walker, Emma. Diary 1883. State Library of South Australia MS D6942(L).

Way, Samuel. Diary letter 1869. State Library of South Australia PRG 30/6.

Way, Samuel. Diary 1897. State Library of South Australia PRG 30/2.

Williams, Thomas. Diary 1860. State Library of NSW B465.

Williams, Thomas. Diary 1881–1882. State Library of NSW B486/B487.

Willis, William. Letters 1889. National Library of Australia MS 3513.

Woodman, H. T. Diary 1855. National Library of Australia MS 4055.

Wrede, Robert William. Diary 1853. La Trobe Collection, State Library of Victoria MS 9208.

Wyndham, Alward, and Frances McInherny, ed. *The Diary of George Wyndham of Dalwood, 1830–1840*. NSW: Dalwood Restoration Association, 1987.

Wyndham, Hugh Leslie. 'Bukkulla Station'. 1957. State Library of NSW ML B1505.

Wyndham, Reginald. Diary 1882. State Library of NSW ML MSS 1946/1 + 2.

Secondary Sources

Adam, J. A. Stanley. 'Some Australian Characteristics'. *Cosmos Magazine*, 31 August 1895: 581–4.

Allwood, John. *The Great Exhibitions*. London: Studio Vista, 1977.

Archer, John. *The Great Australian Dream: The History of the Australian House*. 1987. Sydney: HarperCollins, 1996.

Armstrong, Isobel. 'Transparency: Towards a Poetics of Glass in the Nineteenth-Century'. *Cultural Babbage: Technology, Time and Invention*. Ed. Francis

Spufford and Jenny Uglow. London: Faber, 1996, pp. 123–48.

Bagehot, Walter. *The English Constitution*. 1867. London: Kegan Paul, 1896; Brighton and Portland: Sussex Academic Press, 1997.

Barker, Felix, and Peter Jackson. *London: 2000 Years of a City and its People*. London: Cassell, 1974.

Beaver, Patrick. *The Crystal Palace: A Portrait of Victorian Enterprise*. Chichester: Phillimore, 1986.

Bennett, Tony. *The Birth of the Museum: History, Theory, Politics*. London: Routledge, 1995.

Bindman, David, and Malcolm Baker. *Roubiliac and the Eighteenth-Century Monument: Sculpture as Theatre*. New Haven: Yale University Press, 1995.

Bird, Anthony. *Paxton's Palace*. London: Cassell, 1976.

Boldrewood, Rolf. 'The Australian Native-Born Type'. *In Bad Company and Other Stories*. London: Macmillan, 1901, pp. 351–9.

Boldrewood, Rolf. *Robbery Under Arms*. London: Remington, 1888.

Bolton, G. C. *Richard Daintree: A Photographic Memoir*. Brisbane: Jacaranda, 1965.

Bonyhardy, Tim. *Australian Colonial Paintings in the Australian National Gallery*. Canberra: Australian National Gallery, 1986.

Brisbane Courier, 29 March 1882.

Budge, E. A. Wallis. *Cleopatra's Needles and Other Egyptian Obelisks*. London: Religious Tract Society, 1926.

Burton, Anthony. *Bethnal Green Museum of Childhood*. London: V&A, 1986.

Burton, Antoinette. *At the Heart of the Empire: Indians and the Colonial Encounter in Late-Victorian Britain*. Berkeley: University of California Press, 1998.

Burton, Antoinette. 'London and Paris through Indian Spectacles'. *History Workshop Journal*, 42 (1996): 126–39.

Cantlie, James. *Degeneration Amongst Londoners*. London: Leadenhall, 1885. Rpt. in *The Rise of Urban Britain*. Ed. Lynn Hollen Lees and Andrew Lees. New York: Garland, 1985.

Carter, Paul. *The Lie of the Land*. London: Faber, 1996.

Carter, Paul. 'Spirits of the Dead: A Sound History of "Cooee"'. *The Sound In-Between*. Sydney: New South Wales University Press, 1992, pp. 26–51.

Carter, Tom. *The Victorian Garden*. 1984. London: Bracken, 1988.

Caygill, Marjorie. *The Story of the British Museum*. London: British Museum, 1981.

Chadwick, George F. *The Works of Sir Joseph Paxton, 1803–1865*. London: Architectural Press, 1961.

Chambers, Iain, and Lidia Curti, ed. *The Post-Colonial Question: Common Skies, Divided Horizons*. London: Routledge, 1996.

Chapman, William Ryan. 'Arranging Ethnology: A. H. L. F. Pitt Rivers and the Typological Tradition'. *Objects and Others: Essays on Museums and Material Culture*. Ed. George W. Stocking, Jr. Madison: University of Wisconsin Press, 1985, pp. 15–48.

Clarke, Marcus. 'The Future Australian Race'. *Australian Nationalism*. Ed. Stephen Alomes and Catherine Jones. Sydney: HarperCollins, 1991, pp. 47–50.

Clarke, Patricia. 'The *Other* Harpur, or: How I Stumbled across an Unknown Colonial Poet'. *National Library of Australia News* (March 1998): 18–21.

Clayton, Peter A. *The Rediscovery of Ancient Egypt: Artists and Travellers in the Nineteenth Century*. London: Thames and Hudson, 1982.

Cochrane, Peter. 'Britishness in Australia'. *Voices: The Quarterly Journal of the National Library of Australia*, 6.3 (1996): 63–74.

Colley, Linda. *Britons: Forging the Nation 1707–1837*. London: Pimlico, 1992.

Coombes, Annie E. 'Museums and the Formation of National and Cultural Identities'. *Oxford Journal of Art*, 11.2 (1988): 57–68.

Davison, Graeme. 'Sydney and the Bush: An Urban Context for the Australian Legend'. *Intruders in the Bush: The Australian Quest for Identity*. Ed. John Carroll. Melbourne: Oxford University Press, 1982.

Dickens, Charles. 'The Private History of the Palace of Glass'. *Household Words: A Weekly Journal*, 18 January 1851: 385–91.

Dutton, Geoffrey. 'British Subject'. *Nation*, 6 April 1963: 15–16.

Driver, Felix, and David Gilbert, ed. *Imperial Cities: Landscape, Display and Identity*. Manchester: Manchester University Press, 1999.

Fish, R. 'Enville Hall'. *Journal of Horticulture and Cottage Gardener*, 8 November 1864: 372–6.

Fothergill, J. Milner. *The Town Dweller: His Needs and His Wants*. London: Lewis, 1889. Rpt. in *The Rise of Urban Britain*. Ed. Lynn Hollen Lees and Andrew Lees. New York: Garland, 1985.

Freeland, J. M. *Architecture in Australia: A History*. Melbourne: Cheshire, 1968.

Freud, Sigmund. 'The "Uncanny"'. *The Standard Edition of the Complete Psychological Works of Sigmund Freud*. Vol. 17. Ed. James Strachey. London: Hogarth, 1955, pp. 219–52.

Gelder, Ken, and Jane M. Jacobs. *Uncanny Australia: Sacredness and Identity in a Postcolonial Nation*. Melbourne: Melbourne University Press, 1998.

Gloag, John, and Derek Bridgwater. *A History of Cast Iron in Architecture*. London: Allen & Unwin, 1948.

Great Exhibition of the Works of Industry of all Nations, 1851: Official Descriptive and Illustrated Catalogue. 3 vols. London: Spicer, 1851.

Greenhalgh, Paul. *Ephemeral Vistas: The Expositions Universelles, Great Exhibitions and World's Fairs, 1851–1939*. Manchester: Manchester University Press, 1988.

Greenslade, William. *Degeneration, Culture and the Novel 1880–1940*. Cambridge: Cambridge University Press, 1994.

Habachi, Labib. *The Obelisks of Egypt: Skyscrapers of the Past*. New York: Scribner, 1977.

Hage, Ghassan. *White Nation: Fantasies of White Supremacy in a Multicultural Society*. Sydney: Pluto, 1998.

Hall, Catherine. 'Imperial Man: Edward Eyre in Australasia and the West Indies, 1833–66'. *The Expansion of England: Race, Ethnicity and Cultural History*. Ed. Bill Schwarz. London: Routledge, 1996, pp. 130–70.

Bibliography

Hall, Catherine. 'Rethinking Imperial Histories: The Reform Act of 1867'. *New Left Review*, 208 (1994): 3–29; 'Histories, Empires and the Post-Colonial Moment'. Iain Chambers and Lidia Curti. *The Post-Colonial Question: Common Skies, Divided Horizons*. London: Routledge, 1999, pp. 65–77.

Hepper, J. Nigel, ed. *Kew: Gardens for Science & Pleasure*. London: HMSO, 1982.

Herbert, Gilbert. 'A Cast-Iron Solution'. *Architectural Review*, 153 (1973): 367–73.

Higham, Charles, and Michael Wilding. *Australians Abroad: An Anthology*. Melbourne: Cheshire, 1967.

Hitchcock, Henry-Russell. *Early Victorian Architecture in Britain*. 2 vols. 1954. London: Trewin Copplestone, 1972.

Hix, John. *The Glasshouse*. London: Phaidon, 1996.

Hobsbawm, Eric, and Terence Ranger, ed. *The Invention of Tradition*. Cambridge: Cambridge University Press, 1983.

Horne, Donald. *The Lucky Country*. Ringwood: Penguin, 1964.

Howitt, William. *Land, Labour and Gold; or Two Years in Victoria*. 1855. Kilmore, Australia: Lowden, 1972.

Hoyt, Edwin P. *The Vanderbilts and their Fortunes*. London: Frederick Muller, 1963.

Illustrated Guide of the Orient Line of Steamers between England and Australia. London: 1884.

Illustrated London News, 7 August 1886.

Inglis, K. S. 'Going Home: Australians in England, 1870–1900'. Ed. David Fitzpatrick. *Home or Away?: Immigrants in Colonial Australia*. Canberra: RSSS, Australian National University, 1992, pp. 105–30.

Inglis, K. S. *The Rehearsal: Australians at War in the Sudan, 1885*. Sydney: Rigby, 1885.

J., W. 'Australian Song Birds'. *Australasian*, 22 December 1866.

Jupp, James. *The Australian People: An Encyclopedia of the Nation, its People and their Origins*. Sydney: Angus & Robertson, 1988.

Kröller, Eva-Marie. *Canadian Travellers in Europe, 1851–1900*. Vancouver: University of Vancouver Press, 1987.

Lane Fox, A. 'On the Principles of Classification Adopted in the Arrangement of his Anthroplogical Collection, Now Exhibited in the Bethnal Green Museum'. *Journal of the Anthropological Institute*, 4 (1875): 292–309.

Lewis, Miles. 'The Corrugated Iron Aesthetic'. *Historic Environment*, 2.1 (1982): 49–64.

Lewis, Miles. 'The Diagnosis of Prefabricated Buildings'. *Australian Historical Archaeology*, 3 (1985): 56–69.

Lewis, Miles. 'The Portable House'. *The History and Design of the Australian House*. Comp. Robert Irving. Melbourne: Oxford University Press, 1985.

Littlejohn, R. A. *Richard Teece: A Biographical Note*. Australian Mutual Provident Society, 1979.

McClintock, Anne. *Imperial Leather: Race, Gender and Sexuality in the Colonial Contest*. London: Routledge, 1995.

Bibliography

McGregor, Russell. *Imagined Destinies: Aboriginal Australians and the Doomed Race Theory, 1880–1939*. Melbourne: Melbourne University Press, 1997.

McKean, John. *Crystal Palace: Joseph Paxton and Charles Fox*. London: Phaidon, 1994.

MacKenzie, John. *Orientalism: History, Theory and the Arts*. Manchester: Manchester University Press, 1995.

Mandall, W. F. 'Cricket and Australian Nationalism in the Nineteenth-Century'. *Journal of the Royal Australian Historical Society*, 58.4 (1973): 225–46.

Maré, Eric de. *The London Doré Saw*. London: Allen Lane, 1973.

Marshall, P. J. *The Cambridge History of the British Empire*. Cambridge: Cambridge University Press, 1996.

Maynard, Margaret. *Fashioned from Penury: Dress as Cultural Practice in Colonial Australia*. Melbourne: Cambridge University Press, 1994.

Merrillees, Robert S. *Living with Egypt's Past in Australia*. Melbourne: Museum of Victoria, 1990.

Metcalf, Priscilla. *Victorian London*. London: Cassell, 1972.

Miers, Margaret. 'The Derby and the Grand National as Aspects of British Popular Culture'. Diss. Open University, 1994.

Mitchell, Cecily Joan. *Hunter's River: A History of Early Families and the Homes they Built in the Lower Hunter Valley between 1830 and 1860*. Newcastle West: Estate of C. J. Mitchell, 1973.

Mitchell, Timothy. *Colonising Egypt*. Cambridge: Cambridge University Press, 1988.

Moore, John Hammond. *Australians in America, 1876–1976*. Brisbane: University of Queensland Press.

Morgan, John Edward. *The Danger of Deterioration of Race*. London: Longmans, 1866. Rpt. in *The Rise of Urban Britain*. Ed. Lynn Hollen Lees and Andrew Lees. New York: Garland, 1985.

Mulvey, Christopher. *Anglo-American Landscapes: A Study of Nineteenth-Century Anglo-American Travel Literature*. Cambridge: Cambridge University Press, 1983.

The Museums Area of South Kensington and Westminster. Vol. 38 of *Survey of London*. London: Athlone, 1975.

Noakes, Aubrey. *Cleopatra's Needles*. London: Witherby, 1962.

Olsen, Donald J. *The Growth of Victorian London*. London: Batsford, 1976.

Orient Line Guide: Chapters for Travellers by Sea and by Land. London: Sampson Low, 1890.

Parsons, Neil. *King Khama, Emperor Joe and the Great White Queen: Victorian Britain through African Eyes*. Chicago: University of Chicago Press, 1998.

Perren, Richard. *The Meat Trade in Britain 1840–1914*. London: Routledge, 1978.

Pesman, Ros. *Duty Free: Australian Women Abroad*. Melbourne: Oxford University Press, 1996.

Pesman, Ros, David Walker and Richard White. *The Oxford Book of Australian Travel Writing*. Melbourne: Oxford University Press, 1996.

Phillips, Samuel. *Guide to the Crystal Palace and Park*. London: Bradbury, 1854.

Physick, John. *The Victoria and Albert Museum: The History of its Building*. Oxford: Phaidon, 1982.

Pick, Daniel. *Faces of Degeneration: A European Disorder, c. 1848–c. 1918*. Cambridge: Cambridge University Press, 1989.

'Pioneers of the "Thirties"'. *Dalgety's Review–For Queensland*, 16 May 1933.

Pitt-Rivers, Lieut-General. 'Typological Museums, as Exemplified by the Pitt-Rivers Museum at Oxford, and his Provincial Museum at Farnham, Dorset'. *Journal of the Society of Arts*, 18 December 1891: 115–22.

'Portable Houses . . . What are they?' *Trust News*, 10.7 (1983): 12–13.

Porter, Dale H. *The Thames Embankment: Environment, Technology, and Society in Victorian Britain*. Akron, Ohio: University of Akron Press, 1998.

Pratt, Mary Louise. *Imperial Eyes: Travel Writing and Transculturation*. London: Routledge, 1992.

Preston, Rebecca. *'The Scenery of the Torrid Zone': Imaginary Travels and the Culture of Exotics within Nineteenth Century British Gardens*. Imperial Cities Project: Working Paper 9. Egham: Dept. of Geography, Royal Holloway, 1997.

Quartermaine, Peter. 'International Exhibitions and Emigration: the Photographics Enterprise of Richard Daintree, Agent General for Queensland 1872–76'. *Journal of Australian Studies*, 13 (1983): 40–55.

Reynolds, Henry, comp. *Dispossession: Black Australians and White Invaders*. Sydney: Allen & Unwin, 1989.

Richards, Jeffrey. *Films and British National Identity: From Dickens to Dad's Army*. Manchester: Manchester University Press, 1997.

Robbins, Keith. *Nineteenth-Century Britain: Integration and Diversity*. Oxford: Clarendon, 1988.

Robertson, E. Graeme. 'The Australian Verandah'. *Architectural Review*, (April 1960): 238–45.

Robertson, E. Graeme. *Victorian Heritage: Ornamental Cast Iron in Architecture*. Melbourne: Georgian House, 1960; rpt. Sydney: Ure Smith, 1974.

Robinson, Jeffrey. *The Echoes Fade Not: A History of Toorak College*. Victoria: Toorak College, 1987.

Rothenburg, Marc, and Peter Hoffenberg. 'Australia at the 1876 Exhibition in Philadelphia'. *Historical Records of Australian Science*, 8.2 (1990): 55–62.

Rowland, Percy F. 'The Beginnings of an Australian National Character'. *The Nineteenth Century and After*, 52.307 (September 1902): 400–11.

Ruskin, John. *The Stones of Venice*. Vol. 1. London: Dent, n.d.

Ryan, Jan. *Ancestors: Chinese in Colonial Australia*. Fremantle: Fremantle Arts Centre Press, 1995.

Ryan, Jan. 'Chinese Australian History'. Ed. Wayne Hudson and Geoffrey Bolton. *Creating Australia: Changing Australian History*. Sydney: Allen & Unwin, 1997, pp. 71–8.

Ryan, Simon. *The Cartographic Eye: How Explorers Saw Australia*. Melbourne: Cambridge University Press, 1996.

Sattin, Anthony. *Lifting the Veil: British Society in Egypt 1768–1956*. London: Dent, 1988.

Serle, Geoffrey. *From Deserts the Prophets Come: The Creative Spirit in Australia 1788–1972*. Melbourne: Heinemann, 1973.

Shoemaker, Adam. '"Don't Cry for Me, Diamantina": An Alternative Reading of Pauline Hanson.' *Journal of Australian Studies*, 53 (1997): 20–8.

Solomon, David. *Coming of Age: Charter for a New Australia*. Brisbane: UQP, 1998.

Stepan, Nancy. 'Biological Degeneration: Races and Proper Places'. *Degeneration: The Dark Side of Progress*. Ed. J. Edward Chamberlain and Sander L. Gilman. New York: Columbia University Press, 1985, pp. 97–120.

Stocking, George. W., Jr. *Victorian Anthropology*. New York: Free Press, 1987.

Stoler, Ann Laura, and Frederick Cooper. 'Between Metropole and Colony: Rethinking a Research Agenda'. Ed. Ann Laura Stoler and Frederick Cooper. *Tensions of Empire: Colonial Cultures in a Bourgeois World*. Berkeley: University of California Press, 1997, pp. 1–56.

Stratton, Jon. *Race Daze: Australia in Identity Crisis*. Sydney: Pluto, 1998.

Stratton, Jon. *Writing Sites: A Genealogy of the Postmodern World*. London: Harvester Wheatsheaf, 1990.

Summerson, John. *Georgian London*. London: Barrie & Jenkins, 1988.

Tiffin, Christopher. 'Imagining Countries, Imagining People: Climate and the Australian Type'. *SPAN*, 24 (1987): 46–62.

Times, 18 May 1871.

Times, 24 May 1939.

Times, 25 May 1939.

Thomas, Nancy. *The American Discovery of Ancient Egypt*. Los Angeles: Los Angeles County Museum of Art, 1995.

Tyack, Geoffrey. *Sir James Pennethorne and the Making of Victorian London*. Cambridge: Cambridge University Press, 1992.

Ward, Russel. *The Australian Legend*. 1958. Melbourne: Oxford University Press, 1966.

White, R. B. *Prefabrication: A History of its Development in Great Britain*. London: HMSO, 1965.

White, Richard. 'Bluebells and Fogtown: Australians' First Impressions of England, 1860–1940'. *Australian Cultural History*, 5 (1986): 44–59.

White, Richard. *Inventing Australia: Images and Identity 1688–1980*. Sydney: Allen & Unwin, 1981.

White, Richard. 'The Soldier as Tourist: The Australian Experience of the Great War'. *War and Society*, 5.1 (1987): 63–7.

White, Richard. 'Sun, Sand and Syphilis: Australian Soldiers and the Orient, Egypt 1914'. *Australian Cultural History*, 9 (1990): 49–64.

Whitlock, Gillian. 'A "White-Souled State": Across the "South" with Lady Barker'. Ed. Kate Darien-Smith, Liz Gunner and Sarah Nuttall. *Text, Theory, Space: Land, Literature and History in South Africa and Australia*. London: Routledge, 1996, pp. 65–80.

Woodruff, Douglas. *The Tichborne Claimant: A Victorian Mystery.* London: Hollis & Carter, 1957.

Woollacott, Angela. '"All This is the Empire, I Told Myself": Australian Women's Voyages "Home" and the Articulation of Colonial Whiteness.' *American Historical Review,* 102.4 (1997): 1003–29.

Index

Index

Index

Great Fire of London, 127
Grosvenor House, London, 117
Guardian, 115

Hage, Ghassan, 168, 182–3
Hall, Catherine, 19–20, 29, 79
Handel Festivals, 65
Hannan, Richard, 26–7, 101, 125–6, 131,
 136–7, 140, 185–6
Harpur, Thomas, 96
Hart, Lucy, 52
Haysom, Ida, 174–5
Heliopolis, 128
Hemming & Co. (Bristol iron house
 manufacturers), 54
Henning, Rachel, 91, 93
Hereford, 142
heritage sites and historical discontinuity,
 119–22
Higgins, Nettie, 132
Hill, Lord, 97–8
Hill, Sir Rowland, 97–8
Hindmarsh, Governor, 56
Hitchcock, Henry-Russell, 63, 85–6
Hix, John, 59, 67
Hobart, 147
Hogan, James, 121–2, 136
Holborn Viaduct, London, 124
Holman, Ada, 131
Holmes A'Court, Hon. C., 93
Honiton, 173
Honolulu, 139, 178
Horne, Donald: *The Lucky Country*, 166,
 167, 169
Howitt, William, 53–4, 62
Hudson, Martha, 125, 135, 137–8, 144, 145,
 146, 149, 186
Hull, 141
Hunter Valley, 88, 102, 110, 150
Hyde Park, 95, 96, 97

Illustrated Guide, 46
Illustrated London News, 66, 73–4
India, 4–5, 13, 15, 18, 21, 39, 72, 133, 161
International Exhibition (South
 Kensington, 1872), 85
Inverness, 171
Ireland, the Irish, 7, 11, 13, 16, 17, 49, 99,
 104, 160, 181
 and Australian visitors, 141–2, 145,
 153–8, 173
Italy, 15, 162, 172

Jacobs, Jane M., 48–9, 58

Jamaica, 20, 21, 72
James, Henry, 109
James, Mary, 176–7
Jerrold, Douglas, 59
John Duthie (ship), 149
Jones, Barry, 182
Joy, Alfred, 53, 54–5, 56–7, 62
Joy, Henrietta, 53, 56, 57
Jupp, James, 14

Kater, Mary, 14–15, 16–17, 25, 26, 27,
 100–1, 176–7
Kenilworth Castle, 41, 42
Kent, Duke and Duchess of, 117
Kerr, Edna, 69, 177–8, 179, 181
Kew Gardens, 6, 67, 69, 70, 71
 Palm House, 59, 62, 73–4
Kilgra, 88, 190
Killarney, Lakes of, 153
Knox, Robert, 17
Kokoda Trail, Papua New Guinea, 24
Kröller, Eva-Marie: *Canadian Travellers in
 Europe, 1851–1900*, 4, 46

Labett, William, 69
Labor government (Australia, postwar),
 18
Laing, Samuel, MP, 64, 82
Lake District, 173
Lancashire, 31
landscape, 9, 10–11, 37–9, 42–3, 93–4, 160,
 169, 172, 180
Lane Fox, Col. Augustus Henry, 83–4, 85
 Lane Fox collection, 83–4, 85, 86
language, 142–4, 145, 154, 158–9, 160–1,
 163, 178
La Trobe, Governor, 56
Leaton Hall, Bobbington, 150, 153
Leconfield (Wyndham property), 88,
 89–90, 164, 191
Leichhardt, Friedrich, 92
Light, Colonel, 55
Lime Street Station, Liverpool, 63
Lincoln, 141
Lincolnshire, 43–4
Liverpool, 7, 63, 141, 143, 156
Lloyd, Thomas, 27
Loddiges Botanic Nursery, Hackney, 67
London, 1, 4, 7, 11, 15, 16, 23, 26–7, 28, 30,
 39, 43, 58, 62, 63, 88–9, 91, 94, 95, 97,
 100, 101, 106, 107, 112, 114, 119–33,
 139, 141, 143, 145–7, 153, 155, 160, 162,
 169–70, 172, 173, 174, 175, 179–80, 181,
 184

Index

Index